W9-APK-097

The Calligrapher's Handbook

THE CALLIGRAPHER'S HANDBOOK

essays by

M. C. OLIVER
WILLIAM BISHOP
JOHN WOODCOCK
ALFRED FAIRBANK
M. THÉRÈSE FISHER
SYDNEY M. COCKERELL
MARGARET L. HODGSON
WILLIAM M. GARDNER
DOROTHY HUTTON
BERTHOLD WOLPE
IRENE BASE

edited by C. M. LAMB, M.A.

FABER & FABER LIMITED
24 Russell Square
London

First published in mcmlvi
by Faber and Faber Limited
24 Russell Square London W.C.1
Second edition mcmlxviii
Printed in Great Britain by
John Dickens & Co. Ltd. Northampton

SBN 571 04660 6

Contents

Contents

Plates

Figures in the Text

Figures in the Text

Preface 1968

SINCE the publication of this book in 1956 a number of changes has occurred in the materials available to calligraphers and in the addresses of firms supplying such materials. The following notes are intended to inform readers of these alterations and to preclude attempts to obtain materials which are no longer available from firms whose addresses have been changed.

The revived interest in calligraphy has led to the production of numerous books dealing with the subject, and a list is included on p. 245 of some of those most likely to be of interest and help to students of the craft. These books were written after the chapters which comprise this volume were composed.

The supplies of prepared quill pens have dwindled considerably in recent years, though some are available from artists' colourmen, e.g. Lechertier Barbe, 95 Jermyn St,. London, S.W.1, or L. Cornelissen and Sons, 22 Great Queen St., London, W.C.2. Messrs. Henry Hill of the Swan Works, London, N.8, no longer supply quill pens. Unprepared quills, primary flight feathers of turkeys or geese, can sometimes be obtained from farmers who breed these birds, and the quills can then be prepared as suggested in chapter I.

Many scribes nowadays are using pens with metal nibs, and it should be noted that the pen factory of G. W. Hughes has been closed; but before closing an excess stock of Flight Commander nibs was made and placed with the wholesalers, Messrs. John Heath and Co. Ltd., of 508/514 Moseley Road,

Birmingham 12. Messrs. Dryad Ltd. of Leicester, and 22 Bloomsbury St., London, W.C.1, stock many forms of metal nibs for italic writing. Mr. Alfred Fairbank recommends the Osmiroid italic nib no. 95, which is made both for right and left handers by Messrs. E. S. Perry, of Osmiroid Works, Gosport, Hampshire. The Swan Calligraph and the Swan Perfect Pen are no longer manufactured. The Parker Pen Company Ltd., of Bush House, London, W.C.2, make excellent fountain pens with chisel shaped nibs in various widths for italic writing. The address of the Esterbrook Pen Company Ltd., is now Mowland St., Birmingham, 4. Platignum fountain pens can be obtained from Platignum House, Six Hills Way, Stevenage, Herts.

Supplies of vellum and parchment are obtainable from Messrs. H. Band and Co. Ltd., of Brent Way, High Street, Brentford, Middlesex. It is said that vellum is no longer finished by hand, but that a hard smooth surface is obtained by the use of a special preparation. Some scribes prefer vellum which has not been so treated, and this can be obtained on application to Messrs. Band.

Messrs. W. J. Cowley, of Newport Pagnell, Bucks., have taken over the vellum making business of Messrs. T. R. Loosley and Son, and can now supply both vellum and parchment.

The supplies of paper for calligraphers are good at present, though Arnold and Foster no longer make paper, and Whatman's papers are not readily available. All handmade papers of Barcham Green are obtainable from T. N. Lawrence and Son, 2 Bleeding Heart Yard, Greville St., London, E.C.1, and a variety of hand made papers is supplied by Messrs. W. S. Hodgkinson and Company Ltd., 19 Tudor Street, London, E.C.4.

With regard to the supply of gold and other metallic leaf, and of gilders' requisites, it should be noted that Messrs. Whiley's addresses are now, G. M. Whiley Ltd., Victoria

Rd., Ruislip, Middlesex, and 54 Whitfield St., London, W.1.

With reference to appendix B, page 232, on 'Illumination and Decoration', the author points out that in line 2 the truth has been reversed, and the line should read 'Chinese ink is rubbed down with distilled water, as this produces a blacker shade than when tap water is used'. On page 236 the following note should be added; 'Since contributing this appendix the author has become aware that much exquisite mediaeval illumination shows no sign of an outline drawn either by pen or brush'.

In respect of pigments it should be noted that Genuine Ultramarine, Azurite and Malachite are no longer obtainable. Messrs. Roberson and Co. suggest that Azurite can be replaced by Cobalt and New Blue.

Preface

The essays which comprise this volume constitute a memorial to two craftsmen: one, Edward Johnston, C.B.E., whose eminence as a calligrapher of genius is widely acknowledged; the other, Colonel J. C. H. Crosland, who was a gifted carver, engraver and penman, and had great interest in the calligraphers' crafts and their methods, models and equipment.

The preparation of the volume, whose origin lies in a suggestion by Alfred Fairbank, C.B.E., has been made possible by a generous gift from Mrs. J. C. H. Crosland to the Society of Scribes and Illuminators, and for this gift the Society would again express its grateful thanks.

The essays are nearly all the work of pupils of Edward Johnston, or pupils of his pupils, and may be regarded as a supplement to Johnston's classic work *Writing and Illuminating and Lettering*, first published in 1906 and now in its twenty-fifth impression.

In the preparation of the volume much help and advice has been given by Messrs. Faber and Faber Limited, and guidance and encouragement have been generously afforded by three successive honorary secretaries of the Society of Scribes and Illuminators; Miss Thérèse Fisher, Miss Dorothy Hutton and Miss Heather Child, who has also prepared the bibliography. Particular information relating to the processes of which they have such wide experience has been given to the authors of the relevant chapters by Messrs. Band, of Brentford, the vellum manufacturers, and Messrs. Spicers, the paper makers. To them and to all who have furnished technical details grateful acknowledgement is recorded.

It is hoped the book will be of interest to the expanding circle of those aware of the aesthetic possibilities of formal and informal writing, and of help to those who practise the craft of calligraphy, for it is based on the extensive experience of working craftsmen.

It is worthy of note that the issue of this volume coincides with the fiftieth anniversary of the publication of Edward Johnston's *Writing and Illuminating and Lettering*. This is clear evidence of the vitality of his teaching and the enduring quality of his inspiration of others. *Defunctus adhuc loquitur*.

I

Pens, Pencils, Brushes and Knives

The more working knowledge a craftsman has of his tools the better able is he to design and execute good work. Therefore, it is appropriate that the opening chapter of this book should deal with the principal tools used in the art of writing, calligraphy or penmanship.

The pen is one of man's most useful instruments of expres-

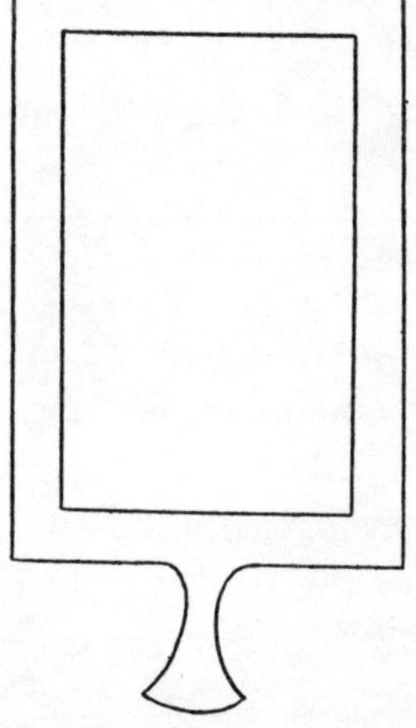

Fig. 1. Roman Wax Tablet

sion: in the dissemination of knowledge and learning and in the shaping of our alphabetic letter forms, whether before or after the advent of printing, no single tool has been of greater importance than the simple pen. This chapter is not intended to give a detailed history of every type of writing instrument, but to mention only those which are important to the calligrapher (although in a wide sense all types of writing instruments have relationship).

Every conceivable substance capable of absorbing ink or liquid colour, or of receiving an impression with a pointed stylus, was used as a writing surface. The earliest plant stem used by the ancient Egyptians has been identified as the *Juncus maritimus*, a rush plant, which grows in the marshy lands of many parts of the world, including England. The ink used by

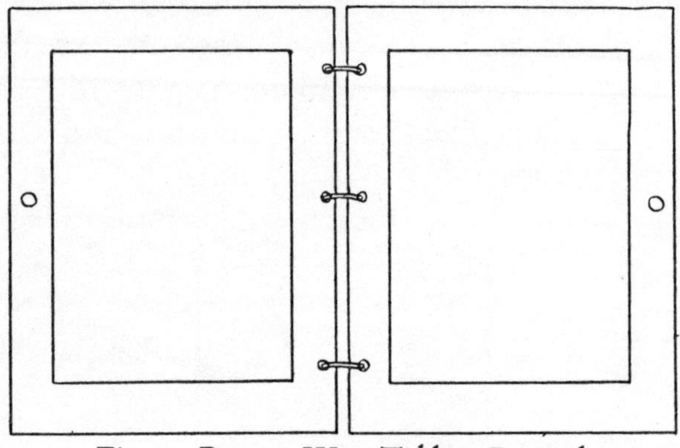

Fig. 2. Roman Wax Tablet, Diptych

the Egyptian scribes was remarkably good in quality and made invariably of carbon obtained from soot, lamp black, or charcoal mixed with gum and water and shaped in the form of solid cakes to fit the ink receptacles of their writing palettes.

The pen made from this rush plant was solid and of varying thickness and used according to the size of writing required, some being as slight as one-sixteenth of an inch in diameter. (See examples in the British Museum.) This rush stem was used for three purposes. Firstly, as a brush, in which case the end used for painting was bruised or macerated to cause the fibres to spread; secondly, for drawing with ink or colour, in which case the drawing end was sharpened to a point without a slit to give a line of equal thickness in whichever direction it was used; and thirdly, and most important, as a pen, which when so used was cut at an angle, also without a slit, the natural fibres of the plant stem absorbing and giving off the ink or colour by capillary attraction. From experiments carried out by the writer there is no evidence to suppose that the end of the writing pen as distinct from the brush was bruised by striking lightly with a heavy object, or by biting and fraying the end between the teeth. Although writing ends of Egyptian rush pens now in the British Museum are frayed, this is more the result of deterioration after thousands of years than of intent. In seeking to discover how a pen is cut, the finish of a stroke is as important as the commencement, and most examples of Egyptian hieroglyphic writing show pen

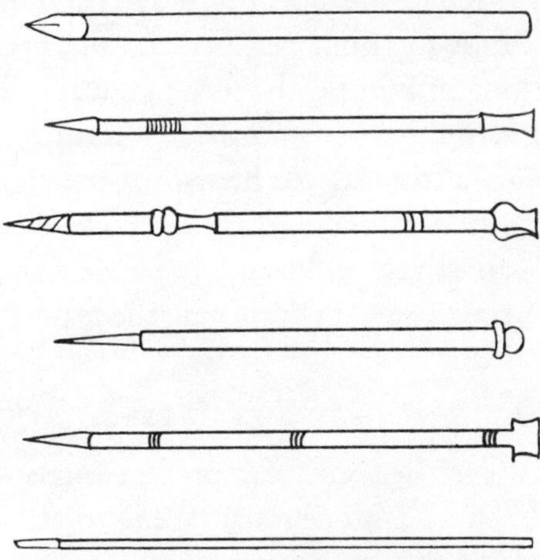

Fig. 3. Reed Pen and Roman Styli

strokes cleanly finished, proving that the pen was cut, and not macerated so as to leave a jagged irregular writing edge.

The other type of pen used later by the Egyptians was the hollow-stemmed reed *Phragmites Aegyptiaca* cut with a slit, in the manner of a modern broad-edged quill pen. It appears that this type of pen came into use about 600 B.C., for examples of writing of this period can be seen showing a definite contrast and graduation between thick and thin strokes upon which simple character has been built the beauty of our letter forms. A thin sliver of wood or bamboo with the writing end cut and shaped like a wood chisel will also produce thick and thin strokes.

One of the most important changes which followed the improvement in the production of animal skins for writing surfaces was the introduction of the quill pen made from one of the large flight feathers of a bird. It would seem that this change took place when vellum and parchment came into use as a writing material, which gradually began to displace the papyrus roll in 190 B.C., although the earliest reference to such a pen is much later. It will be noticed that there is some similarity of shape between a hollow reed and the barrel of a quill pen. Whilst the quill pen became the primary instrument for writing in Europe, the reed pen was still retained for certain letter forms, e.g. Greek cursive writing.

In various countries, up to the end of the eighteenth century, isolated attempts were made to produce metal pens of bronze, copper, silver, gold and bone of shape similar to quills but none succeeded in displacing the feather quill pen.[1]

MODERN METAL PENS

Metal pens were first manufactured in England at the beginning of the nineteenth century. Whilst craftsmen deplore the use of metal pens for writing on vellum and parchment, modern metal pens of different types are of great use for special purposes in the work of the scribe or calligrapher, such as for posters, notices, showcards, certificates, memoranda and correspondence, where cost, speed and time are important factors.

Metal pens for large posters and notices, or for occasions where wide strokes are required, are sold in Europe and

[1] See examples of Roman metal pens in the British Museum and other Museums. Examples of eighteenth-century metal pens are contained in the William Bishop collection of writing instruments.

America under various names, automatic pens, border pens, block letter pens, type pens, parcel pens, poster pens and witch pens, each suited for a different purpose. Pens with wooden holders to which were fixed either a piece of horn or metal suitably shaped were used several hundreds of years ago for writing large letter forms. Of metal pens available to-day Boxall's plain stroke pens are recommended for large lettering. They are of non-rusting metal and made in varying widths from one-sixteenth to three-quarters of an inch, the latter pen making a capital letter of approximately six inches high. Of Boxall pens, the larger sizes are recommended as of

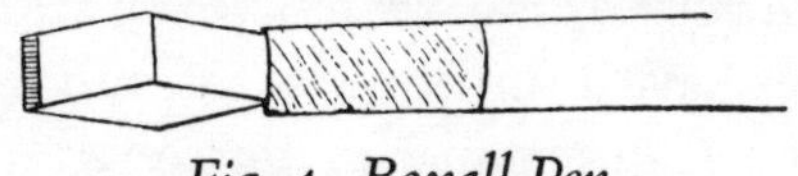

Fig. 4. Boxall Pen

more use than the smaller. For the smaller sizes one can use W. Mitchell's round hand pens or other makes. Instructions for the use of Boxall's plain stroke pens are as follows. A new pen should be filled and worked gently about on a piece of paper until the colour flows; should there be any sign of scratching it will soon wear off with use, or it may be drawn gently on a fine stone. Take care to see that the blade without teeth does not project beyond the toothed blade, however slightly, or the pen will not mark. Careless handling will cause this. If it occurs it must be carefully bent back flush with the other. A slight overlap of the toothed blade does not matter. When writing, the toothed blade should always be uppermost. The best method of filling the pen is by feeding the colour between the blades with a brush. Before use place the pen in a pot containing about half an inch of water for a few seconds. Poster colours used with these pens should be kept stirred and should be chosen with care. Inferior poster colours will clog the pen. A small drop of glycerine can be added or powder colours ground with gum arabic and water can be used. After use clean and dry the blades of the pen.

Mr. J. H. Manwaring recommends Messrs. Dane & Co. Ltd., Sugar House Lane, Stratford, London, E.15, for poster and waterproof colours used with metal pens.

Some of these large pens are constructed to produce a double stroke intended for ruling borders. Letter forms made with these pens which do not rely upon the skill of the hand have the appearance of trick writing and are best avoided.

For the smaller sizes of pen lettering or writing there are numerous types of pens for use with a penholder made in England and on the Continent, in a range of sizes up to a nib width of approximately one-eighth of an inch for straight pen and slanted pen writing. Others which are not so useful to the calligrapher have a turned up square nib and are designed for special letter forms similar in appearance to the printer's Egyptian type face. For lettering and handwriting metal pens can sometimes be improved, and a finer thin stroke obtained, by a few gentle strokes of the pen held underneath-side-up at a chisel angle on a fine stone. Care should be taken to see the edges are not too sharp, otherwise when writing the pen will not move smoothly over the surface of the paper. For handwriting, too sharp a pen is not required, as will be seen from a study of italic handwriting of the fifteenth to sixteenth centuries where the nib appears to be well worn but delightfully manageable.[1]

Metal pens made with the left side shorter than the right are recommended for left-handed writers.

With many types of lettering pens a small piece of metal is fitted to act as a reservoir; if used it should not be placed too near the nib or pen's edge, otherwise it will cause the thin stroke to become too heavy and indistinct. William Mitchell's reservoir pen holder is specially made for use with these pens. When used with colour see that the reservoir does not clog.

For the larger sizes of pens the writing board should be sloped to an angle of 45° to prevent the ink or colour from

[1] See also *A Handwriting Manual* by A. Fairbank.

flowing too freely. Metal pens should always be cleaned and wiped dry after use. When first used, the varnish of metal pens often irritatingly prevents the ink or colour from adhering evenly; this can be overcome by placing and moving the new pen in the flame of a match for two seconds and immediately plunging it in cold water, whereupon the colour or ink will be found to adhere with no loss or damage to the pen nib.

Metal pens most widely used and recommended for formal calligraphy are:

Pedigree round hand pens, size 00 to 6 (square and oblique)
Cursive series 0973
Decro series (somewhat hard)
Rex series (0906)

All these pens are made by William Mitchell.

Similar shaped pens in varying widths are made by:
Perry & Co. (Pens) Ltd.
J. Gillott & Sons Ltd.
G. W. Hughes (Violin pen)
Gilbert & Blanzy (No. 229–230, various widths), France
Esterbrook Hazell Pens Ltd.

For fine line work in pen drawing:
J. Gillott's 303 pen

Use can be made of these metal lettering pens in an old fountain pen holder of the lever type and others. Remove the fountain pen nib and feed bar and insert the shank of the lettering pen; a small piece of wood or match stick can be used as a feed. Higgins's black ink, Swan 'Old English' manuscript ink, and others, work well with these composite pens. Different sizes of metal pens can be used in these holders.

Many types of steel, non-ferrous, and stainless steel pens are available for the contemporary style of handwriting known as Chancery Script, and other italic styles derived from the modernized Italian cancellaresca corsiva of the sixteenth century. These pens are of the edged type, as opposed to pointed pens, with wide shoulders and nibs shaped either square, right

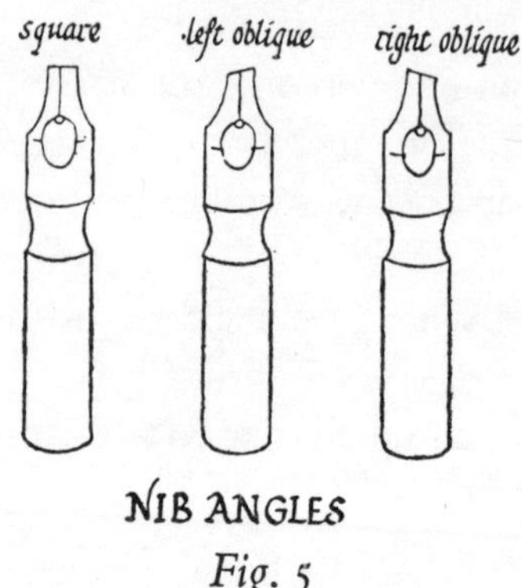

NIB ANGLES

Fig. 5

oblique or left oblique, i.e. stub. Whilst the nibs of some of these pens are fine, medium, broad or extra broad, others are only fine or medium. The thickness of the metal of a number of these pens varies and governs to some extent the elasticity or spring of the pen when writing. Handwriting is easiest and best results are obtained when little or no pressure is exerted on the pen. The thinner types of metal pens are preferred to the thick, the nibs' edges of the former are more cleanly finished and in writing move more smoothly over the surface of the paper. One metal pen specially made for italic handwriting is the Geo. W. Hughes Flight Commander pen No. 1240, obtainable in four breadths, fine, medium, broad and extra broad. The following list of edged pens suitable for cursive or italic handwriting is a short and incomplete selection from the 10,000 different patterns of metal pens made annually in Birmingham for world-wide requirements. A metal pen should be referred to by its name, number and maker, as stamped on the shank of the pen.

The steel pen makers of England, some of whom are the longest established in the world, encourage inquiries from the public in matters concerning metal pens and their uses in relation to handwriting and lettering.

Name of Pen	Number	Particulars	Maker
Flight Commander Pen	1240	Fine, medium, broad, extra broad	Geo. W. Hughes Steel Pen Maker St. Paul's Pen Works, Birmingham, 1.
Senator Pen	365	—	
Durador	1301	In one breadth only	
Reliance	0782B	For left handers	
Violin	1034	For left handers	
Violin	1191 to 1199	From breadth 1 the widest to breadth 9 the narrowest	
Football Series	1321 to 1325	In breadths 1 to 5	
Relief	314	—	Messrs. Esterbrook Hazell Pens Ltd. 2/3 Great Pulteney Street, Piccadilly, London, W.1
Probate Pen	313	Large stub with medium point	
Jonquil Pen	—	Fine Relief	
Chancellor Pen	239	Medium point stub	
Black Stove Pen	284	—	
Queen's Own	570	—	C. Brandauer & Co. Ltd. Steel Pen Manufacturers 124 Newgate Street, London, E.C.1.
'J' Pen	251	Fine, medium broad	
Clan Flora Macdonald Pen	—	—	
Rover Pen	1939	—	Joseph Gillott & Sons Ltd. Steel Pen Manufacturers Victoria Works, Graham Street, Birmingham, 1.
Super Stub	1150	—	
Inqueduct Pen	G–1	Stainless steel reservoir pen	
Golden Quill	0795	Fine and medium	William Mitchell British Pens Ltd. 'Pedigree' Pen Works, Bearwood Road, Birmingham. or 134 Old Street, London, E.C.2.
Pedigree Fleetwing	0528	—	
The Legal Pen	2199F	Fine	
Italic	0284	Breadths 1 to 5 for right handers	
Italic	0290	Breadths 1 to 5 for left handers	

Name of Pen	*Number*	*Particulars*	*Maker*
Durabrite	No. 2	Stainless Steel	Perry & Co. (Pens) Ltd. 36 Lancaster Street, Birmingham, 4.
Roc. 27	—	Iridinoid stainless steel reservoir pen	E. S. Perry Ltd. Pen Manufacturers Pen Works, Angel Road, Edmonton, London, N.18.
Roc. 25	—		
Pan	555	Fine and medium	
Good Luck Pen	1001B	Iridinoid	
Gold Wing	—	Reservoir pen	Macniven Cameron Ltd. Waverley Works, Blair Street, Edinburgh, 1.
Silver Wing	457	—	

FOUNTAIN PENS

Can a fountain pen be of use to the calligrapher fascinated by the beauty of letter forms? Whilst fountain pen makers may not have the educational knowledge of the quill pen and the manner of cutting, some reputable firms will undertake the making of a gold pen nib to suit the writing style of the user. This requires greater understanding of the subtleties of pens, nibs, writing styles and pen hold than is generally realized. For hundreds of years quill pen making for the common use of handwriting was an individual and personal accomplishment, the manner of shaping varying principally according to the choice of style of writing, how the pen was held, and the degree of pressure applied.

The principal function of the fountain pen is for letter form making, the nib, i.e. the extreme writing point, being the most important part of the fountain pen. The nib of a gold pen would, in a short time, wear out if it were not fused and strengthened with iridium, a harder and more durable metal than gold. Formerly, this small piece of iridium was often left unshaped so causing the thin strokes to become too thick in the side movement of the pen in writing, thus losing that delightful contrast between thick and thin strokes which gives handwriting an important quality. In recent years some fountain pen makers have attempted, with success, to shape by grinding the iridium tip to overcome this loss of contrast, so adding to the beauty of the letter forms.

The Swan Calligraph Pen, and the Swan Perfect Pen, (Messrs. Mabie Todd & Co. Ltd., Swan House, Whitby Avenue, Park Royal, London, N.W.10) which are made in three widths of nibs, fine, medium and broad, and shaped right oblique, left oblique and square, have been specially designed with this improved feature and are recommended to those interested in good handwriting. A most useful booklet can be obtained from the firm giving details of the calligraph pen with examples of handwriting in chancery and informal scripts.

Another feature of some modern fountain pens is the interchangeable nib section (that part which is screwed into the

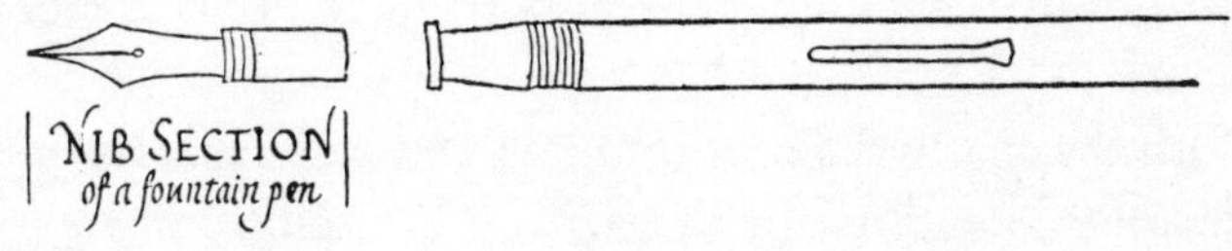

Fig. 6

pen barrel). The advantage of these fountain pens is that they eliminate the delay and inconvenience of factory point repairs. If a pen nib becomes damaged or is in any way unsuitable, unscrew the old nib section and screw in a new one. Instead of buying a new complete fountain pen one buys a new nib section.

The Esterbrook Pen Company—relief pens—produces this type of pen in a wide variety of thirty different point styles; instead of gold, the pen is made of Duracrome tipped with a hard alloy. This firm also produces a 'Relief' fountain pen with fine, medium and broad nibs. One of their latest productions is an unspillable desk pen set, consisting of an ink container filled in the ordinary way from a bottle. The main ink supply in the base is raised by capillary action to the pen by means of a unit containing nylon filaments. One dip of the pen will write about three hundred words. To refill, the penholder is placed in the socket of the ink-container and instantly refills. The nib section, fitted to the barrel of the penholder, is interchangeable and there is a choice of thirty-three pen points. This firm's address is: Messrs. Esterbrook Hazell Pens Ltd., 2/3 Great Pulteney Street, Piccadilly, London, W.1.

Another pen available to those interested in italic handwriting is the Wyvern manuscript fountain pen, made by The Wyvern Fountain Pen Co. Ltd., Leicester. This pen is fitted with an edge nib of gilt steel for Dudley, Marion Richardson and Fairbank handwriting.

There is also the 'Osmiroid 65' italic fountain pen with a choice of six interchangeable italic nib units made by Messrs. E. S. Perry, Ltd., Angel Road, Edmonton, London, N.18.

'Platignum' fountain pens also have interchangeable nib sections.

With the many types of fountain pens available to-day, the reader should endeavour to acquaint himself with the particular performance of each make. All reputable fountain pen manufacturers supply illustrated information about their products.

PENCILS

Modern pencils are usually obtainable in degrees varying from 9H, very hard, to 6B, very soft. For the ruling of writing lines on vellum and parchment it is advisable to use a pencil of the hard variety—6H or 8H. Owing to the abrasiveness of pounce and sandarac used in preparing the skin surface for writing, too soft a pencil leaves a black, furry, indistinct line.

Two HB or B pencils of suitable lengths tied together with

string or secured with one inch gummed paper make a most useful tool for learning and teaching the component strokes of pen letter forms, the two pencils indicating the two outside

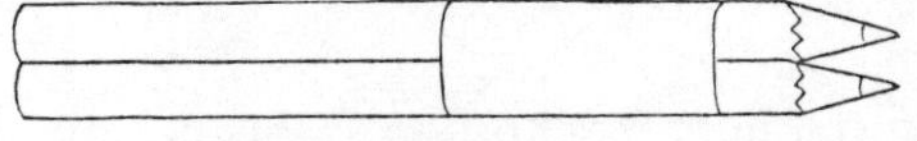

Fig. 7. Double Pencils

points of the pen's edge. The width of the stroke can be varied slightly by shaving the sides of the pencils nearest to each other before tying together.

Where contrast of weight, extra large letters for notices or posters are required, or when large metal, reed or bamboo pens are not available, two pencils with a piece of grooved wood between of a width varying according to the thickness of the stroke required and tied as before make another easy and handy tool for the pen letterer. Other methods are also possible. After the outlines of the letters have been written in with this tool, the letter forms can be filled in with a brush.

For the purpose of making rough pen lettering designs some calligraphers use a flat layout or carpenter's pencil cut with a chisel-shaped edge to give wide strokes. Both ends can be utilized, giving two different widths of pencil strokes, or shaped for different letter forms. Pencils of blue, red, green, yellow are available for colour contrasts. 'Monk' lettering pencils in black and colour made by William Mitchell's are also available for teachers when first introducing pen lettering in schools. Lettering chalk is obtainable from Dryads Ltd., for classroom work, or lecturing, where one needs to demonstrate on a blackboard.

BRUSHES

Brushes used in the art of illuminating should be of the best quality. Red sables, sizes 00 to 2, are those mostly favoured for this purpose. The hairs of the best have a 'spring' when pressed forward with the fingers, and whilst the tips should be cleanly pointed, straggling hairs are to be avoided. If these appear after use they can be removed with a pair of tweezers

Brushes with longer tips known as writers are often needed for painted letter forms and sign-writing. The hairs are of sable, civet or squirrel set in quills and known as lark, crow, duck, goose etc. according to the size of the brush. Sticks or handles are sold separately to fit these quill brushes, or an old brush handle can be used. The quill 'ferrule' should first be softened in water and the stick inserted into the quill and fixed with glue or 'cellotape'.

For applying ink to the quill in writing, it is not necessary to use a brush of the best quality.

Quill camel-hair dabbers are useful for brushing away loose gold leaf when gilding. The brushes are large, round and soft.[1]

QUILL PEN KNIVES

The quill pen knife, used exclusively for the shaping and

Fig. 8. Quill Pen Knife, Eighteenth Century

cutting of quill pens, is an instrument about which very little appears to be known by the public, and for most people, except those who make and mend their own quill pens, has long lost its original use. In fact, to-day, such a knife is un-

[1] For information concerning the making of red sable hair brushes, and the history of silver point, pens, burnishers, etc., see *Painting Materials* by R. J. Gettens and G. L. Stout, D. Van Nostrand Co. Inc., 250 Fourth Avenue, New York, 1943.

For early pens and brushes see *Ancient Egyptian Materials and Industries* by A. Lucas, 3rd edition, Edward Arnold, 1948.

obtainable, except perhaps by the professional quill cutter, of whom there are few, and he probably has the knife specially made. As of many things of the past, including the quill pen, no early written history of the knife exists. Those eager for knowledge have to spend considerable time delving into different channels of research endeavouring to trace the development of this and other writing instruments.

The shapes of the blades and hafts of the knives varied from century to century. The length of the haft or handle was about the width of the palm of the hand and shaped to be held comfortably, whilst the length of the blade was sometimes slightly more or slightly less than that of the haft. Up to about A.D. 1400 the cutting edge of the blade was generally straight although occasionally it is shown to curve outwards.

From 1450, at a period which coincided with the birth of new learning and papal calligraphers, the quill pen knife became very diverse in shape and size. A change in the size and form of manuscript writing also brought changes in the width of the knife blade. Formerly, wide down strokes of the quill of about one-eighth of an inch required pressure from both hands for cutting the nib of the pen owing to the extreme hardness of the quill substance. With the coming of professional writing masters, and the general desire and fashion of educated people to learn handwriting, the width of the knife blade by the seventeenth century became less and was often as narrow as one-eighth of an inch. At this period when letter forms were finer and the downstrokes in writing often obtained by pressure from a pointed pen, it was customary for the final cut of the nib to be done by the right hand only, in one of several ways: by inserting into the barrel of the pen to be nibbed the shaft of another quill, or the pointed haft of a penknife, or by inserting and cutting on a piece of bone or ivory suitably shaped, or nibbing upon the left thumb nail. For the latter a piece of wide bone or ivory, ring shaped, was sometimes slipped over the first joint of the left thumb.

In the early centuries the handles were made usually of bone, wood, ivory, leather and the blades of iron. From about the seventeenth century the knife handle often became very decorative, gold, silver, agate, tortoiseshell, inlaid with precious stones and metals, whilst the blade, either fixed, folding or sliding, was of the finest steel. The cutting edge was either straight, convex or concave according to individual taste and the fashion of pen cutting.

The blades of French eighteenth-century quill knives were sometimes fixed at a slight angle to the handle to facilitate pen shaping and cutting, a characteristic so far as the author knows confined to France.

John Wilkes, pencutter, writing in 1799, said:

'Those who make their own pens have a great advantage provided they keep their knives in the best order possible, otherwise they can never make a good pen, for unless the knife cuts exceeding smooth the pen will make a ragged stroke. The pen knife should be kept free from dust and damp.

'A good penknife, like a musical instrument, should be kept in the highest state of perfection, more particularly when it is remembered that a really good penknife is a scarce article . . . a hone that will suit a razor would be too soft for a penknife that must attack a hard quill which would break the edge of a razor to pieces. Great care should be taken to set the knife so that it will cut smooth and fine and cut off the point in shaving down the sides. The blade for pen cutting should be set most on the outside (i.e. the right edge looking down on the blade), making it a little convex, but not too much so. If made too keen it breaks and will soon be filled with notches. A plain leather strop will always be found to answer the purpose for stropping.'

Although the quill pen knife varied in shape and material from country to country it seems there were three points agreed upon: viz. the length of the haft or handle, the temper of the steel blade, and the utmost care of the knife, for without a sharp blade no one can cut and shape a quill.

In paintings and reproductions of writing equipment from the sixteenth century onwards three types of knives are often shown: two knives for quill cutting, one of which was used for cutting and shaping the barrel of the quill, the other for the final cutting of the nib. (Many writing masters advised the use of two knives.) The third, a specially shaped eraser knife, was used for preparing the surface of the skin and erasing writing mistakes. The blade of this knife was convex in shape and and had a sharp razor-like edge for scraping.

In the seventeenth and eighteenth centuries those learning to write and cut quill pens were often instructed to clean the pen before re-cutting as the obnoxious acid ingredients of writing inks blunted the edge of the pen knife.

It appears that with the introduction of metal pens in the first quarter of the nineteenth century, the quill pen knife gradually fell into disuse and finally developed into the modern desk knife, used not for quills, but for cutting string and sharpening pencils.

At the first attempt to cut and shape a quill pen, one soon discovers the importance of the knife and that 'it should be kept in the highest state of perfection'. The hard or tough coagulated albumen of which the quill-barrel is composed requires to be cut with a very sharp and properly set blade. The knife for quill cutting should not be put to any other use. The modern types of knives favoured by members of the Society of Scribes and Illuminators include the surgical scalpel, the gardener's budding knife and the chiropodist's pedicure knife. Budding knives can be ordered from any good cutler; surgical scalpels from J. Weiss & Sons, Ltd., 287 Oxford Street, London, W.1; and pedicure knives with fairly wide blades can be obtained from chemists' shops.

To sharpen the knife and set it for quill cutting requires a fine stone (preferably Arkansas Stone) obtainable from a toolmaker's shop or ironmonger. Place the stone flat on the table and, after wetting the surface with a few drops of water, rub with a piece of soap. Soap is preferred to oil as oil adheres to the blade and, if carried on to the quill when cutting, will cause the ink to form in blobs on the pen. Hold the knife in the right hand with the cutting edge towards you, rest the blade on the stone at an angle of 45°, and with a to-and-fro circular movement of the hand form a rounded bevel on the right side edge of the blade. When this is finally obtained, place the blade flat on the stone, but with the back of the blade towards you and, with a to-and-fro movement across the stone, remove any roughnesses and give a final set. Looking at the back of the knife, the blade should now be flat on its left side and be slightly rounded on its right cutting edge. The blade can be further improved by stropping on a leather strop and its sharpness tested on the left thumb nail. If sharp, the blade's edge will catch on the thumbnail, if not it will glide over the surface.

It is desirable that the right cutting edge of the blade should be slightly rounded, for if it is not the knife moves in a jerky manner and the shoulders of the pen are difficult to form. Furthermore, the flatness of the opposite side of the blade facilitates a pleasant slicing movement in the final nibbing of the pen.

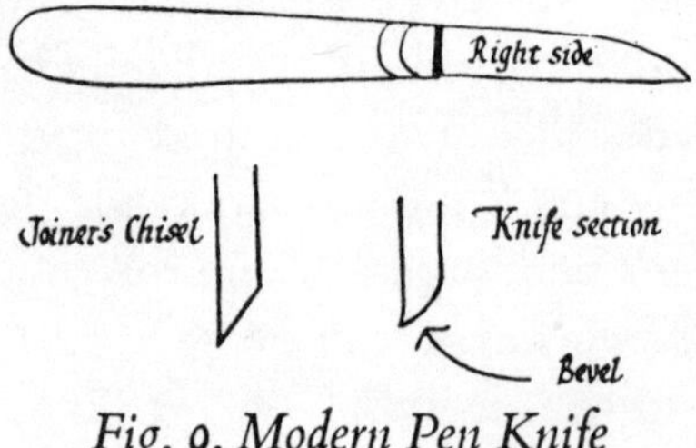

Fig. 9. Modern Pen Knife

QUILL PENS

A quill pen is made principally from the large flight

feathers of birds such as swans, geese and turkeys. It is not known with any degree of certainty when and where the quill pen was first used. In the British Museum there are paintings of Egyptian scribes writing with what appears to be a feather. It is known also that the goose was a very common bird in ancient Egypt and around the Mediterranean, and later in Greece and Rome, and that the Romans also experimented in making pens of metals, with shaft, barrel, nib and slit, all in one piece, similar in shape to a quill, proving that they were well acquainted with the quill pen as a writing instrument (150 B.C.).

It appears safe to assume that the quill pen came into gradual use with the establishment of Roman formal capital letters, of graduated thick and thin strokes, and the supplanting of papyrus by vellum as a writing material about 190 B.C.

In the middle ages, when the quill pen flourished as the principal instrument for writing, different kinds of birds were used to supply the quills of scriveners and scribes in the law-courts and scriptoria of Europe. Mention is made of the pelican, swan, goose, pheasant, eagle, peacock, raven and others. In the course of time pens made from the quills of the swan, goose, turkey, duck, crow and raven came to be accepted as the best for the purpose of writing and drawing. Anserine and gallinaceous birds, which include the swan, goose, and turkey, have the longest-barrelled quills and accordingly the wing feathers from these birds are best suited for pens. The feathers are classified as primaries, secondaries and tertiaries according to the order in which they are fixed in the wing. In the case of the goose and turkey the wings have many flight feathers, but it is usually the five outer wing feathers which are employed for pen making, the remainder being suitable for other commercial purposes. The feathers are termed pinions or firsts, seconds, thirds etc. Sixths and sevenths were sometimes known as flags, and used for fine writing and drawing, as also were the pin feathers of some birds. The seconds and thirds, having the largest and roundest barrels, were usually considered the best for writing.

The shafts of quills which curve to the right when held in the hand for writing are taken from the left wing. Some calligraphers prefer these to the right wing quills which curve to the left. Commercially, the quality of quills is estimated by the size and weight of the barrels, and the term for the weight used is the loth, a German weight of little more than an ounce.

Large bales of quills were imported into England during the eighteenth and nineteenth centuries from various countries including Ireland, Greenland, Iceland, Hudson Bay, Norway, Russia, Poland and Germany. They were sorted according to the length and size of the barrels into primes, seconds and pinions, the best swan and goose quills coming from countries with the coldest climate. For over one hundred years, Hudson Bay goose quills have been well known for their durability and good quality and are distinguished from other quills by their black feathers. Goose and turkey farming in England also supplied thousands of quills for pen making. The time of moulting was considered the best for collecting quills, as the large wing feathers were then in the best condition for making into pens.

The large wing feather of a turkey, swan or goose consists of three parts: (1) the shaft, stalk, stem or scape, (2) the tube, barrel, calamus or quill, and (3) the barbs with their barbules.

In its natural state, the barrel or quill has a greasy external skin or membrane, and an internal pith, and is inclined to be soft. To remedy this, it must first be dressed or cured, by hardening the quill and removing the fatty surface and internal pith. From accounts and documents of the past, preparing the quill for use as a pen by removing the grease and hardening the barrel was an operation carried out individually by the person using the pen. First it was customary to heat the quill in the hot ashes of a fire, and to remove the outer membrane by scraping the barrel of the quill with the back of the pen knife blade, afterwards rubbing smoothly with a piece of woollen cloth or fish skin. Secondly, by wetting the barrel with spittle or water and rubbing vigorously with a piece of fish skin. Or thirdly, by holding the barrel over a charcoal fire and then scraping with a pen knife.

The methods employed were technically called clarifying and dutching.

(1) Clarifying (clearing or making transparent). This consists in removing the outer membrane by rubbing with a piece of coarse material or fish skin and steeping the quills all night in water and then hardening in a pan of hot sand. (This method was formerly used for pens but later used only for tooth picks.)
(2) Steam and hot sandbath.
(3) Hot water and heated stove or oven.
(4) Heated sandbath and friction (scraping).
(5) Dutching (heat and pressure). This method involved the use of a fire enclosed with brick sides and an iron face plate in front having a circular hole about 1½ inches in diameter for thrusting in the quill. A smooth iron or steel plate (heated) and an instrument termed a hook used for applying pressure to the barrel of the quill and scraping off the outer skin.

The following quill-dressing recipes are given to acquaint the reader with some of the methods employed in England and the Continent during the past three hundred years:

1. *Dutching (eighteenth century English)*. The quills are gradually damped either by being placed in a damp cellar for a day or two with the points of the quills in the earth or wrapped in a damp cloth several hours before they are worked upon. A square hole is made in a coal fire in a horizontal direction between the bars about six inches in depth and a proportionate width; the barrel of the quill is then inserted, care being taken that the quill does not touch the fire but

receives the heat alike in all parts of the barrel. When the quill is thus heated (one to two seconds) it is drawn beneath a dutching hook and a thick plate of warm steel with a very smooth surface. This operation takes off that membraneous substance with which the barrel of the quill is covered when in its raw state. The quill is then put in the fire again and the same repeated reversing the position of the barrel. It is then held in the fire again by which means it regains its roundness, the pressing beneath the instrument having flattened it. By these means the grease is extracted and the outer skin removed leaving the quill clear and hard. If before dutching the quills are not sufficiently damp, they are likely to crack on the sides. It requires great attention to give the quill sufficient heat and at the same time to avoid cracking it. After this the quill is rubbed with a piece of the skin of the dog fish to polish it.

2. *Clarifying* (*nineteenth century*). The operation consists in heating the quills in a fine sandbath to 130° to 180° Fahrenheit and scraping them under pressure while still soft from heat whereby the outer skin is removed and the pith shrivelled up. If the quills are kept too long in the sand they become brittle; if too short a time they will not split clear. Finally rub them strongly with a cloth.

3. *Clarifying* (*seventeenth century*). Scrape off the outer film of the quill and cut the ends off, put them in boiling water wherein is a small quantity of alum and salt, let them remain fifteen minutes, then dry them in a hot pan of sand or in an oven.

Of the methods employed, dutching seemed to be most favoured for pens. Quills were sometimes dyed in turmeric acid but it appeared to serve no useful purpose except to add to the cost. The barrels of the quills were often rubbed smooth with a cloth and pumice powder.

To prepare quills at home tie them loosely in a bundle, place them in a steamer of boiling water so that the quills are not touching the water, put on the lid and steam for one hour.

Take out and dry by a warm fire. Next day scrape the barrels with the back of a pen knife and rub smoothly with a piece of woollen cloth. Leave several days before using.

Another method is to hold the quill horizontally by the feather so that the barrel is parallel to and about 1½ inches from an electric fire bar. Keep turning the quill so that the heat is applied evenly to the barrel for about eight to ten seconds. (This softens the quill and shrivels up the pith and surface membrane.) Holding the feather in the left hand, place the quill quickly on the hot plate and pull the barrel beneath the back edge of a pen knife held in the right hand. This flattens and scrapes off the film. Turn the barrel and scrape again. Do not scrape too much otherwise you thin the barrel of the quill. The quill can be cut into a pen almost immediately or left to dry and harden and cut later. If cut immediately one can feel the quill hardening under the knife. The slit is put in last. If done earlier when the quill is soft the slit becomes irregular.

For the plate a smooth piece of steel or iron four inches square and half an inch thick can be heated to a moderate heat over a regulated gas ring. An inverted circular sponge cake tin, which should be held fast, will also serve as a plate. Finally, rub the barrel smooth with a piece of woollen or linen cloth, tie the quills into a bundle and leave to allow the cool air to circulate. Time helps to harden the quills.

CUTTING QUILLS

Edward Johnston, in a letter[1] dated 5th April, 1933, addressed to the late Colonel J. C. H. Crosland, and now in the possession of Alfred Fairbank, writing upon the question of the uncut quill states:

'My experience is not great, but, as since the war it has been more difficult to buy good ready-cut quills, I have got the

[1] Reprinted here by permission of Mrs. P. Gill.

local poulterer to save a bundle of turkey's pen feathers, and have succeeded in making quite satisfactory pens of these.

'I hang up the bundle of feathers (as it is my fancy that they are better for some drying or shrinking—I think *Cocker* says something about *warm ashes*, but slow, "natural" processes are usually safest for the ignorant—and perhaps for the "cunning" as well: I have not proved this fancy by contrary experiment). The quills have usually had about a year's drying, or more, when I cut them.

'1st. I cut off the unwanted length (p. 54).[1]

'2nd. I strip off the barbs (pp. 54–5). Note: this is more easily done by holding them between the *blade* edge *and the thumb* than between finger and thumb as shewn in fig. 26.

'3rd. I scrape off the horny surface—almost like a skin which appears to surround the quill and stick to it very closely. I have noticed that although the end of the pen feather may *look* quite clean and ready, unless this horny skin—or surface—is thoroughly scraped off—or at least well scraped—the pen will usually not split satisfactorily; in fact it is apt to shew a ragged tear in this surface substance or skin, while the "slit" (beneath the surface) appears to be diverted or interrupted.

'I assume the structure of the quill to consist of an inner longitudinally fissile substance and an outer membrane or substance which has a binding effect (i.e. tending to prevent splitting)—comparable to a "wire-wound" gun barrel (if that is the correct expression) or to the remarkable anticipation of that construction to be found in "Mons Meg" in Edinburgh Castle.

'4th. I cut off the end and shape and make the slit exactly as shewn in figs. 17–21 (pp. 52–3) in the cutting of the *cane* pen.

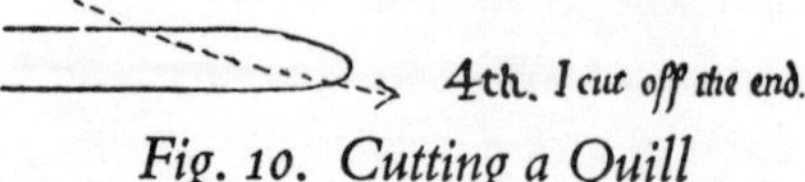

Fig. 10. Cutting a Quill

[1] Edward Johnston, *Writing, Illuminating and Lettering*, Pitman, London, 1929.

'5th. But, *before the final edge cut* (fig. 22) in both cane and quill I hollow out the sides of the tip to give this shape

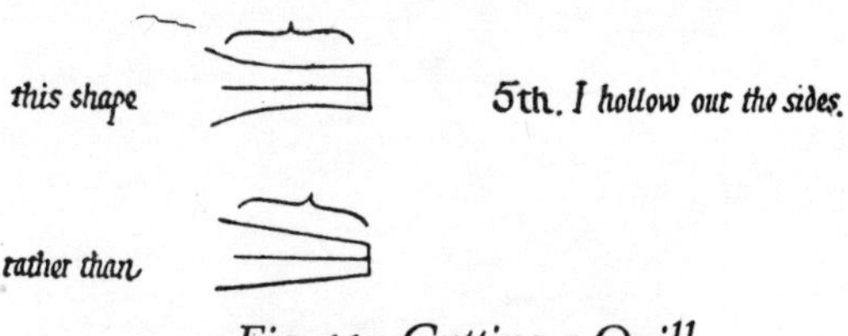

Fig. 11. Cutting a Quill

rather than making it approximately parallel sided and
'6th. Cut a long bevel (compare b. fig. 36) and

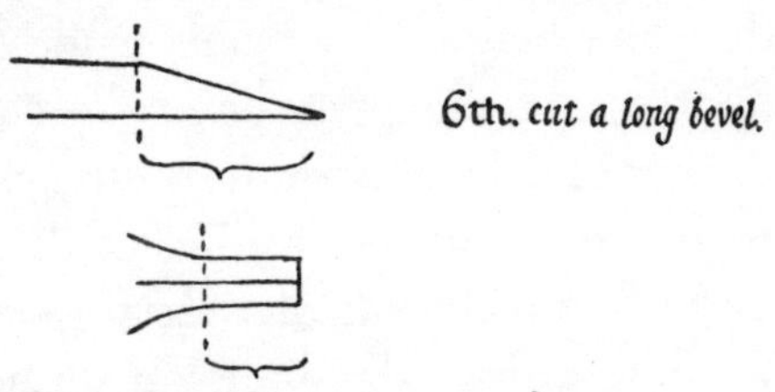

Fig. 12. Cutting a Quill

'7th. Finally cut the nibs-edge (vertically) getting a shape which in side section might be indicated (much magnified) thus . . .

'The *thickness* of the edge (*a*) is so slight that it does not count as long as the true edge (*b*) remains sharp (which sharpness is as necessary, and no more lasting in perfection in a thicker nib).

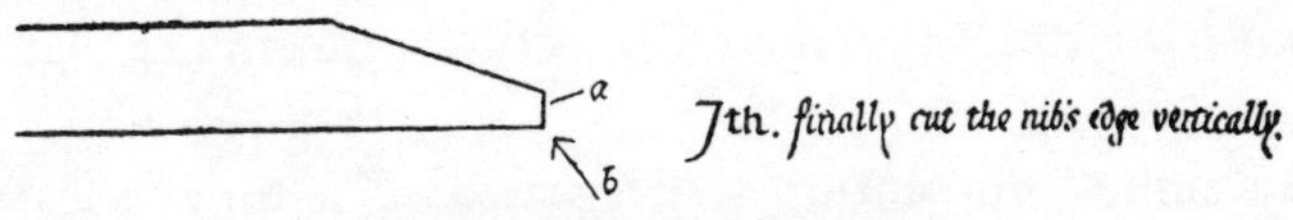

Fig. 13. Cutting a Quill

'The great advantage of this long bevel is that the ink which oozes out of the tip is kept well away from the paper. (*c*) is less likely to ink the thin strokes too heavily than the blunt-bevelled pen may (*d*).

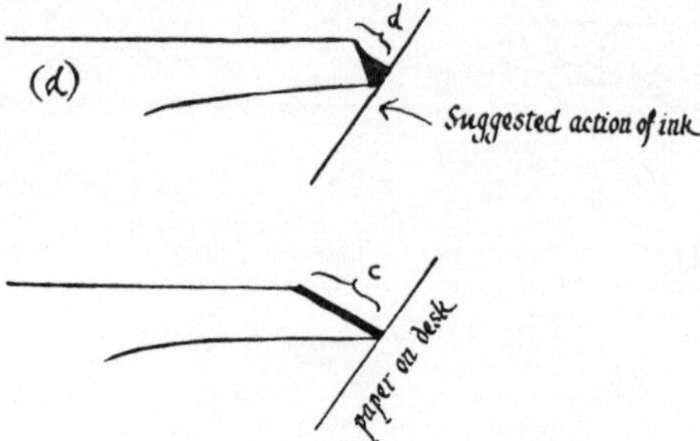

Fig. 14. The Final Bevel

'It has another advantage, that being made by the long bevel, very thin, the nibs edge may be finally cut with great ease and little danger of distortion of the quill (or cane).

'To revert to my 4th, and the making of the slit (I think that you will not find much difficulty after good scraping) I make a *short* slit with a thin edge knife—a surgical scalpel is good—lengthen it, preferably by a jerk with a lever (fig. 27), and sometimes by pressing up both sides with my fingers. In any case it is best to make the split go back pretty far and cut away from the front part all of it in which the slit remains, or tends to remain, open.

'The best rule for length of slit is as long *as is compatible with strength* (i.e. as long as possible).

'For the shaping of the pen, a proper pen cutting blade is most desirable; this professional pen knife is *quite* flat of *even hollow-ground to keep it so on the left side*, and on the "right" side it has a bevel (i.e. the cross section V resembles that of a joiner's chisel).'

An eighteenth-century writer stated: 'The time to learn to make a pen is when you learn to write. The ability of using and the knowledge of making a pen should always go together, he who cuts the grass should be able to whet his scythe.'

Professional quill cutters of the past usually described by diagrammatic sketches the order and number of cuts employed in making a pen. Quill pens from law stationers and art shops are sold cut for ordinary use. Edward Johnston in his book, *Writing, Illuminating and Lettering*, deals fully with the method of re-cutting these pens for 'careful writing'.

The order of cutting a complete quill is as follows:

(1) Hold the quill in the left hand with the feather away from you and with the pen knife in the right hand cut about ¼ of an inch of the back of the quill slopingly to the point.

(2) Slightly scrape the back of the quill with the pen knife, and make the slit.

(3) Reverse the quill and cut the underneath cradle somewhat longer than the first cut about half-way through the barrel—too much weakens the quill.

(4) With the cradle of the barrel uppermost shoulder the right side.

(5) Reverse the quill and shoulder the left side equally to the right side, taking care to make the nib the width of the stroke required. It was considered necessary only with undressed quills to scrape the back of the barrel where the slit was to be made.

(6) Nib the pen.

The cutting slab for nibbing the pen should be smooth and flat, of a size about 1 in. × 1 in. × ¼ in. Too soft a substance causes the cut of the nib's edge to sink into the slab. If instead of placing the cutting slab at the table's edge it is glued or fixed to a piece of thicker wood of similar shape more freedom is allowed for the fingers to nib the pen.

The order of the cuts in making a pen has varied throughout the centuries. It was customary in the middle ages for the first cut to be made slopingly to the point on the underneath part of the barrel, so making the pen with a small cradle, which in this manner was better for holding the ink.

The short incision for the slit can be done in one of several ways:

(1) By holding the pen perpendicularly and making a short cut with the knife blade where the nib will be formed.

(2) By resting the top of the quill on the cutting slab and making a small incision with the point of the pen knife.

(3) In the same manner as (2), above, but using a safety razor blade (M. C. Oliver's recommendation). The slit is lengthened by inserting in the barrel the end of another quill, or brush handle, or the pointed end of a pen knife handle and twitching upwards with the right hand whilst the left thumb nail presses hard on the top of the quill at the point to which the slit is to extend.

When the shoulders of the pen are shaped, the slit can be extended by twitching upwards with the right thumb nail, or by flicking sharply the first or second finger of the right hand upwards against the nibs. The slit should be neither too long nor too short but just sufficient to allow the capillary attraction of the ink.

Quill pens of the following types are usually made in the sizes indicated:

SWAN—small, medium, large.
GOOSE—small, medium, large.
TURKEY—medium, large.
DUCK—yellow-tipped.

They can be obtained cut or uncut from Henry Hill & Sons, Swan Works, Brook Road, Hornsey, London, N.8.

Although somewhat greasy, swan quills are suitable for large letter forms and, for those who like its bigger barrel, are firmer; whilst for general purposes turkey quills are best. Small goose and duck are used for fine writing and drawing. As duck quills are small and difficult to hold, the barrels can be cut off and a piece of wood suitably shaped, inserted as a holder, making the part you hold larger in circumference than that in the barrel. For the purpose of holding comfortably these smaller quills Colonel Crosland recommended the use of a small bamboo or reed. The barrel of the small quill was cut off and inserted securely into the pith of the bamboo or reed.

REED AND BAMBOO PENS

Reed and bamboo pens are obtained principally from the Near East and India, in which parts of the world they are still in use.

Reed pens are of great value for writing on vellum and parchment where the size of the writing required is beyond the range of a quill pen. As reed pens are softer in substance than quills, and more readily obtainable, some scribes advise learning to cut a reed before a quill pen. Reeds can be obtained from the marshlands and riversides of England. They should be cut and allowed to dry before using. Reed pens from India and the Near East can be purchased from artists' colourmen, whilst thin hollow 'canes' used for training young plants can be obtained from seed shops and corn chandlers. They are invaluable for learning the shapes of letter forms, whether straight pen or slanted pen.

One can cut a reed pen with cradle and shoulders in one slice, and slit as a quill. If soaked in water for ten minutes before nibbing reeds will be found to hold ink and colour more readily. For various purposes, one can use many plant stems for writing on different surfaces. Colonel Crosland often used stems of elder for writing out garden labels on wood.

Large bamboo pens which are hard and tough can be partly shaped with a wood chisel, and finally cut with a pen knife.

Plant stems vary in their usefulness as pens because of the fibrous substances of which they are composed; it is wise, therefore, to experiment and attempt to discover those which are of most use in the art of fine writing.

II

Pigments and Media

PIGMENTS[1]

Since the days of the prehistoric cave-painter the search for colouring matter has continued throughout the ages. Whether the final products have improved in richness of hue and depth of tone is open to question. The tendency at the present day is to produce pigments by chemical means rather than from organic sources, and in the latter case to grind by machinery rather than by hand and indeed to cease to prepare those rare pigments of exquisite beauty where the demand is deemed insufficient to justify the labour involved. The illuminator is forced to select his palette from what is available.

Pigments are either:

(1) of organic origin
- (*a*) from plants, e.g. indigo, obtained from the roots of a plant in India.
- (*b*) from animals, e.g. ivory black, obtained from the soot of burnt bones.

(2) of inorganic (mineral) origin
- (*a*) from natural sources, e.g. the earths (raw sienna, yellow ochre, etc.)
- (*b*) from those artificially produced, e.g. cobalt, viridian, French ultramarine.

[1] An asterisk denotes those colours recommended for general use owing to their brilliance and stability.

[ ] Pigments almost unobtainable but recorded for their practical interest.

These classifications are of interest rather than of importance to the scribe. From whatever source the pigments are produced the illuminator requires of them the following qualifications:

1. They should not fade. They should withstand the action of sunlight, and here the calligrapher of the bound book has the advantage over the writer of the framed panel in that his work is not likely to be, and certainly should not be, exposed to direct sunlight at one opening for any considerable time.

2. They should not discolour or darken. This might occur either through the chemical action of the pigment itself, the combining of two incompatible pigments, the introduction of an unsuitable preservative, or the effect of the atmosphere.

3. They should be brilliant of hue and of a luminous quality.

4. They should be free from impurities, dirt, mould, 'doctorings' or fillings.

5. They should be very finely ground, smooth and tractable, having that fluid quality sensed by the hand when mixing them with their medium.

6. When possible they should be of an opaque nature. This desirable property dispenses with the addition of Chinese white which tends towards 'muddy' results.

The leading artists' colourmen supply 'first quality' powder (levigated) colours: it is, however, wise for the scribe to know something of the nature of these pigments. For example, if he cares for the durability of his work he should realize the following facts: that vermilion, cadmium and French ultramarine contain sulphur, either inherent or through the process of manufacture; that owing to the presence of sulphur they are prone to discolour or blacken when in contact with an acid; that therefore both medium and preservative must be free from acid. Should he also be so fortunate as to possess powdered azurite or malachite he should remember that they will undoubtedly fade or discolour unless enclosed within a suitable and acid-free binding. The medieval scribes were aware of these facts, indeed many references to the appropriate tempering of the differing pigments occur in their books of recipes.

The extensive variety of pigments available may bewilder the student. It is wise, however, for him to restrict his palette to a few dominating colours, for uses on title-pages, in headings, for initials and rubrics, and later to extend his range when exploring the infinite possibilities of decoration and miniatures. A well-planned book will have a system in colour throughout, even as it has a system in lettering; this plan in colour statement will contribute towards unity and dignity. It is as well, therefore, to fix on a red, a blue and a green and adhere to them consistently throughout the work on hand, with perhaps a subsidiary colour to form a liaison. Should gold be used it should be considered here as a colour, in which case the colour scheme should be simplified to avoid over-elaboration of effect. Blue in conjunction with gold frequently looks better than vermilion with gold, which sometimes gives a 'hot' appearance, though on such matters it is unwise to dogmatize. Colour illusion and the complimentary shades of red to green, blue to orange and yellow to violet should, however, be recognized, for the illuminator may be presented on occasions with such problems. As an instance, he may be painting a coat of arms with the shield quarterly red and blue with gold charges; the vermilion will take on a pinkish hue and the blue a purplish, requiring careful adjustment. Always it should be remembered that colour is not absolute but relative, varying with its surroundings.

The following brief list of pigments is suggested from which to select an adequate palette. Other colours are on the market and could be used if they conform to the requirements already stated. Three colours, genuine ultramarine, azurite and malachite are recorded as valuable pigments though the supply is negligible.

REDS

**Vermilion.* This is a compound of mercury and sulphur. It can well be considered a basic pigment for the illuminator, as it unites most of the desirable qualifications; it is intense, brilliant, opaque, tractable and reasonably permanent. The method of manufacture has altered little since the eighth century A.D. It is obtainable in several shades—in vermilion, scarlet vermilion, orange vermilion and Chinese vermilion; this latter, being the deepest shade, is considered the more reliable. Scarlet vermilion is that variety most favoured by scribes, but a mixture of vermilion and orange vermilion is also good. If desired, a little Chinese white may be added for extra body. The brilliance of hue diminishes slightly when the pigment dries. Vermilion should not be exposed to direct sunlight owing to a tendency for black spots to appear, nor should it lie adjacent to emerald green, a 'copper' colour, as the edges of the vermilion may blacken. With these reservations it remains the outstanding pigment for the scribe's use.

Cadmium red. Modern improvements in the reliability of this pigment make it a possible substitute for vermilion should the latter be unobtainable. Containing sulphur, it, like vermilion, is liable to blacken when next to emerald green.

Alizarin crimson. This modern product, a coal-tar derivative, is reasonably permanent and hence replaces the vegetable madders and crimson lake of doubtful stability. Carmine, of cochineal origin, will unfortunately discolour rapidly when exposed to light.

Venetian red and light red. Both pigments are native 'earths' containing iron oxide; like most earths they are permanent to light.

BLUES

Of all colours blue was the most highly prized by the medieval scribes. Neither expense nor effort was spared in its production. It was the colour for the Virgin's robe, the colour for the celestial firmament. Numerous references to blue pigments occur in the medieval books of recipes, and the subject has been extensively dealt with by Professor D. V. Thompson.[1] The two mainly in use in medieval times were genuine ultramarine (lapis lazuli) and azurite (azzurro della magna). It is unfortunate that both colours are almost unobtainable today. Other blues formerly in use were indigo and bice, of which latter little is known.

Genuine ultramarine. This rich pigment is made by grinding and purifying the semi-precious stone lapis lazuli. The supply has come exclusively from Persia since the earliest times but recipes for its manufacture in Europe date only from the twelfth century A.D. Even as at present produced it possesses a deep intensity of hue and is to be recommended for work of special importance. Should the colour appear purplish a touch of black or viridian with white may improve it.

Azurite (blue verditer). Is a native copper carbonate. The late Graily Hewitt stated that this true blue was mainly in use between A.D. 1250 and A.D. 1400; it is frequently referred to in documents and ranked next to ultramarine in value. It is a colour of peculiar beauty of hue, being neither too green nor too purple if correctly ground. At the present day, as sold in pans, tubes or cakes, it is useless, the colour having been destroyed owing to the presence of acid, and for this reason the artists' colourmen no longer stock the ground pigment. Should it, however, be both correctly ground and rightly tempered with parchment size free from acid the result appears to be entirely satisfactory.

Ultramarine ash, is a delicately pale blue containing frag-

[1] Daniel V. Thompson, Jr., *The Materials of Medieval Painting*, George Allen & Unwin Ltd., London, 1936.

ments of lapis lazuli and can be used if strengthened by the addition of another blue, such as prussian blue.[1]

**Artificial or French ultramarine*. First produced in France in 1828 this pigment has proved a useful substitute for genuine ultramarine. It is light-resisting but owing to the use of sulphur in its manufacture it may discolour in the presence of acid. Its purplish tinge can be moderated by the addition of viridian or cerulean and Chinese white.

Cobalt blue. This is permanent, but by itself is somewhat insipid for the piercing colours required in illuminating.

**Cerulean* is reliable and permanent and of considerable body. At full strength it has a somewhat greenish metallic appearance but should a purplish blue be mixed with it a pleasing result may be obtained.

Prussian blue. This pigment is not generally considered permanent and therefore should not be used by itself.

Indigo is a fine deep colour, which for artists' purposes is still produced from the root of a plant, but is known to be fugitive.

Monastral blue. This being a dye is scarcely suitable for the scribe's use. The colour tends to streakiness and has a metallic tinge.

The following *Mixed Blues* are here recommended though all, being mixed with white, suffer from a degree of muddiness:

(i) French ultramarine + viridian + Chinese (zinc) white
(ii) French ultramarine + viridian + a little black + Chinese (zinc) white
(iii) French ultramarine + viridian + a little alizarin crimson + Chinese (zinc) white
(iv) French ultramarine + cerulean + Chinese (zinc) white.

These four mixed blues have been recorded as used in recent manuscripts by members of the Society of Scribes and Illuminators.

[1] Edward Johnston, *Writing, Illuminating and Lettering*, chap. 10, Pitman, 1906.

GREENS

Emerald green. A basic copper arsenite, was first made in 1788. This intense colour is highly poisonous. It will blacken any adjacent sulphur colour such as vermilion and French ultramarine. It should only be used by itself.

**Emerald oxide of chromium or viridian.* This most useful pigment has no connection with emerald green. It is both brilliant in hue and permanent to light. Being transparent it requires the addition of lemon yellow, an opaque pigment, or aureolin with Chinese white, to give it body.

Malachite is a carbonate of copper. This splendid and luminous colour, which is usually found in mineral deposits close to azurite was much used by medieval scribes. Being both brilliant and translucent it is to be preferred to emerald green which it resembles. Owing to the cost of grinding it is almost impossible to obtain and, like its copper neighbour azurite, must be tempered with size when applied.

Cobalt green. This light green is slightly heavy and gritty; when mixed with lemon yellow it has a useful body. It is permanent.

Monastral green is a dye and as such not highly suitable. It has, however, been used with some success mixed with cerulean and white.

Verdigris is fugitive, and *terre verte*, though useful for the modelling of flesh, has little strength of colour.

PURPLES

The somewhat raucous purple known today has no place in the medieval manuscript. Sometimes a mixture of blue and red was used but among the more frequent variants were brazil wood, haematite and even whelks. For present-day use, indian red with white or purple madder with white is advocated. Indian red is an iron oxide and is therefore akin to haematite. The shades, however, vary considerably; the one recommended is the pre-war product which changes to a subtle lavender when white is added. Lettering in this colouring, used with discretion, forms a harmonious liaison between blue and vermilion on a page. Indian red as supplied to-day appears to be merely a deeper shade of Venetian red.

Cobalt violet resembles purple ink and is to be avoided as a colour though reliable as a pigment.

YELLOWS AND BROWNS

The various earth pigments of *yellow ochre*, the *siennas* and the *umbers* are permanent but are too heavy and dull for use except in decoration or miniature work. *Vandyke Brown* is fugitive.

**Lemon yellow*, possessing body, is a useful clean yellow for adding to viridian or white. Some scribes prefer *aureolin*, though more transparent. Both are safe colours. *Gamboge* is impermanent. *Chromes* are made from lead and will blacken.

BLACKS

**Ivory black, lamp black and vine black* (*charcoal*), are each satisfactory. They consist of carbon obtained in the form of soot from burnt objects, such as bones, oil or vine shoots.

WHITES

**Chinese white* (*zinc*) is permanent to light and will not darken. To obliterate the bluish shade when painting fine lines and dots a touch of lemon yellow can be added. Being smooth of texture Chinese white mixes well with other pigments.

Titanium white, of recent discovery, possesses considerable covering power. It is a compound of titanium oxide and barium sulphate, the proportion of these being worked out to obtain the maximum density and permanence. It is non-poisonous, and is supposed neither to be affected by acids nor darkened by sulphur compounds and gases.

Flake white should never be used; it is composed of lead and will quickly 'brown' when exposed to sulphur.

In the interests of the craft it is emphasized that only first-class colours should be used; tints, dyes, coloured inks, 'process white' and poster colours are unsuitable for use.

This survey of pigments for the use of the scribe and illuminator is merely a sketch; for further information the reader must refer to books mentioned in the bibliography. While of necessity the writer must warn against the attendant dangers to the various pigments, the executant should not be unduly apprehensive, though always avoiding those known to be unstable.

Artists' colourmen recommended

Messrs. Chas. Roberson & Co. Ltd., 71 Parkway, London, N.W.1.

Messrs Lechertier Barbe Ltd., 95 Jermyn Street, London, S.W.1.

Messrs Winsor & Newton Ltd., 51/52 Rathbone Place, London, W.1.

Messrs George Rowney & Co. Ltd., 10 & 11 Percy Street, London, W.1.

MEDIA[1]

Having the requisite information as to which pigments are suitable for use, the problem for the illuminator is in what form to buy them and how to apply them. First-quality colours should be purchased from one of the leading artists' colourmen, who supply them in:

(*a*) Tubes
(*b*) Pans
(*c*) Cakes
(*d*) Powder 'levigated' colours.

[1] Unless otherwise stated all methods mentioned of tempering pigments have been used by the author.

Water colours, ready for use, contained in tubes or pans, though convenient in form, include in their composition a percentage of glycerine. This glycerine, owing to its hygroscopic nature, is liable to attract mould on vellum. Better than tubes or pans are the old-fashioned 'cake' colours which are bound together by gum. Chinese white should be purchased in a bottle or in a tube, which thus provides protection from extraneous colouring matter. Cleanliness in all details should be observed if brilliance of hue is to be obtained. Cake colours should rest each in its own saucer, and when not in use be covered from dust. The main colours of red, blue and green should have their own brushes, palettes and waterjars. For tubes, pans and cakes no medium except water is required, and the beginner is therefore free to struggle with the preliminaries of the craft whilst employing these simple methods.

Coloured drawing inks are unsuitable for the scribe, being transparent and thin.

The application of colour by the pen presents some difficulties not experienced when using ink, the colour being inclined on the one hand to dry and thicken in the quill's slit and thus not to flow, and on the other to flood to the base of the letters, giving uneven tone. To overcome these troubles, the pen should be frequently wiped with a clean rag, the tin strip removed altogether, whilst the desk angle should be greatly reduced. For versals the quill's slit should be lengthened. Right judgment for maintaining the colour's consistency will develop with experience, but a rich, milky texture is generally found good.

As the beginner proceeds it is right that he should make his own medium for his colours. His knowledge of his materials will thus grow, and the brilliancy and clarity of the illumination to which he aspires will then increase. He should purchase finely levigated powder colours. A reliable artists' colourman will supply any pigment on the market in powder form made up in glass test tubes. For convenience these can be kept in a flat box (e.g. cigar box) lined with cotton wool to avoid glass breakage. They may even be separated with advantage into two boxes, one to contain the 'cool' colours (blue, green, black and white), the other the 'warm' colours (red, yellow, brown).

Implements required will be a palette knife (ivory rather than steel, and one not previously used for oil painting), a frosted glass mixing slab, a small glass muller, and a china receptacle to hold each colour when mixed. An excellent form of china palette contains a number of small wells with a covering lid to keep colours both clean and moist. If no lid is provided a piece of glass will serve. Plastic and enamel palettes are available but china ones are to be preferred. A glass stopper, or agate pestle, is also required.

Whatever vehicle is used for binding, the powdered pigment must be completely and permanently enclosed within it, otherwise the colour when dry will dust off. Nor must the medium be too tenacious or it will shrink and crack the pigment as it dries. Experience rather than accurate measurement will dictate the correct strength.

The manner of mixing the medium and the pigment can be either:

(1) To shake out a very small quantity of the powder colour on to the frosted side of the glass slab. Add whatever medium is to be used, and grind gently by a circular movement with the glass muller. Remove this mixture with a palette knife, transferring it to a small jar or china well, or

(2) The powder colour can be placed in a china well and some of the medium dropped on top of it. With the glass stopper or agate pestle the powder colour and medium are thoroughly mixed. Should the powdered pigment be sufficiently ground by the maker this procedure is more economical of pigment, the transfer operation being omitted.

In either case the mixture, if covered, will remain liquid from a few hours to two days according to the day's temperature, and should be stirred as used.

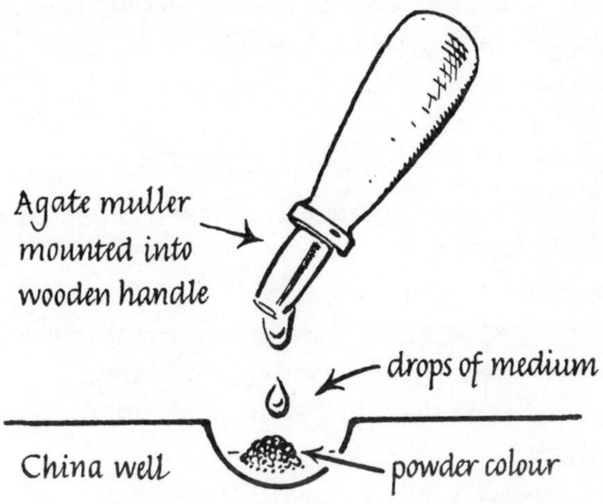

Fig. 15. Mixing Medium and Pigment

For the calligrapher's purpose the following binding materials are sufficient to temper pigments on vellum: gum, or egg, or glue or parchment size. All these binders were used in the great period of medieval illumination, sometimes indeed a mixture of two together. On this subject much light has been thrown by Professor D. V. Thompson Jr.[1] in his reprints and translations of old manuscripts and by his comments thereon. It should be remembered that whatever be the vehicle employed each medium gives its own inherent quality to the work, that of egg differing from gum, and gum from size. It remains for the practitioner to discover his individual preference, unless the pigment dictates otherwise.

GUM

The use of gum is the simplest of the methods here suggested. It is known to have been used in manuscripts as early

[1] See Bibliography.

as the eleventh century and by the sixteenth century it was superseding other methods.

Gum-water is required. This product as sold by the artists' colourman is likely to contain acid as a mould deterrent, and this may eventually harm both 'sulphur' and 'copper' colours. The following recipe is therefore given:

Gum-Water:

1 part gum arabic (or senegal). For this choose clear, clean crystals.

2 parts water.

Leave to dissolve, next day strain through muslin, add a small amount of a preservative which must be acid-free.

(Suggested Preservative: 5% Beta Naphthol dissolved in boiling water.)

This gum-water solution when kept in a glass jar with glass or wooden top can be used as needed diluted with water to the required strength.

Method. Mix in an egg-cup water and gum-water. Proportions may be $\frac{1}{3}$ water to $\frac{2}{3}$ gum-water varying to $\frac{2}{3}$ water to $\frac{1}{3}$ gum-water. Experience will decide. If the gum is too strong the colour will not flow easily in the pen and will crack or curl off the vellum. On the other hand if it is too weak the pigment will not be held by the medium and the powder will dust off. A trial should be made by passing the finger over the test specimen. Once made this gum medium can be mixed with colour by either of the methods previously described, either on a glass slab or in a china well. It is a clean, clear medium, but has two slight disadvantages: first, it is not waterproof and should another coat be painted over it, as may occur in miniature work, the ground coat will 'move'; and secondly, the medium is inclined to be brittle and crack. Early recipes suggest the slightest addition of sugar or honey.[1]

[1] This addition of sugar or crystalline honey can be added plain or as a solution. The solution, as recommended in the anonymous fourteenth-century

EGG

(1) *Glair* (*white of egg or 'clarea'*). It is known that this medium was largely employed from the eleventh to the thirteenth centuries. The process of making the 'glair' was similar to that given by the fourteenth-century monk Cennino Cennini,[1] but is quoted here from the translation by Prof. D. V. Thomson, Jr. of a fragmentary treatise written at least two hundred years earlier.[2]

Method. 'Both colour and glair, therefore, should always be handled very neatly; nor are beautiful things made by any other means than by clarifying and selecting the preparations. Now if you mean to handle them so, have a very clean platter in which you may always prepare the glair . . . reserved for this alone . . . prepare furthermore a whisk . . . when you are ready . . . you separate the white of the egg from the yolk;[3] and placing the white on the platter you beat that white of egg strongly, unintermittently . . . until it is converted as it were into a water froth or into the likeness of snow and sticks to the platter, and loses the power of running or shifting in any direction, even if you turn it bottom side up, that is, the bottom of the platter on top and the glair underneath. But still you should know this: that if you were to beat it seven or ten times, in beating or whipping the glair,

treatise, *De Arte Illuminandi*, chap. 19, translated by Professor D. V. Thompson, Jr., can be rendered thus:

1 tablespoon crystalline honey.

2 tablespoons water—boil gently, skimming off the froth as it appears. When clear add 2 more tablespoons of water and boil. Remove to cool. Add 1 teaspoonful 'glair' to which previously has been added 1 dessertspoonful water. Stir well. Return to boil, continue to remove froth. When clear and about the same quantity as at first, remove and strain into a small pot.

(Acknowledgments to A. V. H.)

[1] *The Book of the Art of Cennino Cennini*, chap. 131. Trans. Christiana J. Herringham, George Allen & Unwin Ltd., 1899, see *Il libro dell' Arte de Cennino d'Andrea Cennino*. Trans. Daniel J. Thompson Jr., New Haven, U.S.A., 1933.

[2] 'De Clarea' of the so-called anonymous Bernensis MS. Berne A 91.17. A fragmentary extract from a lost work of the second half of the eleventh century. Trans. D. V. Thompson Jr., 1932.

[3] Here the thread or chicken of the white would be removed.

after it sticks to the platter it would be improved. Indeed that insufficient beating of the glair proves a pitfall to many; and when it is whipped too little it becomes practically a glue and when mixed with colour it makes that colour run like a thread, and the colour is utterly ruined, and cannot even flow from the writer's pen without great difficulty; and when it is laid on parchment, it appears very unsightly. . . .'

The plate is then sloped, and the next day the liquid, now distilled, is poured into a vessel. It will keep a few days, then thicken and dry up. A small amount of honey or sugar solution or size can be added to counteract its strong contractile power. The author of *De Arte Illuminandi* recommends glair as the medium for vermilion with a touch of honey and earwax added.

2. *Glair and gum.* The following recipe from the fifteenth-century Strasbourg MS. translated by Lady Herringham[1] is contributed in practical form by Miss Ida Henstock:

Method. 'To the liquid from one white of egg (after beating stiffly and leaving overnight to run off) add ½ teaspoon gum arabic, ½ teaspoon French white wine vinegar; dissolve and strain. Add ¼ teaspoon sal ammoniac previously dissolved in a minimum amount of warm water; strain. In use it should be diluted with distilled water.'

The medium lends clarity and purity to the colours; it will work well in thin gradations and is excellent for finest white hair lines.

3. *Yolk of egg. Method.* Make a hole at either end of the egg to allow the white to run out, carefully pierce the sac containing the yolk which then escapes without skin or 'chicken'. To this add water varying from one third to twice its quantity as experience dictates. Mix well with a wooden instrument, strain through muslin.

Although pleasant to manipulate, this medium is more

[1] Lady Herringham, *Notes on Medieval Methods: Explanation of the Tempera Painting of the Trattato*. George Allen & Unwin Ltd., London, 1899.

suited to decoration and miniature work than to lettering, being liable to thicken in the pen slit. Any yellow tinge from the yolk quickly disappears. Caution should be observed in the consistency of the medium, for excess of fatness gives a greasy appearance. It is excellent for any modelling, giving solidity to the form, and the underpainting will not move.

Though tender until dry, it finally becomes hard and tough.

GLUE AND SIZE

1. *Fish glue.* The late Allan Vigers, the illuminator, successfully used Lepage's fish glue as a medium. Mr. Graily Hewitt writes of his manner of handling:

Method. 'He took clean saucers for his several colours and put little mounds of powder colour thereon and glue as he reckoned enough; mixed water with these, guessing how much, stirred up and made brush trials of results; and let these dry. Then with a brush and plain water he made some brush strokes and again let these dry. Then with his finger through a clean handkerchief he rubbed the strokes. If colour came off on the handkerchief he had too little glue and added a little more, till no colour came off. He then of course kept the palette away from dust, and it was all ready for future use when required, when he used a brush and plain water, treated it in fact like a dry cake colour from the shop.'

It must be remembered that there would be a preserving acid, probably either carbolic or acetic acid, in the bought fish glue, and that any 'copper' colours used might be affected. No signs of deterioration, however, are apparent in his panel for the Art Workers' Guild after more than thirty years of exposure to light and damp.

2. *Stale parchment size.* For calligraphers, the many possibilities of this excellent binder have only recently been explored, though its use for painters has been known[1] or

[1] A recent instance appeared in a letter in *The Times*, 16 February, 1931, from Mr. Noel Heaton. 'Some few years ago I had the opportunity of making

suspected from early days. References to the use of size in medieval recipes are few and vague. Size used sufficiently warm for fluidity inevitably cockles the vellum.[1] In 1933 a valuable extract appeared from *The Art of Limming* 1573 in a note on *De Arte Illuminandi*:[2]

'Sett the sise . . . in some seller or shadowyd place, or under the earthe where it may stand moyste by the space of vii daies untill it be perfecte clammy and rotten . . . and you shall wel understand that al the sises the elder they be and the more clammy, and rotten they be, the better they be.'

A few years after the publication of *De Arte Illuminandi* Mr. A. Victor Hughes writes in his manuscript volume 'For his Children's Guidance':[3]

'But if parchment size does go bad that does not mean that its usefulness is at an end, for it goes liquid and gets more and more sticky as it goes liquid, until finally it attains a condition in which it can be worked as a liquid medium both for colouring and gilding and it is possible that it was used in this state by former craftsmen. If some of the putrid liquid is strained and a little preservative added in that state, it seems to retain the property of size as a medium, without giving rise to further mould or decay. I have experimented with small quantities of "old" size and it appears to me to work exceedingly well and once dried out it does not appear to me to be offensive.'

As the revival of this little-known medium for calligraphy

detailed analysis of some pigments of Chinese paintings from the Stein collection . . . the vehicle used for fixing the pigment was size.' He states that of the seven pigments used one was azurite and another malachite.

[1] In 1921 the writer experienced this difficulty when illuminating Blake's 'Sun descending in the west', though on re-examining the manuscript recently the brilliance of colour appeared so surprising as to encourage further experiments. That size could remain fluid when cold had not then seemed possible.

[2] *De Arte Illuminandi*, note 107, by Prof. D. V. Thompson, Jr. giving extract from *The Art of Limming* fol iir, reproduced in facsimile from the original printed in London 1573. Ann Arbor. Edwards Brothers 1932.

[3] M.S. Book in two parts by A. Victor Hughes. Copies in the possession of the MS. Club.

is in its early stages, its history has been dealt with here at some length.

Method. 'Take a handful of clean parchment shavings cut up small. Place them in a "*bain-marie*"[1]; well cover the shavings with water. Simmer several hours until the water is reduced by at least one third. Strain off through muslin. Next day register the strength with the finger. It should be tough. Leave this in a covered jar in "some seller or shadowyd place". In the course of a few weeks a mould will form on the top. When the mould has made a surface all over decant it back into a pan, add a pinch of Beta Naphthol to the warm liquid,[2] scald the jam jar and filter the hot size back through an old handkerchief folded in four. It should be clear and pink, should stay liquid and become more so, but eventually it will dry up unless water is added now and again. It should last three to five weeks without needing new size.' (A. V. H.)

This size is suitable for many purposes, but should be kept in a moist atmosphere (such as in a bathroom). It is good for use with all pigments. There being no acid in its composition, the 'copper' colours azurite and malachite can safely be used without fear of discoloration, and indeed they are tractable in this medium when not in others. The basis of the medium being parchment, its affinity for the surface on which it is written or painted is obvious. White need rarely be added, as pigments acquire an opaque quality; a mixed muddiness is therefore avoided. If one pigment overlays another the under-coating does not 'move'. It will be noticed that the surface of lettering written with size appears slightly raised, this being specially the case with azurite. To the heraldic artist its value

[1] *Bain-marie:* a vessel containing the substance to be cooked standing within a saucepan of water that boils.

[2] There is however a stage in the ageing of the size, if sufficiently strong and before the mould film appears, when preservative does not appear to be necessary. Indeed if the pinkish colour caused by Beta Naphthol is objected to, the risk can be taken of omitting the preservative altogether provided the liquid appears clear. It is important that the size should be very strong before it is permitted to liquefy.

is considerable as the pigment so mixed will lie happily on a gold surface. To the gilder on vellum it offers surprising possibilities.

In addition to the media of gum, egg and glue, *casein milk* and *starch* can be used but these are more generally required for wall decoration or for commercial purposes than for the craft of lettering and illuminating.

A few additional points should be considered regarding all media for use on vellum.

I. OFFSETTING

If by misadventure colours offset from insufficient strength of any of the binding media here considered, size or glair, weakened by water, can be painted over the offending part, taking care that the liquid is not so strong as to give an ugly gloss. A binding medium which is too weak is less of an evil than one too strong, which may cause cracking.

2. CONSISTENCY OF PIGMENT

A thick chalky substance is not only unsightly but unwise, as the late Professor E. W. Tristram wrote: 'the thinner the pigment applied the better, because the tension, contraction, and pull of the pigment are less when it is thin. If the vehicle—gum or size—is too strong and the pigment too thick it will pull away from the ground. Contraction is reduced by mixing sugar or honey or glycerine with the vehicle.'

3. APPLICATION OF COLOUR

For miniature work on vellum it is advisable to use the colours in a dryish consistency and apply by stippling. A wash on vellum is difficult to manipulate.

4. PRESERVATIVES

The purpose of a preservative is to destroy bacteriological and also fungoid growth, though not all bacteria are harmful. Preservatives which guard against one growth may not be effective against another. It is better to use no preservative than one harmful to a pigment. As a precautionary measure vellum should be kept in a dry room, being sensitive to damp which nourishes mildew. When tempering powder colours with egg (glair or yolk), for immediate use, a preservative is unnecessary, as the medium will dry out hard and tough. The liquid yolk of egg medium without preservative will last three to four days, and will then thicken and become useless. It is true that a drop of acetic acid or oil of lavender will extend its life, but on vellum the oil is undesirable and the acetic acid might discolour certain pigments.

Should a medium, such as gum, be stored for future use a preservative is desirable. Chloroform or pure alcohol are alternative preservatives to that given on page 56. (When in store, chloroform and alcohol, being volatile, must be well sealed and kept in a cool place.)

As has been seen, Beta Naphthol is a safe preservative for both size and gum. Formalin, so frequently suggested, will make the size stringy and unworkable; it is also an acid and therefore should be avoided. The late J. D. Batten when lecturing to the Society of Scribes and Illuminators on 20th April, 1928, stated that 'mildew grew on paintings only in the presence of moisture and that they could safely be washed with pure alcohol or methylated spirit, without risk of damaging the gum, that on paper this would be a safe procedure though perhaps not on vellum'.

Honey and sugar solutions will not keep indefinitely in their liquid condition. It is therefore advisable to make only a small quantity at a time.

Brushes. Fine red sable brushes should be used, but old and fat ones that have lost their point are suitable for the purpose of feeding quill pens with colour. Modern sable brushes have not the resilience of pre-war days when the hair came from the wild animal of Russia and not from the domesticated species of Canada. It is therefore best to buy the shorter-haired brush rather than the long, as the latter soon lose their vitality. The size of brush ranging from No. 00 upwards is a matter of personal preference. Brushes should be well washed in cool water as the media recommended in this chapter are inclined to rot the hairs.

Records. The value of keeping records of successes and failures cannot be too highly stressed, both as a guide to the scribe himself and to others. Where one experimenter may fail in his results another may succeed. In this way some further knowledge may come to light and assist all in a nearer approach to the amazing beauty of execution of the medieval craftsmen. It is for the scribe to select that medium most suited to his needs and whereby he can express himself with most fluency.

III

Ink

'Ink is the great missive weapon in all battles of the learned'

JONATHAN SWIFT

Ink is the term for any fluid with which records are made on parchment, paper or similar substances. The importance of the part played by the ink used in writing a manuscript is often disregarded. On the right choice of ink depend the legibility, permanence and beauty of the writing. The student should take care to ensure that any ink employed has the following qualities.

It must flow freely, be permanent, and be even in colour. It should have a grittiness rather than a stickiness. It should be non-corrosive, non-poisonous, not easily erased and non-fermentable. This last requirement can be fulfilled by the addition of some antiseptic such as phenol or thymol (see Recipes 2, 4 and 7). All ink should flow freely from the pen used, but in hot weather, overheated rooms and hot climates it is not the fault of the ink if this is difficult to control. Ink which flows easily in an even temperature becomes temporarily thick and intractable in too warm surroundings.

There are only two methods of preparing ink given in classical and medieval recipes.

1. Mixing gum with lamp-black: this is permanent and unchanging.

2. Treating salts of iron with tannic acid: such ink fades to that brown tint familiar in western manuscripts. Iron gall inks require a small proportion of strong acid to render them

stable and for that reason may bite through the paper or parchment in time. Judging by appearance some ink has been a mixture of both kinds and so faded unevenly.

Carbon Inks can be classified thus:

Carbon blacks consisting of practically pure carbon in amorphous condition	Gas black—derived from incomplete combustion of gases and substantially free from grease. Lamp black—derived from the incomplete combustion of oils. Used for centuries before gas black was obtainable.

To prepare Chinese ink (lamp-black): the Chinese never kept liquid ink in bottles or ink wells but prepared as much as they needed at a time. For this purpose they had a slab of marble or other stone which had a small round cavity at one end. A few drops of water were poured over the finely polished surface and the stick or cake of ink was gently rubbed against it, the ink flowing into the cavity.

Distilled water should always be used or, if it cannot be obtained, rainwater that has been boiled and run through a single filter paper, or ordinary potable water which has been brought to the boil and allowed to cool.

Liquid preparations of Indian ink are sometimes made by grinding up with water fragments of Chinese and Japanese sticks which have been broken in transit.

Lamp black has been superseded to a certain extent by carbon black which is now manufactured on an extensive scale from the natural gases issuing from the oil-wells of the U.S.A.

Inks which will not be affected by water when dry are called waterproof inks. They are too heavy and sticky for ordinary use and do not flow freely but are convenient for outlines if the outlined forms are to be coloured afterwards.

Ink can be removed from skins or paper by very careful scratching with a sharp knife, or better still by long and careful use of a soft rubber. The surface can then be smoothed and polished with a flat ivory paper knife after which it should be possible to write again without the ink floating; but it is advisable to use very little ink or colour in the pen for such corrections. Ink that is diluted with vinegar cannot be easily erased. There are one or two good English and American typists' erasers, including one in pencil form, on the market now which are effective when handled with great care and if a soft rubber is used gently after, always with the grain and never against it. Palimpsests are vellum manuscripts from which the writing has been erased by rubbing the surface with pumice stone so that it can be used again. Many writings of classical times were undoubtedly lost this way, and as many preserved.

Ink	*Comment*
1. *B.C. 2697.* Chinese stick ink consists of lamp black baked up with some glutinous substance; the finer oriental kinds are delicately perfumed, often with musk.	Improves with keeping. Should never be used until at least 3 years old, should be frequently rubbed with the hand to preserve the polish which is its protective coating.
Graily Hewitt gives the best and simplest method of preparing it: 'Into a clean palette slant put a salt-spoon of water and then, by watch, rub the stick for 3 or 4 minutes. If it then gives a good black, that is your gauge. If not black enough rub another minute. So then you know your need of water and amount of rubbing to repeat exactly the same density. Of course the water should be rain or distilled.'	New stick inks now being imported are of doubtful quality and fade after much exposure to light. Only good Chinese stick ink rubbed down according to the requirements of the scribe using it is absolutely reliable and endures the test of time without change.
Another authority advises that it should always be rubbed down in a palette with a tooth matt, i.e. roughened surface.	

Ink	*Comment*
2. *A.D. 1540.* Palatino's Recipe made and used by the late Colonel Crosland who writes: Soak 3 oz. galls coarsely crushed in $1\frac{3}{8}$ pints rainwater. Leave in the sun 1 or 2 days. Add 2 oz. copperas, finely crushed, stir well with a fig stick. Leave in the sun 1 or 2 days. Add 1 oz. gum arabic and leave one day in the sun.	I found $\frac{1}{2}$ oz. gum sufficient. The mixture should be carefully strained, bottled with India-rubber corks—re-bottled after sediment has settled. Phenol should be used to prevent mould. When I had it prepared by a careful chemist the mixture was finally warmed (not boiled) for 15 minutes. This infusion (without boiling) is advised in *L'Arte di Scrivere dell Encyclopedia Methodica*, Padua, 1796. It is unlikely to fade for a long time.
3. *1672.* Edward Cocker's prescription from *The Pen's Transcendency.* Pour 2 gallons of rainwater into an earthen stand or vessel that is well leaded or glazed within; and infuse in it 2 pounds of gum Arabic, 2 pounds of Blew-galls bruised, 1 pound of Copperas and 2 oz. of Roch Allum: stir it every morning with a stick for 10 days and then you may use it. You may vary the quantity observing the same proportions.	Greyish when first used, turns black after a few days. Fluid and easy to use but inclined to eat into the skin or paper. Fades a little after long exposure to light.
4. *1904.* Dr. Ainsworth Mitchell's ink made, used and praised by the late Colonel Crosland, who writes:	

Ink	*Comment*
(i) Dissolve $1\frac{1}{2}$ oz. of tannin in 1 pint of warm water. (ii) Dissolve $1\frac{1}{2}$ oz. of copperas in $\frac{1}{2}$ pint of water. Mix (i) and (ii) and add 1% (say $\frac{1}{2}$ oz.) of gum arabic also $\frac{1}{2}$ drachm phenol (Calvert's carbolic acid). Expose to air and sun for darkening and stir frequently. Keep in an earthen vessel covered with muslin and stir every day for a week. After darkening add 1 in 1,000 parts of hydrochloric acid. Let the ink settle for a week and decant. Warming accelerates the darkening but the ink should not be boiled.	'This ink is superior to Palatino's in appearance and permanence.'
5. *1927.* Edward Johnston's Recipes from the S.S.I. Record Book.	
Black ink	
Yellow ochre + ivory black water (a little vermilion) + gum water. Ivory black has a remarkable quality of absorbing colours (Church) and so makes mixtures darker than you would expect. The yellow ochre powder is a gritty 'earth' which helps. As Edward Johnston said to the Society: 'A gritty ink is better than a slimy one.'	Easy and convenient to make and has not been known to fade at all even after long exposure to light.
6. *Red ink*	
Scarlet vermilion + water + gum water.	Is unlikely to fade, vermilion mostly improves with age.

Ink	*Comment*
Edward Johnston writes: 'I find a very little (solid) Oxgall a help, it has the objection of being dark but it lasts much longer than the liquid and I am used to it. Very little must be used or it will make the colours spread and soak.'	
7. *1935*. Ingredients of an ink made by William Bishop. 8 gas black 2 gum arabic 1 teaspoonful formalin mixed with distilled water to desired density. Care should be taken in using the gas black as it is very flocculent. A puff of breath will cause the black to fly all over the place. Mix black with the dissolved gum and add the water.	Seventeen years after the specimen was written, no fading seems to have taken place.
8. *1952*. Higgins' General Drawing Ink (U.S.A.).	Owing to Board of Trade restrictions unobtainable in the U.K. at present but there is hope that it will be imported again soon.
9. *1953*. Two mixtures suggested by users of Higgins' Inks. $\frac{1}{2}$ Waterproof } $\frac{1}{2}$ Eternal } and $\frac{3}{4}$ Waterproof } $\frac{1}{4}$ Eternal }	They flow easily and are a good colour. Insufficient time has elapsed to gauge the possible rate of fading.

Palatino's, Cocker's and Dr. Ainsworth-Mitchell's recipes can be made up cheaply at any chemist. It is as well to ask that the stoppers of bottles may be either glass or real cork.

Recipes which are so often quoted that they should be reliable are:

1660. Dr. Peter Canneparius of Venice wrote the popular Italian proverb,

> *Una due tre e trenta*
> *A far la bona tenta*

i.e. one part gum, two of vitriol and three of galls in 30 parts of water.

1825. For making Indian ink. Put six lighted wicks in a dish of oil, hang an iron or tin concave cover over it so as to receive all the smoke; when there is a sufficient quantity of soot settled to the cover, then take it off gently with a feather upon a sheet of paper, and mix it with gum tragacanth to a proper consistence.

N.B. The dearest oil makes the finest soot, consequently the best ink.

Waterproof ink. This consists of black or colours dissolved in a solution of resin in alcohol or other suitable medium which on evaporation leaves the resin and pigment attached to the surface of the paper. The resin protects the pigment from the solvent action of water. They are too sticky for calligraphers and were intended for draughtsmen.

Boil 4 oz. shellac and 1 oz. borax in 30 oz. water, then strain. Grind colours with this such as Indian red, vermilion, indigo. For small quantities the colour may be rubbed in a mortar.

Ink for writing on wood. Brush surface of wood with boiling solution of gelatine and then sponge with a mordant containing 10 parts of alum, 2 parts of hydrochloric acid and 10 parts of tin chloride in 50 parts of water.

Writing in different colours may then be done on this prepared surface with solutions of various pigments, such as cochineal (red), decoction of Persian berries (yellow), decoction of anacardium seeds (black), potassium permanganate (brown) and decoction of logwood (blue).

To restore faded writing. Brush over the writing with a feather or camel-hair brush dipped in tincture of nutgalls. This easy process will bring out the manuscript as clearly as if newly written.

The origin of ink is still a matter of dispute, as ancient records differ. There were only a few kinds, but in composition and appearance they preserve a remarkable identity, though belonging to countries and epochs widely separated. The basis of ink both in China and ancient Egypt was carbon derived from lamp black. A manuscript written by Chien-ki-Souen dating back to 2697 B.C. in which the entire process of making ink is described and illustrated was discovered in China some years ago and translated into French by Jametel in 1882.

In ancient Egypt there is a roll dating from about 2500 B.C. which is probably the oldest extant writing on papyrus. One of the earliest Greek parchments dating back to 2200 B.C. relates to the sale of a vineyard. The carbon ink of ancient Egypt was prepared in solid sticks as in China, and was used down to the fifth century: remains found in inkstands would seem to confirm that it was available in fluid form also. Among the coloured inks the Egyptians used were red ochre, yellow ochre, malachite, and to make a blue colour they ground down fragments of sapphire, haematite, emerald and topaz. They were made into cakes, presumably with gum, to permit emulsification of the pigment in water and to act as a fixative. The Hebrews reserved carbon inks for religious writings. Dioscorides, 40 B.C., physician to Anthony and Cleopatra, in a dissertation on the medicinal use of herbs gives the proportion of lamp black and oil to be used as three to one. Vitruvius, 30 B.C.–A.D. 14, describes a method of preparing soot from pitch-pine mixed with gum and dried in the sun.

It is to the female wasp that we are indebted for gall ink. This was probably invented in the anterior orient, for the species of oak on which the gall wasp deposits its ova that form the excrescences known as galls grows in Asia Minor, Syrial and Persia. It seems to have come into existence only during the first centuries of our era, and was used by the Persians, and mentioned by Philo of Byzantium in the second century. Byzantine ink was a different tint and may have been a bituminous preparation, probably semi-liquid bitumen used directly and without further preparation. Possibly the earliest extant document written with iron ink is an Egyptian parchment of about the seventh century A.D. From then the use of iron inks spread to Europe but the transition from carbon ink, often erroneously called Indian ink, to that of galls and iron was very gradual. Astle, Keeper of the Records in the Tower of London 1803, found that black ink used by the Anglo-Saxons in documents of the seventh, eighth and ninth centuries had preserved its intensity better than that used at later dates. He came to the conclusion that it was because the earlier inks contained carbon. The earliest reference to it is made by the monk Theophilus who wrote *Diversum Artium Schedula* in the eleventh century. He describes an ink prepared from thorn wood: an aqueous extract of the wood was evaporated to dryness and the powder was mixed with green vitriol.

The word ink was derived from the Latin *encaustum*, the name given to pigment first used in baking tiles. Later it was restricted to the purple ink with which Roman emperors signed their names, the black ink being called *atramentum*, *ater*—black. Ink made from the pigment of the cuttle-fish, i.e. sepia, was used by the Romans, and from the Murex mollusc was obtained the famous Tyrian purple. They used also gold and silver inks which consisted of finely divided metals incorporated with gum and covered with beeswax. Plutarch, 46–120 A.D., mentions red ink (to which we owe the word rubric) which was compounded of minium or vermilion. Sidonius says that red ochre was used. Wecker of Basle in

1612 describes an indelible ink compounded of lamp black and linseed oil. Various methods of preparing coloured inks were mentioned by Canneparius of Venice in 1660; Persian berries for yellow, logwood mixed with copper acetate and alum for purple. Various substances were used by the Chinese as the original source of lamp black, e.g. rice-straw, pine-wood, haricot beans, tung-oil and sesame oil. To-day European lamp black is made from impurities obtained as by-products in the manufacture of turpentine, oil, tar, etc.

Permanency in colours generally has reference to their ability to withstand sunlight and ordinary atmospheric conditions; carbon black excels all others in this respect. There are two inks most pleasing to modern scribes: Chinese stick ink which must be rubbed down, and Higgins' Drawing Ink from which the scribe's quill or pen is filled from a quill in the cork of the bottle. Of recipes there are a great many, a few of these are included here. It must be remembered that the test of ink is in contact with the skin or paper and not by itself. Innumerable inks are on the market, but only by trial and error, and by constant experiment, can the one be found which expresses the craftsmanship of the individual.

IV

Skins, Papers, Pounces

The materials on which human ideas have been recorded have in the past shown great variety; but roughly tanned skins, cloth, silk, palm and other leaves, the papyrus first made by the ancient Egyptians and adopted by the Classical world, together with the thin metal plates, and ivory and waxed wooden tablets of the Romans, have long ago fallen into disuse. On the other hand the methods discovered by Greek workmen at the court of a Pergamene king in the second century B.C. for preparing the skins of sheep, cows and calves are substantially the same as those used to-day in the preparation of vellum and parchment.

The art of paper making, a Chinese discovery of the second century A.D., has been practised in Europe from the eleventh or twelfth century onward, the knowledge of its technique having been transmitted by the Arabs. Paper eventually superseded skin for all ordinary purposes, but vellum and parchment held their place for the production of majestical and legal documents, and the vellum-maker's craft has never died. It would be a fascinating study to trace the history of the workshops and the men through whom the skill in preparing such materials has been handed down, but the inquiry is beyond the scope of this work. We may take it for granted that all the firms now making vellum and parchment have received their knowledge from practical workers whose teaching has formed part of an unbroken tradition.

This chapter, then, is concerned with vellum, parchment and paper. These materials are of so many thicknesses, surfaces and colours that no one scribe could exhaust their possibilities in one lifetime, or successfully exploit more than a few of them.

Occasional excursions have been made into writing with a pen on linen or on gessoed or plain wood, but these are unusual. The brush is the natural tool for use on textiles, while the chisel, the graver or, failing these, the brush is better suited to wood. Linen has too rough a grain for writing and is too absorbent for ink, unless the appearance of its surface has been spoiled, as in engineer's tracing cloth. The brush can carry, as the pen cannot, a pigment able to lie on an open-woven ground, and one which will not spread on a partly absorbent surface.

Gessoed and plain wood present *rigid* surfaces. In all writing a certain amount of 'give' or 'spring' is needed between the tool applying the pigment and the ground receiving it. On a rigid surface this can be provided by the 'spring' of a brush. A pen—even the most flexible—is a hard-edged tool, and the 'give' of the vellum or paper plays an important part in securing freedom and rhythm in writing. Thus, every calligrapher prefers to write on an unstretched skin: when circumstances make it necessary that vellum or paper is strained before use, it is best stretched from the edges only and not pasted down on a mount; but even when pasted down some slight amount of 'spring' remains.

Writing vellum is made from the skin of cows, calves, goats and sheep. Only a small proportion of skins is selected from numbers of the highest quality. These fall into two classes from the scribe's point of view. First, the skins which can be prepared for writing on one side only (the outer or hair side). Secondly, those which, after careful preparation, can be used on both sides. The preparation by the vellum-makers and the scribe's own finish minimize the difference between the surfaces, but the dissimilarity remains, giving the beauty of variety and naturalness to the script and calling out of the scribe all his experience, judgment and skill.

The skins, freshly flayed from the animals, are sent to the vellum factory where they are first washed and then placed in tanks of weak, old lime-water until they are ready to be depilated by hand; they are then treated by a machine which cuts away all the surplus flesh and fat on the inside surface; after further liming in liquors of increasing strength they are once more scraped on the flesh side and then, well washed, are stretched on frames and punched down with a blunt half-moon-shaped knife used with a liberal supply of warm water. The flesh side is sprinkled with fine, powdered lime to ensure a hard clean surface. Then, still on their frames, the vellums are taken to a room where one of the most skilful of English craftsmen is at work. With a sharp semi-circular knife mounted on a short staff, he shaves away the hair side of the skin to a clear writing surface. It needs experience gained through many years of apprenticeship and practice to teach him when the desired result is achieved. The vellums are then damped and straightened, dried, cut out of their frames and finished with pounce. Any further treatment is the business of the calligrapher himself.

Parchment, which is made from the inner side of a split sheepskin, requires different treatment from vellum. The skins are limed and split[1] by a band knife in a splitting machine. The flesh splits are then taken and re-split to remove any surplus fat, re-limed, tied into frames, punched down with a semi-circular knife and hot water to remove the grease still further, dried, shaved level on the split side of the skin, and then painted with whitening and placed in a hot drying room to draw out any fat they may still retain. They are then washed again and cleaned with a semi-circular knife and hot

[1] The splitting of a sheepskin is made easy by a layer of fat which runs through the middle of the skin.

water to remove the whitening, dried, cut off, pounced, and are then ready for sale.

All parchment skins are prepared for writing on both sides, but, as with vellum, the surfaces of the two sides are dissimilar. The manufacturers whose products are known to members of the Society of Scribes and Illuminators at the present time (1955) are:

Messrs. H. Band & Co. Ltd., Brent Way, High Street, Brentford, Middlesex. (Telephone, Ealing 9254/5.)

Messrs. T. R. Loosley & Son, 8 Avery Hill Road, London, S.E.9. (Telephone, Eltham 1458.)

Messrs. Elzas & Zonen, Celebridge, Ireland. (Telephone, Celebridge 70.)

These three firms make both vellum and parchment.

Messrs. W. J. Cowley, 100 Caldecott Street, Newport Pagnell, Bucks. (Telephone, Newport Pagnell 38.)

This firm makes parchment but not vellum. The parchment made by Messrs. Stallard of Havant, Hants., which is praised in Graily Hewitt's book has not been produced since 1939. An interesting and detailed account of its manufacture appeared in *The Times* of 16th October, 1928.

CHOOSING VELLUM AND PARCHMENT

Once the decision between the three possible forms—panel, scroll or book—has been made, the choice of material is conditioned by this, by the matter and purpose of the writing, and by the estimated cost of the finished work.

The finest and most sumptuous materials should be reserved for subjects worthy of them and never be wasted on trivialities. When fine vellum is desirable but too expensive, a fine handmade paper is the best substitute and has its own beauties. All imitation vellums are worthless. However finely an occidental scribe may write on paper, writing on vellum will always have an added elegance due to the conjunction of the ink, the scribe's touch and the more sensitive surface. The triumphs of the oriental calligrapher on his particular paper do not enter into this essay.

For framed panels, scrolls and broadsides written on one side of the sheet, thickness and weight of skin are no obstacle. Indeed it is an advantage when a large manuscript has to be strained and framed. 'Grained vellum' provides the largest skins. It is made from the large calfskins and though the size of the skins does not usually exceed 42 in. in length and 30 in. in width, larger skins can be secured when specially required. It is a very handsome vellum, and shows great variety of tints, from deep brownish or brown-mottled skins of a coppery colour, through all sorts of buff and yellowish tints, to a pale warm cream.

Next in size, and running to 42 in. in length and 30 in. in width, but no larger, is 'classic vellum' or calfskin, of the same structure as 'grained vellum' but much finer in texture. This is probably the favourite vellum for framed work, for its delicate colour and fine grain give full value to the inks and colours used on it.

'Manuscript vellum' is also made from calfskin with the top surface removed by scraping: its sizes are therefore the same as in 'classic vellum'. For framing and straining it is well to choose a fairly stout specimen unless the inscriptions are very small.

Of a smaller size again and quite different in surface are the vellums made from goatskin, such as 'grained goat' and 'yellow goat', whose qualities are suggested by their names. These are of a more open grain than calf vellums and are sometimes rather rough and coarse. Running to 34 in. in length by 28 in. in width they are the most varied in colour of all the skins, and their yellows brighter than in any other kind. Being rather cheaper too, they may be satisfactorily employed for work of secondary importance, and are also useful for making temporary covers to protect small booklets. A 'manuscript goat' is made, but it is less flexible than calf vellum, and is not suitable for making books.[1]

It stands to reason that in choosing coloured or variegated vellums we should make sure that the readability of the script should not be unduly reduced by its background: very large writing can stand up to a considerable variation of colour; the smaller the writing the more evenly tinted the background needs to be. In general it is well to choose evenly coloured skins, the *slight* variation in these being one of the special beauties of vellum and parchment, and one which can never be imitated by any manufactured article. Skins of all kinds vary in thickness, the animals' necks, backs and the outer parts being stoutly protected, while the skins gradually become thinner towards the animals' underparts, where they are thinnest. Sometimes in otherwise beautiful skins this transition is sudden and increases the difficulty of working on them and mounting them.

There are three materials made from sheepskin:

1. 'Roman vellum.' When William Morris brought sheep vellum from Rome he asked Messrs. Band to imitate it, and their 'Roman vellum' was the result. It can appear to be of a beautiful egg-shell smoothness, but it is not always dependable in working, being sometimes too shiny or too absorbent. The flesh side is the easier to write on. It is an excellent vellum for printer's use. Its length runs to 32 in. and its width to 24 in.

2. Parchment (Greatest length 36 in., width 28 in.) Its extreme fineness and smoothness make it particularly suitable for gilding provided that it does not cockle. These very fine skins should be mounted by the edges only, the sheet

[1] The reader is referred to Mr. Graily Hewitt's book *Lettering*, p. 261, for a note on kidskins which are very rare, and also for an exhaustive and authoritative essay on parchment.

being drawn drum-head tight but not stuck down on to wood or millboard, as there is a danger that if they are pasted down they may take on the surface of the underlying support and lose something of their own quality.

3. Forel. This is an inferior quality of parchment, produced in white and in a variety of tints. It compares with parchment rather as goatskin compares with calf vellum. The split side is often quite good to write on.

When a piece of writing exceeds the size of any obtainable skin, the work, if for framing, may be executed on two or more panels separately mounted and placed beside or above one another in the same frame; or several skins may be mounted on linen, as, for instance, in a large heraldic scroll. The joining of skins is best done professionally; it is very difficult to paste them on to the linen evenly and to make them permanently secure.

The choice between 'manuscript vellum', 'Roman vellum' and parchment for books is a matter of personal preference. 'Manuscript vellum,' with its firmer texture and slightly nap surface is more responsive to a sharp, hard-edged pen; the smoothness of parchment appeals to gilders; while 'Roman vellum' is less dependable than either, but has an egg-shell-like beauty of its own.

The thinnest calfskins usually available come from still-born calves. Uterine vellum (or unborn calf) is said to be beautiful by those who have tried it. It is very rarely made, but can be supplied to order. It is sometimes a mistake to choose the very thinnest of thin skins if a rubbed surface is desired. A skin with a little body to it, if sufficiently flexible, will better stand the preparation.

Dr. Plenderleith, lecturing to the Society of Scribes and Illuminators on the 10th of May, 1949, said:

'We are all aware that vellum is a type of material made from calfskin and that parchment is from sheep. I wonder if you could be sure that you would recognize the difference in old manuscripts? It has been suggested that in medieval times vellum was much thinner that it is to-day. I went with a micrometer and measured some of the finest manuscripts the British Museum could produce—I found that one was four-thousandths of an inch thick. I took the opportunity of visiting a manufacturer and checked his thinnest parchment with the micrometer—it was four-thousandths and a half. So it would seem that there is very little difference between the thinnest varieties of old and new.'[1]

In choosing either skin or paper for books their weight and thickness must be adjusted to the size and bulk of the intended volume. This is discussed by Mr. Johnston in his *Writing, Illuminating and Lettering*, p. 98 *et seq.* (see page 92). The wise scribe, having digested Mr. Johnston's advice, will further observe the golden rule: '*Always consult the bookbinder before the skins or papers are cut.*'

Vellum and parchment are frequently bought cut to size, but when whole skins are supplied they must be cut up with a very sharp knife on a very hard surface. Professional cutters place their skins on a board made of limewood blocks, place brass-bound patterns on the skins and cut with a boot repairer's knife. When cutting up skins we need a collection of weights to hold the skins and prevent them from slipping. It is impossible to overstress the importance of absolute cleanliness. When starting an important job it is a good plan to wash all T-squares, set squares, etc. quickly with cold water, and then polish them with cotton wool, chamois leather or tissue paper.

The placing of the sheets needs to be considered. It may be a matter of anxious thought to decide which way up a skin should go to enhance the design of a broadside. Planning a

[1] Of ten representative scribes answering the question, 'Do you prefer to work on vellum or on parchment?' only one opted wholly for parchment, saying 'I like the limpness of parchment'. Eight definitely preferred vellum, and one replied 'Vellum for framing, parchment for books'. But in contradistinction see W. Graily Hewitt's notes on parchment on pp. 260–5 of his book *Lettering*.

book and matching page to page, not only fleshside to fleshside and hairside to hairside, but seeking with eyes and fingertips the greatest similarities between like sides, and choosing the most beautiful sheets for special pages (title-pages, book-openings and so on), are tasks that cannot be done hurriedly or in a poor light, for on them the steady flow of the writing will largely depend.

PREPARING THE FINAL SURFACE

Each craftsman must make his own experiments to discover the surface best suited to his needs according to his own trick of hand and cutting of pens, his exact degree of pressure or absence thereof and all the imponderables involved in personality: but of course some general advice can be given.

Parchment presents surfaces so delicate that no preparation beyond pouncing is possible. The following materials are recommended:

(1) Law stationers' pounce ('Oyez' pounce, for example).
(2) Fine pounce powder (Messrs. Band's powder is good).
(3) Gum sandarac alone.
(4) Or one part of gum sandarac and two or three parts of powdered pumice.
(5) Powdered cuttlefish and pumice in equal proportions with a second dusting of sandarac.

(3), (4) and (5) should be sifted through muslin unless bought 'levigated'. Before gilding, a slight pouncing with whitening helps to prevent the gold from sticking to the skin. These pounces may be applied by hand, or with a soft flannel and afterwards dusted off.

Scribes differ considerably in their methods of finishing their vellum surfaces, but it should be remembered that their one object is to make the ink or colour go on to the vellum with a clear edge and an even tint, and stay there.

Vellum tends to retain more flesh albumen than is required

when it is received from the manufacturers. The removal of this surplus and of any remaining traces of grease, coupled with a refining of the textures, is all that need be attempted. Large and highly glazed vellums may be quickly washed with a damp sponge and dried immediately. They should never be allowed to become at all wet or they will cockle. When bone-dry they may be scraped and pounced or simply pounced. Each process of scraping or pouncing will tend to lighten the colour, so, when a deep-tinted effect is aimed at, scraping should be avoided. Scraping instruments, whether knives or specially shaped tools, must be absolutely clean-edged and very sharp and must have rounded corners: dents, chips and angles will produce scratches. The scraper must be used at a steep angle to the skin—between 75° and 90°—for if at all flat it would cut the skin when moving forward and smooth instead of scraping it when moving back.

Erasers should contain just enough roughness to do their work, but no lumps of glass or metal to tear the surface. The green American rubber, Faber's Emerald III U.S.A., is especially good. Rowney's make a good hard green tracing eraser.

Superfine sandpaper, glass paper, emery paper, lump cuttlefish and erasers manufactured with indiarubber, are all suitable abrasives.

Pounces may be divided into two categories:

(1) To remove grease: (*a*) Powdered pumice, (*b*) Powdered cuttlefish (these two are also slightly abrasive), (*c*) Whiting, (*d*) French chalk (these two are grease removers only).

(2) To finish the surface and hold the ink, preventing it from spreading: Gum sandarac.

These may be used separately or in conjunction. The craftsman must be prepared to make experiments and learn by experience. In assessing results the vellum should be scrutinized when held at a sharp angle to the light and also felt with the finger-tips. It is well to have an extra inch of margin, to be cut off in binding, and on it to write a few words to test the state of the skin. But it is the entire page of writing that counts, and it is necessary to keep knife, eraser and pounce close at hand to deal with an unsatisfactory patch if it should occur.

Scraping and sandpapering should follow the grain of the skin, which varies in different parts and must be felt for. Erasers are best used with a circular motion: if used up and down they tend to produce shiny streaks. Sandpaper should be used over a smooth wooden block, and pounce and gum sandarac may be applied by the block when covered with old, used sandpaper, or by means of a rag, preferably flannel. Pouncing by hand, except in small patches, may break the skin of the worker.

Some idea of individual variations may be gained from nine workers' answers to the question, 'What pounce do you use for vellum?':

(1) and (2) Powdered sandarac.
(3) and (4) Fine pumice powder brushed off completely, followed by finely powdered gum sandarac.
(5) Band & Co's pounce.
(6) Fine glass paper and a little sandarac on the hairside, and on the fleshside Faber's Emerald No. III U.S.A. rubber.
(7) Fine glass paper then pounce—'Oyez' if possible.
(8) Hairside, scraped surface and sandarac: fleshside, sandarac only.
(9) Superfine pounce from Band's, with a second dusting of sandarac.

It will be seen from this that the flesh- and hairsides often need different treatment. The hairside is easier to write on, while the fleshside has possibly a better gilding surface. But the greater beauty of pattern on the hairside often makes it desirable for the more elaborate pages. The fleshside is easily spoilt if too much rubbed. It is just here that the price for experience may be exacted from the beginner, who should proceed with great caution, working on small pieces of skin at the start.

Just occasionally a sheet of vellum is found which requires no treatment after leaving the factory and is delightful to work on if used at once. But if it is kept unused for any length of time it will be affected by grease working up to the surface, especially in any warmth. Skins prepared and laid aside require a final pouncing before use. In order to secure smoothness and opacity vellum manufacturers often cover the fleshside of their skins with a preparation which chokes up the pores and has an artificial appearance. This prevents the attainment of a sharp writing surface. Scribes who value the nap on their vellum should make sure when ordering that the fleshside has not been artificially coated.

Recently my own procedure when using Band's manuscript vellum has been: (1) A long and very steady preparation with knife and fine sandpaper, or knife and green rubber, or sandpaper and green rubber, according to the state of the skin when I receive it; (2) The use of powdered pumice alone. and in several applications, each in turn being shaken off to carry away all the grease it has absorbed; (3) A final rub with powdered sandarac alone, to restore the nap[1] after pouncing and to hold the ink, preventing it from spreading. I then hold up the sheet by the fold (or the edge, if a single sheet) and hit the lower edges smartly with my finger nails to flick away all unnecessary powder, and sometimes also dust it with a silk handkerchief. After ruling and before writing I give a very light rub with sandarac applied with the finger-tips. Even after this unsatisfactory patches sometimes occur and call for a fresh scrape with the knife and a new touch of sandarac.

Where there are any parts to be gilded I use very little or no

[1] The nap referred to above is the velvety surface giving 'bite' or 'tooth' to the skin and crispness to the writing. It is a very slight affair, a mere texture, but highly valued by those accustomed to it. It should never be attempted on parchment or Roman vellum whose beauty is of a different nature.

sandarac, as its gummy quality is inclined to make the gold leaf stick to the background.

There are several dangers to avoid in preparing vellums:

(1) Overscraping is quite irreparable: it is better to stop too soon than too late.

(2) It is not so easy to over-pounce, but too much pounce left on the skin will choke the surface; insufficient pouncing will allow the ink to run; too much sandarac means that the ink will not take, while a little too much forces the nib-tips apart and produces a white line down the centre of each letter which may have to be filled in with a finer pen; even a specially hard pen used on a highly sandaraced surface may fail to avert this white line. Also, sandarac in excess will spoil the quality of the ink by adhering to the writing.

(3) If the hand strikes the edge of the skin when pouncing an incurable creasing may occur. A slip of the rubber or scraper may damage the skin in the same way.

(4) It is necessary to work over an absolutely smooth surface. Like Hans Andersen's 'Real Princess and the Bean', vellum feels the slightest irregularity beneath it. Even a grain of pounce under the blotting-pad will cause a mark in the skin. Several sheets of good blotting paper are desirable as a pad over an absolutely smooth board.

These are dangers to avoid in the use of vellum and parchment:

Well cared for skins are most durable. Two real dangers come from excessive heat and from damp. Exposed to undue heat they will curl and shrink; exposed to damp they will expand and in drying—except when in process of straining—they will shrink and cockle.

Work should be kept well away from any heating element and the workroom should be well aired. Owners of framed works on skin should not hang them above radiators. However, above chimneypieces they seem adequately protected by the mantelshelves. Vellum books should never be handled near a hot fire, and should be kept away from damp and dust.

If an erasure is made the friction between rubber and skin will produce heat. It is necessary to stop rubbing at short intervals and so prevent cockling.

All washes put on to skins should be kept as dry as possible.

A blot or smudge should not be washed off—(though a small one may be *instantly* removed by a clean rag over the forefinger moistened with spit, or even licked off)—the blot must be allowed to dry and should then be removed with a knife or eraser. Any attempt to wash it away will stain the skin and fix the stain.

The worker should be careful not to cut himself. The edges of paper, skin or pen, or the tin spring, can give nasty cuts and blood marks are indelible.

THE MANUFACTURE OF PAPER

The process of paper-making consists of disintegrating the fragments of various cellulose materials and saturating them with water until they form a pulp which may be calculated to produce, when thinly spread and dried, the substances which we recognize as drawing paper, writing paper, packing paper and so forth. These differences in kind and quality depend on the component materials and the extent of cutting and bruising to which they are subjected, as well as on the amount of size and other matter added during the manufacture, and finally on the finishing or calendering by rollers which determines the surfaces. Originally paper was made entirely by hand. Now even handmade paper is partly produced by machine, the materials for the pulp being broken down to the fibrous state by machinery and then re-composed by hand.

All paper is made by spreading the pulp on to wire-cloth so

that the water may drain away and allow the fibres to combine. The hand-craftsman uses a mould of wire-cloth with a removable wooden frame called the deckel surrounding it. He dips this mould, with the deckel in position, into a vat where the pulp is already at the required colour and lifts out just enough pulp to make one sheet of paper: as the water begins to run through the wire he gives a shake to the mould, which helps the felting of the fibres and spreads them in all directions. This shake is a knack which takes years to acquire. The deckel is then removed and the mould is inverted on to a felt and pressed down so that the sheet adheres to the felt.[1] A pile of wet sheets with felts between is then put under strong pressure to squeeze out more water; the sheets are then removed from the felts and pressed again. Each sheet is then dipped into a tub containing size, which for handmade paper is gelatine normally mixed with alum and a small amount of formaldehyde to act as a preservative. The surfaces of the sheets are then finished with hot or cold rollers.

For machine-made paper the principle is the same, but the pulp flows on to a wide continuous moving band of wire-cloth at the wet end of the machine and is guided initially by moving sidestraps, called deckel straps. It is then pressed and dried on the same remarkable machine and is finally reeled up as paper.

Artists think of paper as divided into two classes: the partly absorbent, open-textured, NOT HOTPRESSED paper suitable for water-colour, and the less absorbent, close-grained HOT-PRESSED paper made to receive ink. It is with the second class that calligraphers are concerned. We have also to recognize another division into two classes: papers are described as being either wove or laid.

[1] The fine hairs which sometimes catch in pens come from this felt. If there are only one or two on a sheet of paper they may be raised by a needle-point and carefully pulled off: if there are many the sheet should be discarded.

Paper called wove is made on a plain wiremesh and when held up to the light shows no interruption in its texture. Laid paper is made over a wiremesh woven in a series of fine vertical lines. Thicker wires are fixed across the mould at regular intervals and over these the pulp lies thinly. A laid sheet, when dry, shows a series of fine chain marks with stronger semi-transparent wire marks crossing them. These wire marks were originally intended to keep the writing straight. Nowadays they have mainly a decorative value. The use of laid or wove paper is a matter of taste: when laid paper is used the chain marks look best placed vertically.

For many purposes a good machine-made paper is as pleasant to write on as a handmade sheet. But it may not be so durable nor stand an erasure. If the work is intended to last, handmade paper should be selected for it is always made from rags of good quality blended according to the type of paper required; protected by its coating of fine size it should last indefinitely. The word handmade may usually be found as a watermark.

Of other materials used in paper making, esparto grass will long outlast woodpulp. As these are often mixed, durability will depend on their proportions—a very cheap paper, mainly composed of woodpulp, cannot be expected to last long.

Handmade paper is skilfully imitated by paper *mould made* on a special machine, and it is difficult for a non-expert to recognize the difference. Therefore it is wise to buy papers manufactured by firms of repute and supplied through trustworthy agents.

Paper should be bought with some to spare: the colour varies slightly with each vatful of pulp, and it may be impossible to match the sheets after an interval. Paper improves with keeping. It is a good plan to lay in a stock of it and use the oldest sheets.

Here are the standard sizes of paper which may vary slightly according to the make of paper:

Royal	24 in. × 19 in.
Super Royal	28 in. × 18 in.
Imperial	30 in. × 22 in.
Double Elephant	40 in. × 26 in.
Antiquarian	53 in. × 21 in.

Hotpressed Whatman paper is supplied in the two largest sizes, and Hotpressed Unbleached Arnold paper in Double elephant size. Other papers seldom exceed 30 in. × 22 in., and usually run at about 28 in. × 18 in. or slightly less. White H.P. Whatman has a much better writing surface than the vellum finished variety which is made in Imperial size. Thus for very large work we are left with white H.P. Whatman in several weights, H.P. Unbleached Arnold paper, and a wide variety of machine-made cartridge papers. Some of these are kept in continuous rolls and are sold by the yard, and others are made in extra large sheets for architects' and engineers' use. If we use other handmade papers we must divide our work into panels not exceeding 28 in. × 18 in.

When posters and notices are required on coloured paper a certain amount of experiment is necessary. Ingres and Michallet papers will take ink and are satisfactory for large writing but are too rough for small work. Coloured papers obtainable must be tested with different kinds of ink and paint. If it is necessary to use a rather soft-surfaced paper in order to obtain a particular colour it is advisable to write with gouache or with postercolour containing size.

Some good handmade papers available at present (1955) are:

Arnold & Foster's Plain Toned Laid paper in three weights.

Arnold & Foster's W. King Cream Laid Large Post, almost white.

Arnold & Foster's Reinforced Toned Vellum (too thick for books but good for panels and coats of arms), a pleasant warm tone.

Barcham Green's Lettering paper, white, or only just off white.

Arthur Millbourn's Reinforced Vellum Parchment toned, in several weights.

Head's Handmade Lettering paper, in three tints.

J. A. Jones's Handmade Vellum Parchment, white or toned.

Whatman's Hotpressed paper (the best is white).

Hotpressed Unbleached Arnold paper.

From among these and others papers of a suitable size and weight for bookmaking may be chosen. The weight of the paper must be adjusted to the size of the page and the thickness of the book, so that when the book is opened each page may bend over and lie flat. A distinguished bookbinder, in a discussion with members of the Society of Scribes and Illuminators, especially drew their attention to the advice given by Edward Johnston in Chapter VI of *Writing, Illuminating and Lettering*: 'Cut a small sheet the size of a page of the book and clip it between two small pieces of wood (holding it as it would be if bound). If the page will bend over and stay down by its own weight, it is thin enough; if it stands up it is too stiff.'

The question of opacity as opposed to semi-transparency is one of design and correspondence between material and matter, and also one of legibility. The fabric must be opaque enough to keep each page of writing clearly readable. A paper which will carry delicate writing on both sides can be useless under a blacker, heavier hand. For a firm and solid effect we choose a fairly opaque paper; while books of poetry and *belles-lettres* seem to me to gain in elegance when written out on semi-transparent paper, this matter must be adjusted to the liking of the writer of the book and of its owner also.

Some machine-made papers found pleasant for writing on are:

Goatskin Parchment, made by Wiggins Teape & Co. in white and cream shades. A good paper for students' exercises and for working out designs to be shown to clients before the finished work is done. It is improved by a touch of gum sandarac. Spicer's Whitewove, Dominion Bond, Vellum and Cream Laid—all 33 in. × 44 in. These are papers suitable for students' work and for drafts. They cannot be expected to stand erasures.

For very rough drafts and layouts drawer-lining paper is cheap and useful. More careful planning may be done on architects' detail paper (continuous) which has the advantage of semi-transparency. When submitting schemes and designs to clients it is always an advantage to use good paper.

When cutting paper it should be folded over the edge of the T-square, flattened down, and cut with a sharp knife inside the fold, or it may be cut on glass like vellum. (The natural way to fold paper is, of course, to bring the edges of the sheet together, flatten down the fold and cut inside it, but on account of the slight variation and give in handmade paper, the check with the T-square is helpful.)

A good paper will stand a considerable amount of cleaning with rubber, breadcrumbs or pounce. If a sheet has become slightly bent and dented through clumsy handling, a folded old cotton sheet may be laid on the work bench, and over it a piece of damp white blotting paper, over that again a clean dry sheet of plain paper. The crumpled sheet may then be placed on the pile with another dry sheet (or more) above. A moderately warm flat iron may then be carefully passed over the whole. As soon as the injured sheet lies slack and loose it should be removed from the neighbourhood of the damp blotting paper and quickly ironed on a pad of clean, dry material. If the paper is cracked there is, of course, no remedy; an ugly mark will remain when the ironing is finished.

Opinions vary as to the value of pounce used on paper. In general it is best to choose paper free from grease and use it as it comes from the mill. Sometimes, however, scribes are asked to write in bound books and find in them sticky or greasy surfaces: then a judicious use of fine pounce may save the situation, and some few papers are decidedly improved by it.

[When called upon to write in a valuably bound book, the cover may be protected by means of a sling made by sewing an old blanket over a drawing board and turning up the bottom to form a deep pocket in which the book can rest. Bands of soft stuff must be fastened over the sides of the book and across the top. The board can then be safely propped at a writing angle. It may be necessary to ease up one side of the opened book and place a block under it in order to make the other side lie flat.]

SOME TECHNICAL HINTS ON RULING-OUT

Ruling a large broadside on a drawing-board is plain sailing, but on a sheet mounted on a card or a stretcher the work must be set out from the edge, checked with a set square, measured down both side margins and ruled with a straight edge.

When ruling out a paper book the measurements may be made down the front page of each section and pricked through the rest with a fine needle. (A blob of sealing wax over the eye makes the needle easier to handle.) A specimen sheet may be kept into which succeeding sections may be slipped: pricking through the same holes too often will enlarge them and make the ruling irregular.

It is often possible to rule across both sides of an opened folded paper sheet in one operation. But on account of the give it is necessary to check each page by squaring it with the fold. I have found it practical to begin by making a fine needle-prick into the fold at the level of the top writing line. In measuring out vellum books in which every page must be separately set out and ruled the prick is a useful guide, and it should be a help to the binder in sewing up. It is best to rule first the two outer pages of a folded skin sheet and prick through the top writing line in the outer margin of each. Levelling this with the prick in the fold will save time in adjusting the inner pages. A guide made on stiff paper and fastened down on the left-hand side of the board is the easiest way of ruling vellum sheets.

Ruling out the inner pages of a vellum folder is always an awkward job. I have asked various workers how they fasten the folder down. Some say 'with half-inch white elastic', others use movable weights, and others again put strips of card or vellum across the corners and fasten these down with drawing pins, and also put little overlapping wedges on the top edge towards the fold or wherever they seem needed. All these methods have the same disadvantage—i.e. the collision between the fasteners and the rulers, and here each one of us must work out his own salvation.

Lines are ruled with a very hard pencil, a scratching tool or a fine pen and pale ink or colour.

For further information see Edward Johnston's *Writing, Illuminating and Lettering*, pp. 89, 99, 108: and Graily Hewitt's *Lettering*, pp. 174, 184, 193 and 271.

V

Gilding

The fine books of the middle ages were made splendid with the help of burnished gold. They were 'illuminated' by it; their magnificent pages sparkled with this precious metal. We find large areas of gold in twelfth-century initials, tiny patches in fifteenth-century ivy-leaf patterns, thin bars enclosing foliage in borders of the Winchester School, and, at any time from the twelfth century onwards, gold backgrounds to initial letters and miniatures. The effect of this gilding was to brighten, and sometimes to harmonize, small pieces of colour, and to add to the gaiety and liveliness of the page. Then, as formal handwriting declined, the art of decorating it deteriorated, and burnished gold, if it was used at all, was generally used unskilfully. But when calligraphy was revived by Edward Johnston at the end of the nineteenth century, it brought with it opportunities for the illuminator, and Graily Hewitt, after a long series of experiments based on Cennino Cennini's detailed but confusing instructions for gilding, recovered the practice of this difficult craft.

The gilding which decorates the medieval manuscripts is very brilliant and is raised a little from the surface of the page on a thin cushion of gesso: the actual gold is generally used in the form of gold leaf.

There is another kind of gilding which is less bright, produced by the use of matt gold (often called shell gold because it is sold in mussel shells ready for use), and gilding with this material is not difficult. It is either painted on the page or put on with a small quill, and as soon as it is dry it is rubbed lightly with an agate burnisher, which is better than a haematite burnisher for shell gold.

If the craftsman wishes to prepare it himself he may mix real gold powder with a solution of gum arabic or with gelatine. If gum arabic is used, the gold powder should be ground into the liquid gum arabic on a piece of plate glass with a muller, or in a fine pestle and mortar; an agate pestle and mortar is good for this. It is important to use no more gum arabic that is necessary to fix the gold powder to the page. Test by painting a little on a scrap of vellum to see whether it brushes off when it is dry. If it does brush off, add a little more gum until the gold, when it is dry, is securely attached to the page.

Gold powder is never very bright when it is tempered with gum arabic. A better medium is gelatine. A piece of leaf gelatine should be dissolved in one dessertspoonful of hot water, and if the thickness of the leaf is $\frac{1}{32}$ in., a piece that is $\frac{1}{2}$ in. × $\frac{1}{4}$ in. should be large enough. Add to this $\frac{1}{4}$ dwt. of real gold powder, stir until it is cold and then pour it in a flat china palette or plate, which must stand on a level surface. Cover it with a piece of stiff paper to protect it from dust and leave it to dry. When it is dry moisten a little of it with a brush dipped in distilled water and use it like paint. The leaf gelatine must be white and transparent, and free from cloudiness when it is dissolved in water. It is better to use powdered gelatine than leaf gelatine of a poor quality.

Shell gold is useful for fine patterns and small details, but, while gold powder remains at its present price, the illuminator may find this kind of gilding expensive. With care, however, the cost may be kept within reasonable limits, for the method is generally used for tiny forms which are painted most easily with a miniature brush; so two or three new miniature brushes, of different sizes and all very short, should be kept exclusively for shell gold, and never on any account used for anything else. They should be dipped in distilled water kept in a small wide-necked bottle, and afterwards washed in the same water. The bottle should never be emptied, but, as the level of the water sinks through use or evaporation, more distilled water should be added, and when it is not being used the bottle should be closed. When the gold on the plate is finished, at least half of it will have been transferred to the bottle. This gold will be quite clean, since it has been protected from dust and the brushes have been used for nothing else; so the water may be poured off, and the gold, which will be left behind, may be mixed again, using this time less gelatine. The process can be repeated until no gold is left, and in this way most students will find that they can afford to use matt gold, even at its present price.

Shell gold, charming though its effect may be, would never be suitable for the chief decoration of an important work, which needs the other, more brilliant, kind of gilding, where gold leaf is laid on a thin coat of raising preparation (the asiso or gesso) and then burnished until it is very bright. Gilding by gold leaf is a more difficult and far longer process, but the result is well worth the extra trouble it involves.

Success depends to a great extent, but not entirely, on a good gesso. The gesso must form a perfectly smooth cushion on which the gold leaf, when attached, will take a bright burnish; it must be pliable enough to bend without cracking as the page turns; and it must have a slight latent stickiness, so that, when it is breathed on, the gold leaf will adhere to it. Permanent success is impossible unless the gesso is made from a good recipe.

Two kinds of materials are used: hard materials such as slaked plaster of Paris, gilder's whiting, white lead, Armenian bole, and powdered eggshell, to make the hard smooth cushion on which gold leaf will take a fine burnish; and sticky materials, sugar, glue, candy, honey, parchment size, glair and gum, to make the gesso hygroscopic, i.e. sensitive to moisture, and also to make it pliable enough to bend with the page. Slaked plaster of Paris consists of needle-shaped crystals which, entangling, help the sugar and glue in their work of preventing cracking when the page is bent.

A good burnish may generally be obtained for a time if the right touch is used and the burnishing is done at the right moment; but the permanence of the brightness depends on the composition of the gesso. Gold leaf, being extremely thin, is porous, and so, if the gesso contains too great a proportion of hygroscopic materials, on a damp day it will absorb moisture from the atmosphere through the gold leaf, which will, naturally, become dull. A second coat of gold leaf helps to prevent this, but there is always danger that bad weather may affect the burnish unless a gesso is used in which the hygroscopic ingredients are reduced to the smallest amount necessary to make the leaf stick. As the gilder acquires more skill by practice he will be able to use a harder gesso than at first.

The gesso for a great deal of modern gilding is made from slaked plaster of Paris, powdered white lead, sugar, glue and Armenian bole. On these materials Mr. Graily Hewitt based the experiments to which we owe so much; and these, except that parchment size was used instead of glue, are the materials recommended by Cennino in his Treatise. They make a gesso that is as reliable as any that we know, especially for a long piece of work that will have to be carried on to its conclusion through different seasons and varying weather.

In recipes that give successful results the plaster and white lead together are generally six or seven times the sum of the sugar and glue. For the proportion of white lead to plaster Cennino seems to lay down the rule that it is to be about one third, and this works very well.

A beginner might start with the mixture, measured by capacity, 20 parts of slaked plaster of Paris, 6 of white lead,

3 of sugar, 2 of glue. This mixture is easy to use but the gilding will not keep its burnish. After a little practice he should try to reduce the amount of sugar, and he will probably be able to use 18 parts of plaster, 6 of white lead, 2 of sugar, and 2 of glue: and his work will usually remain fairly bright. Later he may be able to use less glue, and then he should obtain good results from 16 parts of plaster, 6 of white lead, 2 of sugar and 1 of glue. This gesso, mixed with glair, has given a burnish that is as bright after twelve years as on the day it was done. A mixture of 20 parts of plaster, 6 of white lead, 2 of sugar and 1 of glue has also given a permanently good result.

Gilder's whiting is often used. In any of the recipes mentioned above it may be substituted for part—less than half—of the plaster; for instance, instead of 20 parts plaster, 11 parts plaster and 9 parts gilder's whiting.

Two of these materials, the plaster and the glair, should be prepared by the gilder. The others can be bought ready for use.

The plaster required for gilding is the finest dental plaster and before it is used it must be slaked. A gallon and a half of water should be put in an enamelled or galvanized pail, which must be free from rust. Add one pound of plaster very slowly to this, allowing it to trickle through the fingers to make sure that it contains no lumps, and stirring it constantly with a wooden spoon. When all the plaster has been added to the water, continue to stir it for at least one hour. The object of the large quantity of water and the long period of stirring is to keep the plaster from setting. Leave it until the next day, when it will be found that the plaster has dropped to the bottom of the pail and the water is clear. Pour off the water, disturbing the plaster as little as possible, fill the pail with fresh water and stir for ten minutes. Do this every day for a week, and, after that, every other day for at least four more weeks. Then pour the water off for the last time, put the plaster into a linen cloth and squeeze it dry. Turn the plaster out of the cloth and leave it for a few days on a piece of white paper in a place where it is protected from dust but not shut away from fresh air. While it is still soft the lump may be cut into two or four pieces for convenience in storing, but it must not be reduced to powder. Slaked plaster of Paris should be kept in a tin lined with paper.

When the plaster is slaked and dry the gesso can be made. A piece of ground or plate glass and a heavy muller will be necessary, also a palette knife, a pen knife with a stout blade, a piece of 'silver paper' (very thin tin foil) burnished smooth, and lastly something in which to measure the ingredients. A small salt-spoon is good for this, but it should not be very shallow, as that makes it difficult to measure accurately.

The following is a convenient way to make the gesso, taking as an example the third recipe mentioned above. Scrape a little plaster from the lump that has been slaked, press some of this firmly into the salt-spoon and level it across the top, then turn it out on the glass. Measure 15 more spoonfuls in the same way, keeping each spoonful separate from the others to prevent any error in counting. If more has been scraped from the lump of plaster than is needed it should be thrown away and not kept to use in the next mixing of gesso, for it will not be quite as good as freshly scraped plaster. Then measure six spoonfuls of white lead, always filling the spoon as tightly as possible and levelling it across the top with the knife. With the muller crush some sugar to a fine powder and measure two spoonfuls of this. (Of course the muller and the patch of glass where the sugar was crushed must be washed immediately.) Centrifugal sugar or sugar candy is best, but if they are difficult to get, loaf sugar is probably the next best thing.

Le Page's glue sold in a bottle labelled 25 is good. An easy way of measuring is by dipping the point of the knife in the glue and letting it drop from the knife into the spoon until the spoon is full. Then wash the knife carefully and with its point, scrape all the glue out of the spoon on to the middle of the sheet of glass. With the palette knife scrape all the other ingredients into a heap over the glue, make a hollow in the top of the heap and into it pour eight spoonfuls of distilled water. Add a little Armenian bole for the sake of colour, but only enough to make it a pale pink. Mix it well with a palette knife and grind it with the muller for forty-five minutes. If it is too stiff to grind easily, a little more distilled water may be added, but it is an advantage to keep the mixture thick.

When the grinding is finished, scrape all the gesso together and put it on the silver paper, arranging it smoothly in a circle about 2½ in. in diameter. The lid of a small cardboard box with holes in the side is useful to protect it from dust without excluding air while drying.

After two or three days, when the gesso has set but has not become very hard, with a pair of scissors cut the circle of gesso and the silver paper together into eight sectors. It is important that it should be cut in this way to ensure that each piece of gesso has its correct proportion of the ingredients, because the gesso at the edge contains more glue than that in the middle. Strip the silver paper from the back of the pieces of gesso and keep them in a ventilated box.

A week after the gesso is ground it should be ready for use, when it must be mixed with either distilled water or glair. Glair has several advantages; it makes it easier to attach the gold leaf, it adds to the brightness of the gilding, and it helps to make that brightness permanent.

Cennino tells us how to prepare glair for gilding. He says we are to put the white of an egg into a basin, to beat it with a broom of twigs cut equal, until the basin is full of thick froth, to pour a glassful of water on the white of egg and to let it stand from night until the next morning to clarify itself. Instead of his broom of twigs we may use an eggwhisk, and it is not necessary to mix as large a quantity as he suggests. The white must, of course, be very carefully separated from the yolk; if any yolk is mixed with it, the glair will be spoilt. When it is beaten to a very stiff froth, a level tablespoonful of the froth—or more—may be put in a cup and an equal quantity of water poured on it. Next morning a clear liquid will be found in the cup with, perhaps, a small wisp of froth left on the surface. The liquid should be poured into another cup, and then it is ready for use. The glair will keep fresh without a preservative if it is left uncovered and no water is added but, of course, it grows stronger through evaporation. In order to counteract this, do not dilute the glair in the cup with distilled water, but put the water straight into the gesso; for instance, instead of mixing the gesso with eight drops of glair, use seven of glair and one of water, or six of glair and two of water.

When mixing the gesso with glair or water, it is very important to avoid making bubbles, for they will rise to the surface and, bursting, leave holes that spoil its smoothness. While it is not possible always to keep work free from them because they may be caused by many things, such as the roughness of the vellum, the gilder, by slow and careful mixing, can at least see that there is none in his gesso when it is applied to the page.

To mix the gesso, break one piece of it into crumbs and drop them into a glass or china egg-cup. An old-fashioned egg-cup of pointed shape is best because it keeps a little liquid in a small space which delays evaporation. A bone penholder slightly rounded at one end makes a convenient tool for mixing.

With a pipette add to the crumbs of gesso two drops of glair or one of distilled water, and leave this to stand for a quarter of an hour. While the gesso is softening, a quill may be cut and the vellum prepared. Then, without adding any more moisture, pound the gesso to a paste, make sure that it contains no hard lumps or air spaces, and press it down firmly so that the surface is level. Add six or eight drops of glair or water from the pipette, keeping a note of the number. Then mix slowly and carefully with the penholder, moving it lightly over the surface of the gesso which lies below the liquid and gradually working deeper. If the penholder is allowed to dig into the gesso, or if it is taken out of the liquid and put back, a bubble will probably be made.

When it is thoroughly mixed, the gesso should be thin enough, but only just thin enough, to flow through a pen. The number of drops of glair or water needed to give this result depends on the size of the salt-spoon used in measuring the ingredients of the gesso and can be discovered only by experiment. When the number is known it should be noted, so that the exact amount can be added with confidence on later occasions. If a stiffly cut quill is used and the gesso is pushed well up the barrel this will help to control the flow.

Whenever it is possible, gesso should be laid with a pen; but sometimes a brush must be used, and then the brush should be dipped first in distilled water and squeezed dry, or bubbles will be formed.

The surface of the vellum may need attention. It should be rubbed thoroughly with finely powdered pumice to get rid of any stickiness, especially if it has been prepared with sandarac before the page was written. All the pumice should be brushed off the vellum or it may clog the pen. Gilder's whiting is sometimes used instead of pumice. When the gilding forms part of an elaborate drawing, the drawing should be made on the vellum in a very fine line with pale ink.

The board must be flat while gesso is being laid. This increases the difficulty of writing, for the scribe has to lean uncomfortably over his work to avoid looking at it in perspective; but, clearly, there is no alternative because, if the board were tilted, the gesso would flow to the bottom of each letter instead of drying flat.

1. The position of the hands just before the gilder leans forward to breathe on the so. The left hand turns back a corner of the folded silk to uncover the gesso to be led. The right hand holds the gold leaf high and away from the gilder's breath. On the is the crystal parchment, on the right the pencil and the large burnisher, with scissors keep it from rolling off the table. Further away are other agate and haematite burnishers useful shapes, and extra pieces of gold leaf overlap the edges of the board so that they may be picked up quickly if they are needed

2. Two ways of handling gold leaf. On the left a book is open at the last page. The ners have been snipped to attach the leaf to the paper. On the right, a leaf of gold has n removed from a book to the gilder's cushion, and cut in four pieces with the knife which is shown. One of the pieces is being lifted with the gilder's tip

The pen should be filled by dipping it in the gesso and pushing the liquid up the barrel with the bone penholder. The gesso left on top of the pen may be flicked away with a finger and then the pen will write sharply. When the letter has been written, and while it is still wet, retouch the thickest part of each stroke, with the pen turned at right angles to its original position to avoid spoiling the shape; at the lightest, quickest touch gesso will flow from the pen into the letter, and will prevent its being too flat when it dries. Then wipe the pen clean, and with the corner of it, draw some of the gesso from the thick strokes into the thin strokes, in order to make the surface level.

Naturally it is easier to lay gesso for letters that are written simply than for built up letters like versals, but versals should be successful if they are executed without hesitation. It seems best to draw first the two strokes outlining a stem or a curve, then, before either can dry, to fill in the space between, adding a little gesso if more height is necessary, and, while the stem is still wet, with a corner of the pen pull out from the top and bottom of the stem the fine finishing lines. Before the letter dries it will be necessary to pull out a little more gesso from the thick stroke into these fine lines, which will otherwise be very flat.

The height of the gesso can, of course, be easily regulated. If it is to be flat, use thin gesso; if it is to be raised high, mix stiffer gesso and flood more of it into the letter.

Sometimes the gesso dries with a hollow down the centre of each letter. The chance of this may be reduced by working in a cooler room, or by laying the gesso more quickly. The hollow, if it does appear, can generally be burnished out or, if it is too deep for this, the gesso may be scraped with a sharp pen knife or fine sandpaper before it is gilded.

Whether gold letters should be kept rather flat or well raised is an important and interesting question, and one that cannot be answered without considering the conditions in which they will eventually be seen. Gilding that is to be shown in a frame always needs to be raised higher than gilding in a book, but whatever we may decide to be the perfect height for the gilding of any piece of work, one thing is certain; the height must be constant throughout that piece of work. For this reason it is necessary to measure carefully the liquid, either glair or water, that is used, so that in a long piece of gilding it will be possible to make the gesso the same strength on different days. When the gesso has been laid for the whole piece of work, or for as much as it is convenient to do in one day, it should be left until the next morning before being gilded. If the weather is not unduly damp, this will ensure its being thoroughly dry, so that when it is breathed on, the surface of the gesso will become sticky and therefore will hold the leaf, while the core will be firm and hard, and strong enough to stand pressure in burnishing. If it is gilded on the day when it is laid, the gesso will probably have a hard surface over a softer core and, in burnishing, the surface may be cracked or broken.

If the gesso has been mixed with glair, it is best to gild on the day after it is laid, but if no glair has been used, the gesso may be left for several days before the gold leaf is applied, and often this is worth while, in order that a suitable morning may be chosen for the work.

Weather makes a great deal of difference to the ease with which the gilding may be done. The best time of year is the autumn; the best time of day is early in the morning, as soon as it is light enough to see clearly. As the air dries, the gilder's difficulties increase rapidly, and if he can gild very early in an unheated room he will find that this, however uncomfortable it may be at the time, will save trouble in the end. A damp morning is best, especially if it grows clear and bright later on. The direction of the wind should be noticed; when it is in the south-west, conditions are generally good for gilding; when it is in the east, they are generally unfavourable. A hygrometer gives the most accurate measure of the moistness of the atmosphere.

Gold leaf is sold in books which contain approximately 25 leaves, each about 3½ in. × 3½ in., and the kind that illuminators use is called Single (or Double) Fine Illuminating Gold Leaf. 'Single' and 'double' refer to the thickness of the leaf. Single is easier to use because it is thinner and therefore sticks more readily to the gesso. The final coat may be of double if the illuminator wishes.

Gold leaf for illuminating is packed between the pages of the small book and is not attached to the paper. The book must be opened carefully, for the slightest breath of air may crumple the leaf or even blow it away.

Illuminators have two ways of handling gold leaf. The first is by cutting through the leaf and the corresponding paper page with a pair of scissors. This has the effect of attaching the leaf lightly to the paper so that the two may be picked up together with the fingers. The scissors must be sharp and they should be carefully wiped with a piece of silk before use, for if they are at all rough or sticky the gold leaf will adhere to them and will be spoilt.

If the gilder starts with the last page in the book of gold, he will find it easier to avoid damaging the other leaves. These should be curled safely out of the way and caught by the left thumb, while the spine of the book is held firmly between the first and second fingers of the left hand, and the paper cover is curled back in the other direction and held by the little finger. Then it will be possible to cut the last page with its piece of gold leaf without crumpling any of the other pieces of leaf in the book. If a small piece of paper and leaf together is cut off the corners, the gold leaf will be held in position on the page, and then it will be possible to cut out the whole page or as much of it as is needed, allowing it to fall on the drawing board, slightly overhanging its edge, so that it may be picked up easily.

The second way needs a little more practice, and it can only be employed in a place that is free from draughts, even those caused by the movement of other people; but few craftsmen, having grown used to it, would willingly return to the first method. A gilder's cushion, a tip, and a knife with a long straight blade, are required. It is still best to begin with the last page of the book of gold leaf, holding the other pages out of the way as before, but now the page to be used may be turned back with the cover and placed face downwards on the cushion. When the book is lifted the gold leaf will be left lying on the cushion, smooth and uncrumpled.

The leaf is cut in pieces of the required size with the special knife, which is held at right angles to the surface of the leaf and pressed firmly down on the cushion, then drawn back a little towards the handle. The knife, of course, must be kept very sharp, and it should be wiped frequently with a piece of silk or it will make the edges of the gold leaf ragged.

The piece of leaf which is to be used may be picked up with the tip (a thin flat brush of sable or badger's hair). The gilder should stroke the tip two or three times over his own hair, and then touch the edge of one of the pieces of gold with it, and the gold may be gently lifted from the cushion and held in the air or moved slowly towards the piece of gesso it is to gild.

Besides gold leaf and the scissors, or knife, cushion and tip, it is necessary to have a piece of very soft silk folded to four or eight thicknesses (an old silk handkerchief that has been washed many times is good), a small piece of the smooth transparent paper known as crystal or glass parchment, a sharp pen knife, a pencil, and one or two burnishers. The burnishers are of very great importance, and a really good burnisher is the gilder's most precious possession. He needs at least one large one, about half an inch wide, with a flat surface at an angle of 30 degrees to the line of its handle. It is best to have this large burnisher made from haematite, though agate is almost as good. In addition to this an agate claw burnisher is useful, and so is a pointed agate if it is possible to find one that has no facets and is smooth enough at the point.

All tools should be arranged in their own places in relation to the work that is being done, so that the gilder can pick up the one he needs without taking his eyes from his work. A burnisher that will roll must be placed between other things that will prevent its falling off the table and being broken.

It is good, if possible, to work with the vellum on a piece of plate glass; the glass keeps the work cool, and its hardness makes burnishing easier. The glass should, however, be at least as large as the vellum; if it is smaller its edge may crease the vellum and do irreparable damage. It is better to work on a drawing board than to take this risk.

The gesso may be scraped to a smooth surface before it is gilded. Until the gilder acquires enough skill to lay the gesso quite evenly it is best for him to scrape away any irregularities in the surface before gilding it. After a little practice he should be able to lay it so that it dries level; but even then he will find a scraped surface easier to gild because the slight roughness left by careful scraping catches the delicate leaf and helps to keep it in place.

Scraping must be done very carefully, either with a sharp pen knife or with the finest sandpaper. The knife should be wiped frequently with a piece of silk and the sandpaper often renewed or heavy scratches may appear, scratches that are too deep to burnish out. As little gesso as possible should be removed, only enough to make the surface level, or, if it is already level, to roughen it slightly.

The gesso should be gilded immediately after being scraped. Cover the letter to be gilded with the folded silk, cut a piece of gold a little larger than the letter and pick it up with the fingers or the tip held in the right hand. With the left hand turn back the corner of the silk and hold it so that it can be dropped quickly over the letter again. Then, with the mouth an inch or two away from the gesso, breathe on it hard about a dozen times, drawing deep breaths. From this moment everything must be done as quickly as possible; hesitation for a fraction of a second may make a great difference to the result. As soon as the breathing is finished, cover the letter with a piece of gold leaf (if the first method of handling gold leaf is being used, flick away the piece of paper), drop the corner of the silk over the letter, and hold it firmly in place with the thumb and forefinger of the left hand; rub the silk hard with the burnisher to press the gold leaf firmly on the gesso and make it stick. Remove the silk, and a pattern corresponding to its texture will probably be seen on the gold. Cover the letter with the small piece of transparent crystal parchment, and run the point of the pencil round the edge of the letter, for this is the place where it is most difficult to make the gold leaf adhere. Then, still keeping it covered, and using the flat surface of the largest burnisher, burnish with a feather-light touch, moving the crystal parchment frequently to reduce the danger of its sticking to the gold. The pattern of the silk will then be erased, leaving the letter smooth but not bright. The first light burnish should be done with the greatest care, for the gesso is still soft and easily damaged, and once the surface has been made smooth it is safest to leave it for a few minutes before touching it again. After a few minutes, rub the burnisher vigorously on the silk to make sure that it is perfectly clean and dry, and, with the lightest imaginable touch, pass it slowly backwards and forwards over the surface of the gold. At first there will be a feeling of slight stickiness but this will gradually disappear, and then the burnisher may be rubbed more firmly, but still not heavily, on the letter; until at last, when it is clear that all is going well and the surface feels slippery, a good deal of pressure may be exerted.

During this part of the work the burnisher must often be

rubbed on the silk to prevent its sticking, and if the crystal parchment is held in the left hand between the letter and the light it will be easier to see if the letter is being damaged. This is the most critical time in the whole process, and at the first warning, either by sight or feeling, that the surface is being injured, the burnishing should stop, to be resumed a minute or two later, unless the damage is serious. If the surface is badly damaged another piece of gold leaf should be applied, and the burnishing should be started again, at first very gently and then more firmly.

When the letter is smooth and fairly bright, a second coat of gold should be laid. It is not necessary to breathe on the letter before applying this, and it is better not to press it with the silk; the leaf should stick to the first coat quite easily. The second coat should be burnished, slowly and lightly at first, and then more and more heavily until the letter is very bright.

Burnishing helps to attach the leaf, so it is a good thing to lay and burnish the second coat before brushing away the loose gold, however anxious the gilder may be to know whether the leaf has stuck or not. There is also an advantage in leaving the loose gold round the letter as long as possible, because, after it has been brushed away, the burnisher may touch the vellum, and picking up from it pounce that has been used in its preparation, rub it over the surface and make a dull patch. This can usually be remedied by rubbing the burnisher on the silk and reburnishing, but sometimes scratches cannot be removed.

When the second coat of gold leaf is laid and burnished, the loose gold round the letter must be brushed off with the silk or a very soft brush. This is the gilder's most anxious moment. It will show whether his gilding is clean and sharp at the edges, or ragged, with gesso showing in places where the leaf has not been held. If there is any part of the gesso that is not properly gilded, he should cover the rest of it with pieces of silk to protect it, and re-gild the part that looks ragged. With rather longer breathing than before, rather more speed in carrying out the work, and rather more force in rubbing the silk down on the gold leaf to press it home, the second attempt will probably be successful.

When a design has been gilded, the drawing of details, such as the mane of a lion or the veins of a leaf, may be impressed on it, in the form of shallow grooves which catch the light. Grooved lines should be made before the gesso has hardened. The safest tool to use is an HB pencil. Cover the gilding with crystal parchment and mark on it the line to be grooved. Then, holding the crystal parchment firmly in place, move the pencil backwards and forwards along this line, increasing the pressure when it is clear that all goes well. This is a safe method to use because the pencil will probably break before it damages the gilding. A deeper groove may be made by using a steel knitting needle instead of a pencil. Then the line must be made through the crystal parchment with one bold, rather quick stroke, and a little practice is needed before this can be done successfully every time.

The vellum round and inside the letter must be examined for any pieces of gold leaf that have stuck to it, and they should be removed with care by the point of a knife or a paper stump.

The work should be burnished again after about half an hour, and once more later in the day. If no glair has been used it may be burnished again a week or a fortnight later, but if the gesso has been mixed with glair it is safest to gild and burnish it on the day after it is laid and not to touch it again.

It is very important that gilding should not be breathed on after the last coat of gold leaf has been laid. Folded silk should be used to protect it while other work is being done on the same page.

If gilding goes badly on a day when the weather seems favourable, it is worth while to ask the following questions.

In the answer to one of them the cause of the trouble may perhaps be found.

(1) Was the gesso stirred very thoroughly every time the pen or brush was filled?

(2) When the gesso was ground, were the ingredients measured with sufficient care?

(3) Was the gesso ground long enough, and yet not over-ground?

(4) Was the silk freshly washed and ironed?

(5) Was the burnisher perfectly clean, with no specks of gold leaf attached to the surface?

Sometimes it is necessary to represent silver. Silver itself, or white gold, will turn black in a few years unless it is varnished, and it is better to use aluminium or platinum. Miss Vera Law has kindly written for this chapter the following note on the use of platinum.

'The application of platinum leaf is similar to that of gold leaf, but, owing to the fact that platinum leaf is both thicker and stiffer than gold leaf, the laying of it is more difficult.

'In order to make the platinum leaf adhere to the raising preparation it would seem that a slightly stickier asiso than that used for gold leaf is necessary. The following preparation has been found to give sufficient stickiness, and has also resulted in a laid ground remaining uncracked when bent round the rim of a sixpenny piece: 8 slaked plaster of Paris, 3 white lead, 1–1½ ground centrifugal sugar, 1 fish glue (Le Page's), 4–5 distilled water, pinch of Armenian bole (for colour). The above measurements are by capacity. It is advisable to buy fish glue in a bottle as the strength of that sold in tubes is apparently reduced in order to keep it moist and squeezable.

'It may be found that some platinum leaf is unevenly beaten. For easier attachment it is best to choose the thinnest parts.

'If, after burnishing, a sort of tarnish, with a blueish tinge appears, the affected part should be carefully wiped over with a very soft piece of wash leather. It is the opinion of certain manufacturers that exposure to coal gas would cause such a blemish.'

The method of gilding that has been described is the safest and easiest. As the student gains command over it he will find that he can leave out part of the process. First he will probably omit running the pencil round the edge of the letter; instead, he will press the gold leaf into place as he burnishes. Then, as his touch grows lighter, he may be able to discard the crystal parchment and burnish the leaf itself as soon as it is laid. He will find it a good exercise to try occasionally to gild without even the silk, allowing himself no tool but the burnisher. This is not an easy exercise but it is invaluable for developing a sensitive touch.

It is interesting to try burnishing the gesso before gilding it; some people find that this makes it easier to attach the leaf, others think it is more difficult. A further useful experiment is to lay the gesso in two coats, a first coat scraped very flat, and a second coat of thinner gesso. This often gives a good result, but it takes a longer time, and the gilder will probably discard the method very soon. After a good deal of practice he may find that he can gild gesso on the day it is laid, and even drop the leaf on the gesso while it is still wet, leaving burnishing until later, but if he attempts it too soon one lucky success will be followed by many failures.

The gilder should make as many experiments as possible. If they lead to nothing at the time, they add to his knowledge of the way materials act in different circumstances; and they provide him with a number of tricks which, held in reserve, may be valuable on a difficult day. Steady success in gilding can never be attained by a fixed rule, for the work does not behave in the same way twice, even on consecutive days under apparently exactly the same conditions. Success is most likely to come by flexibility in method, by resourcefulness in getting out of difficulties, and by a willingness to go back on special occasions to methods long discarded, such as burnishing at first through crystal parchment.

Though it is good to try as many new methods of gilding as possible, experiments with the gesso itself should be made with caution. It is best for the gilder to have a reliable mixture that he understands and can manage reasonably well, and to use that for all commissions; new recipes for gesso should only be tried on work that it is possible for him to keep. He cannot say whether a new gesso is successful or not until he has found out how it behaves in different kinds of weather. Sometimes a mixture that works well in April leads to disaster in August, and sometimes one that gives a brilliant result immediately may have lost its burnish completely in a few months. A recipe can only be pronounced good after it has been used successfully for at least a year, and after work gilded with it has survived a few English winters without any serious loss of brightness. A record should be kept of all experiments, and even when work is being done by the usual method, notes should be made of the date, the weather, the direction of the wind or the reading of a hygrometer, the mixture that was used, the time of day when the gesso was laid, the time when it was gilded, and whether it was burnished immediately, or after a short interval; for all these affect the result. If the work is done in a different room from the one in which the gilder usually works, that should be noted too; because, when it is impossible to gild in one place, the work may go fairly well in a room on the opposite side of the house. Keeping such a notebook will prove very valuable; if a piece of gilding is satisfactory after several years it is useful to know exactly how it was done; if it grows dull the notebook may reveal the cause.

It is not always the fault of the gilding if it loses its brightness, for it cannot be expected to keep its burnish if it is exposed to damp, and until it is protected by a frame or binding it is safest to keep it covered with crystal parchment, between strawboards, and wrapped in several thicknesses of brown paper, opening the parcel once a week to ventilate the manuscript. Nothing but silk or crystal parchment should be allowed to touch the surface of the gold. Great care is needed when it is being bound or framed, and, if it is framed, the protecting glass must be blocked away from it. No successful gilding is ever produced without very hard work, and it is a great pity for it to be spoilt by careless or ignorant handling after it leaves the gilder's studio.

The student will be helped considerably if he is able to examine good examples, especially medieval examples, of the craft. He will find many opportunities of seeing illuminated manuscripts in libraries and museums, in parish churches and private collections. He may have the good fortune to be allowed to handle a book himself, or to watch while its owner turns the pages, and then he will see the work as the artist intended it to be seen. As the light ripples from one piece of gold to another over the curving page, he will understand why only a manuscript decorated with gold or silver is, in the strict sense of the word, illuminated.

VI

The Design of Formal Scripts

The problem of the design of an alphabet is at once made difficult by our inheritance of the traditions of the Roman letter forms. It is never the invention of a new form of script but a variation or development in the process of evolution from a basic form. A knowledge of the history of lettering which, in its periods of slow development perceptible only to later generations and its periods of comparatively marked changes, is a reflection of the social history of mankind, is necessary not only for a study of basic forms of letters but in order that our own design may have a contemporary quality. Lettering will obviously not express this quality as easily as many other art forms but nevertheless the fine alphabet will in a subtle way be distinguishable as of its particular age in the way that the gothic black letter is supposed to have relation to the architectural forms of its period (although the original development of that letter form was due to practical reasons of economy). A background of tradition is as necessary as a feeling for the aesthetic movements of our own time.

The history of lettering may be divided conveniently by the invention of printing. In the preceding period, the development of letter forms was almost entirely influenced by the pen and conditioned by contemporary reading habits. In the second period the printing press perpetuated the best of the Renaissance calligraphic forms and quickly changed reading habits. These facts are especially important to the designer of an alphabet—type has set us a standard of legibility which cannot be ignored. The legibility mentioned here is that of the letters of a normal page or mass of text—obviously lettering in a wide sense must consider a wide variety of standards of legibility and even the script alphabet may have quite a number of varying standards for different occasions. There is little connection between the standard of legibility which may be applied to the letters to be used for pages of text and that applied, say, to a road sign, except the connection which arises from their common ancestry. Considering the mass of text, then, the ordinary person's eye is conditioned in what it accepts as the norm of legibility by what it is used to reading, that is the printed page not the written one, and we may base our standard on the best of these printed pages which are composed in type of Renaissance origin with their calligraphic ancestry.

The importance of this argument has changed considerably during the last half-century. Calligraphy at the turn of the century was much more a leader and educator in legibility and fine letter forms than it is to-day.

This is not to suggest that our pen alphabet should be bound to the typographic form from other points of view than this broad standard of legibility. The type form has properly subdued its calligraphic ancestry to the needs of the material and process—the pen is one of the most clearly formative of tools and the greatest possible use should be made of this fact.

It has already been stated that our standard of legibility will vary according to the occasion. For a mass of text a Roman type of letter (and a particular variety of a Roman letter) will be more readable than, say, a Gothic black-letter, because we are more used to the former (a fourteenth-century reader would, no doubt, find equal difficulty in reading the Roman form). Despite this, not more than a few words of Gothic black letter might do a very useful job in contrasting against a mass of more readable text, and by its difference of weight and pattern focus attention on a heading or some important word.

The greater the degree of informality in the alphabet, the more obvious becomes the dependence on what we are used to. We are entitled to expect a great deal more legibility from a formally written alphabet than an informally written one, for in the latter case various considerations such as speed (and all it implies in the construction of the letters) and the character of the writer are bound to intrude. As Alfred Fairbank says 'our own bad handwriting may be more legible to oneself than the other fellow's scrawl' although even in the most speedy and informal writing the standard of 'a certainty of deciphering' must be applied. Generally, any amount of Roman lower case letters is more readable than a similar amount of capitals, not because we are unfamiliar with the shape of the capital letter but because we do not normally read it in any quantity. In a way the capital letters are more distinctive as units than the small letters but our normal quick reading habits lead us not to see consciously each letter that we read, but to recognize each word or even sometimes a whole phrase by the peculiar shape given to it by its own unique combination of letter shapes. Capitals, then, are perfectly legible on any occasion where the speed desirable in reading several pages of text is not of importance and the eye may linger a little more to distinguish the word letter by letter. For similar reasons capitals remain perfectly legible even when widely spaced to form a particular texture in a heading but lower case letters spaced in a similar way become relatively much more illegible than when spaced closely enough for the distinctive word shape to be quickly identified. Italic letters with their ligatures and typical arch-forms and flourishes are generally less quickly identifiable than the Roman lower case forms and thus are generally considered suitable for such forms as poetry where speed of reading is not usually desirable.

Each letter and thence each word is made up of a certain unique combination of straight and curved strokes, thin and thick, and of serif forms. Any movement of the pen which detracts from this uniqueness of shape of the letters results in confusion between letters and, therefore, loss of legibility within the word. This aspect of legibility is well illustrated by comparison between such a word as 'minimum' written in Roman and Gothic black-letter characters. In the latter case the over-simplification of the structure of the individual letters results in almost complete illegibility of the word as a whole.

minimum

minimum

Fig. 16. Loss of Legibility

A slight emphasis on the first and last serifs of the compound letter forms such as m and n helps the legibility of the word

The combination of shapes within the word is further distinguished by the letters which have descending or ascending strokes, such as b, d, p and q.

Thus, the designing of our script alphabet becomes a balance of distinction and unity. Letters of closely related shape, such as c and e, must have their similar parts made with a similar pen movement, so that a family likeness runs through the alphabet, but this must be balanced against the basic requirement of legibility which is that the utmost distinction shall be retained for each individual character. Therefore the serif of the c and the upper bowl of the e must be as dissimilar as possible within the limits of the pleasant balance of the letter as a whole.

Except when occasion allows the playfulness of flourishing in such a place as not to disturb the pattern of the mass of text no letter should be so unusual in shape as to draw undue attention to itself at the expense of the eye's easy movement along the line.

The quality of unity in the main strokes and the proportions of the letters may be enhanced by the serif forms, but great care is required in the design of details such as the serifs and the height of ascenders and descenders in relation to the height of capitals. The scale of serif in relation to main letter form is very important—if the balance is right the serifs help the movement of the eye along the line and aid legibility by decreasing irradiation. The broad pen naturally makes very distinctive serif shapes but this distinguishing characteristic is very often over-emphasized at the expense of the legibility of the letters: the detail is given more emphasis than the main strokes with sad results. Comparison of the horizontal serif-stroke which the pen naturally makes in a slanted pen alphabet with the serifs of an inscriptional form will show that the pen tends to make a wider, heavier serif than the brush or chisel and, particularly when writing freely or in small sizes, the pen must be used with sensibility if the serifs are not to become unpleasantly Gothic in character or weak in form.

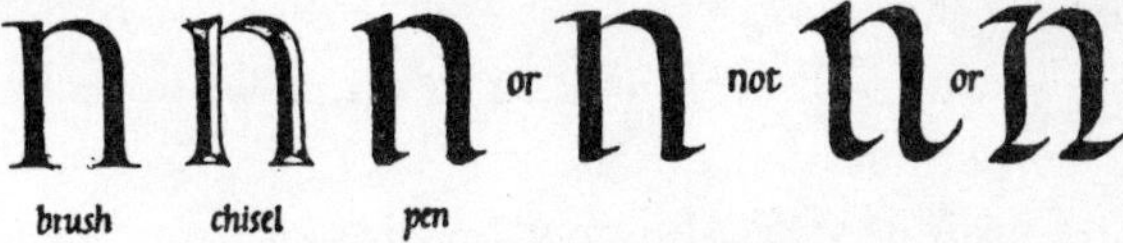

Fig. 17. Scale of Serifs

Each tool gives a serif of different character. The pen-made serifs should bear the same relationship to the whole letter as do those of brush and chisel forms. They are commonly over emphasized by wrong movement or angle of the pen

In semi-formal or condensed writing, curved serif-forms may easily become confused with the main arch-forms of the letters. The angle of the edge of the pen to the horizontal line is important in this respect; if held at an angle of 30°–40° the broad edge will naturally give a greater degree of emphasis to the main verticals of the letter forms than to the serifs or minor horizontal strokes.

Fig. 18. Pen Angle and Main Verticals

The first part shows the relationship of minor strokes of the letter to the major strokes when the pen is held at the correct angle. The second part shows how the minor strokes become too heavy for the major ones when the pen is held at too steep an angle

When writing freely and with speed the pen angle easily suffers and there arises a weakening of curved strokes due to the angularity which results from the pen's tendency to strike off in a line of least resistance to the broad edge. Too much pressure of pen against paper may also result in such a tendency. The pen angle may be increased slightly in writing a less formal italic hand for the sake of ease in moving the pen and keeping the ligatures of a hair-line quality, but the angle should never be so increased as to result in verticals becoming less emphatic than horizontals.

The designing of an alphabet consists of due consideration and sifting of all these aesthetic and practical problems and the rejection of those qualities which are superfluous to the particular purpose of the script. This conscious reduction to a simple form and the use of that form as an expression of penmanship doing a practical job of work may result accidentally in that indefinable quality of fine writing, beauty. That other abstract quality of calligraphy, personality, most obvious in informal handwriting, less obvious in, but equally essential to, a fine formal script, is equally indefinable as beauty and equally a quality not to be consciously striven for but one which will naturally develop with taste and sensibility and the conscious application of the practical qualities of calligraphy—of legibility, good letter forms, unity of letter forms, good arrangement, simplicity and precision, and controlled freedom.

THE ALPHABETS

The provision of alphabets as models is an attempt to provide illustrations of the considerations already discussed, but some of the qualities suggested as essential to fine writing are unavoidably emphasized at the expense of others. The alphabets attempt to illustrate the more practical qualities such as good proportion and construction and legibility at the expense, perhaps, of freedom. They may be considered as models of formal letters, yet of a degree of formality which does not exclude, once their forms have been mastered, the development of pen character and a personal style of writing. The study and mastery of such alphabets should help the student to appreciate the pen as a tool and through it the appreciation of drawn and typographic forms of letters.

The pen is a difficult tool to master—its essential simplicity and forthrightness, the degree to which it gives form and proportion to a letter by its very shape make it at the same time one of the most direct and most difficult of tools to use well. The slanted pen alphabets shown suggest forms of alphabets technically fairly simple, of general usefulness, which retain a definite pen character without departing too far from contemporary standards of legibility.

FORMAL ROMAN CAPITALS AND VERSALS: ALPHABETS. FIGS. 19, 20 AND 21

These three alphabets are all based on the same classical inscriptional proportions but vary in detail of construction.

ABCDEFGHIJK

LMNOPQRST

UVWXYZ

Fig. 19. Roman Capitals, Compound Form

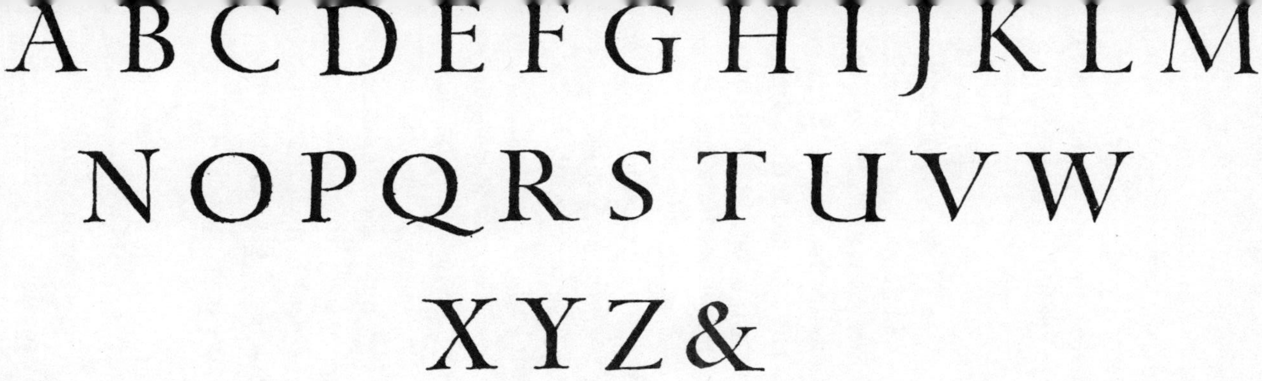

A B C D E F G H I J K L M

N O P Q R S T U V W

X Y Z &

Fig. 20. Roman Capitals, Simpler Written Form

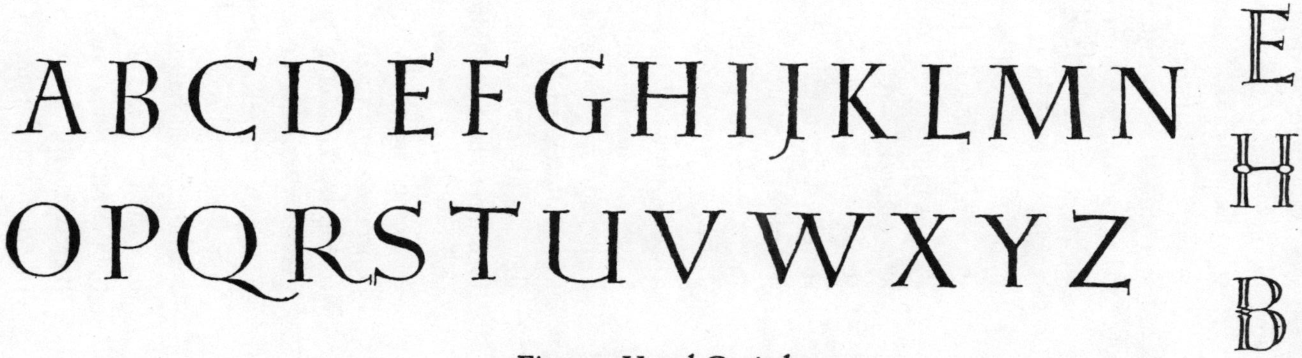

A B C D E F G H I J K L M N

O P Q R S T U V W X Y Z

E H B

Fig. 21. Versal Capitals

Both alphabets of Roman capitals are slowly written but the second is rather more direct and characteristic of the pen than the first which is a compound form, rather more drawn than written. The first is very similar to the versals in construction and differs from the versals only by reason of its serif-construction and form of its curved strokes. In the second alphabet the pen is held constantly at right angles to the writing line except in the case of diagonals and thin uprights; in the first alphabet and the versals the pen is held parallel to the writing line for the construction of straight horizontal strokes and its full width also shows in the case of thin vertical and diagonal strokes. Thus the incidence of thick and thin strokes in the first alphabet is less consistent than in the more simply written second alphabet. The first has forms, such as M and N, in which the contrast between thick and thin is not so marked and which, therefore, might be considered more suitable, say, for a large initial. The compound structure of the first alphabet makes it more generally useful for larger forms and the simpler construction of the second for smaller forms and larger masses of words. The contrast of thick and thin is illustrated in about its maximum convenient degree in the first alphabet. The thick strokes are made in compound form from two outlining strokes of the full width of the pen and filling-in. The width of pen is chosen so that the horizontals of such letters as E and F are not too emphatically contrasted against the thin strokes of such letters as C and D (made by a different angle of the pen) and so that for the greater part of a thick stroke not more than one filling-in stroke of the pen is required—more is inconvenient for any amount of writing.

In the second alphabet the contrast of thick and thin may be varied more. The thins are all made with the thin edge of the pen, the thicks all with the full width of the pen. But this means that the thin strokes are the same whatever the size of pen or whatever the size of letter, and this must have a limiting effect on the size of letter which can be made in this way if the contrast between thick and thin strokes is to be kept within reasonable limits.

The main distinction between the Roman capitals and versals is that the former has the rounded serif-form of its inscriptional model, whereas the latter has a hair-line serif almost at right angles to the two outlining strokes of the upright. The form of curve in the compound Roman letter follows the form of curve in the more simply-written one, that is the increase from thin to thick is gradual, whereas in the versal letter thickening is more concentrated in one place and the flattening of the inside of the curve, the first of the two outlining strokes, is generally more marked than in the Roman. These characteristics of the versals are reminiscent of its Gothic origin. They are illustrated in excess in 'Lombardic' capitals. All straight-pen alphabets, including these three, are difficult for any but the practised penman and are best left until a certain facility has been acquired in the formation of the slanted-pen forms in which the pen is held at a much more normal and comfortable angle. To make the writing position easier the pen is best cut to a more oblique angle than normal for slanted-pen forms. An added difficulty in the case of the two Roman alphabets is that serifs at the end of thin strokes must be finished off with a pen movement which needs some sleight of hand—not a direct stroke of the pen's edge but of its corner. Three simple decorated letters are shown, the decorative quality being achieved by a formal application of the method of constructing the versal alphabet.

SLANTED-PEN CAPITALS AND LOWER CASE: FIGS. 22 AND 23

The capitals are based on the same basic proportions as before but given a quite different character by the use of the slanted pen instead of the straight pen. Both capitals and lower case are written quite quickly by reason of their more

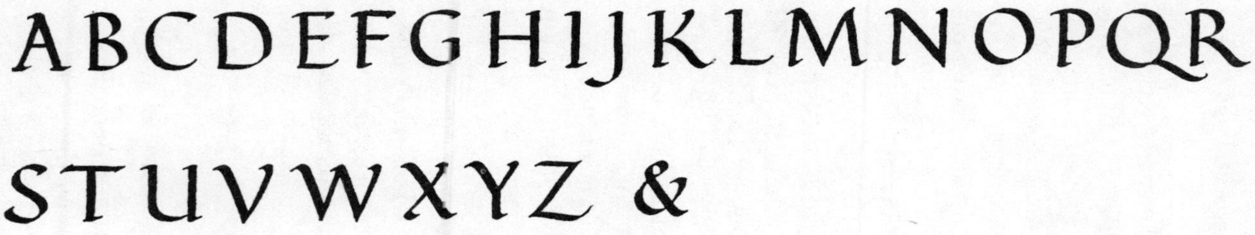

ABCDEFGHIJKLMNOPQR

STUVWXYZ &

Fig. 22. Slanted Pen Capitals

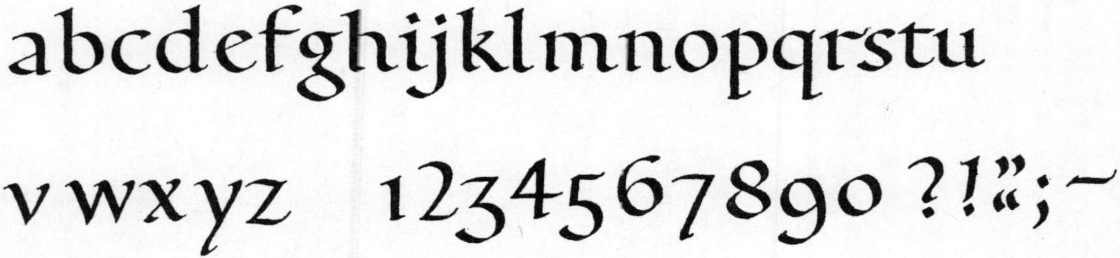

abcdefghijklmnopqrstu

vwxyz 1234567890 ?!";—

Fig. 23. Slanted Pen Lower Case

comfortable pen angle and marked simplicity of construction. Owing to the different pen angle there is less contrast of thick and thin than in the previous alphabets. The angle of the pen must be carefully chosen to preserve the proportion of detail (to avoid over-stressing of serifs, for example) and to avoid badly modulated placing of thick and thin strokes throughout the alphabet. The main strokes of the letters are simply written in one pen stroke (a downward, horizontal or diagonal stroke pulled rather than pushed) and the serifs are combined in the same movement of the pen that makes the main letter-stroke. Thus the pen makes much more of a direct statement than in the compound forms of Roman capitals and versals. The methodical formation of similar strokes throughout the alphabet and a certain speed in writing them are an advantage in keeping consistency and simplicity of statement, but speed and freedom must not be overdone at the expense of strength of structure of the individual letter forms. Speed often has the effect of coarsening such small but important details as the serif strokes and the relationship of size between capitals and lower case.

The lower case alphabet, particularly, may usefully be broken down into a number of similar component parts, and these parts studied in themselves in order to appreciate the architectural strength of construction of individual letters and as an aid to keeping a marked sense of unity and consistency within the whole alphabet. The usefulness of this when studying models or when designing a particular alphabet must not be overstressed—it must be remembered when actually writing that each letter, each word even, is an entity, and this breaking down of letters into parts may lead to over-simplification of those elements and a monotony in the writing. (This is illustrated in certain eighteenth- to nineteenth-century writing masters' copy books.) Similarly, it is useful to relate in one's mind the shapes of letters to certain simple geometrical forms whilst remembering that when actually writing the aim is to write freely, although with consistency and precision, and not to emulate perfect geometrical shapes.

Thus, in the lower case alphabet, one may bear in mind the circle and the semi-circular Roman arch-form in writing the

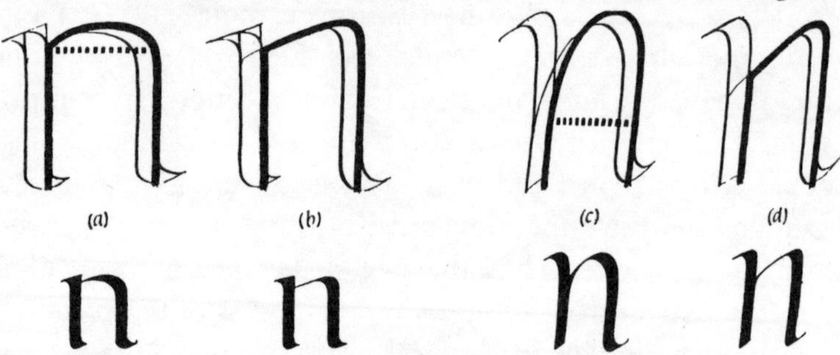

Fig. 24. The Construction of Arch-Forms of Slanted Pen Alphabets

(*a*) *The arch is almost symmetrical and a strong construction and a legible letter result. Note that the arch springs from the point where serif and upright meet.*

(*b*) *The same letter with an asymmetrical arch-form resulting in a weaker and less legible letter.*

(*c*) *and* (*d*) *Illustrating the same argument in the case of the Italic arch-form, but note that the arch springs from a different position in this case.*

round and the arched letter forms. The architectural strength of construction of the upright stroke of a Gothic black-letter character, although quite different in feeling from these Roman alphabets, gives us a picture of a form of construction,

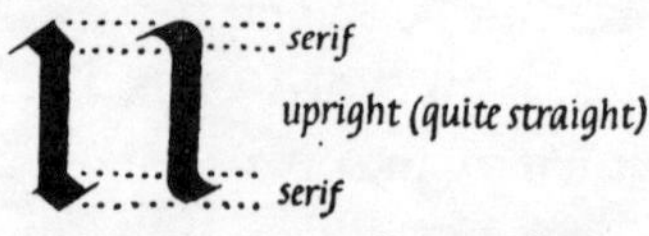

Fig. 25. Upright Strokes

and an idea of the relationship in proportion of serif to the main part of an upright stroke which we may usefully keep in mind in writing the uprights of this slanted pen alphabet. If the curve of the serif stroke is carried into the upright, as commonly happens, the letter will be weakened in construction.

ITALIC CAPITALS AND LOWER CASE: FIGS. 26, 27 AND 28

The difference between these capitals and the slanted-pen Roman capitals may be easily summarized as a difference in proportion due to the italic alphabet being based upon an oval O instead of the Roman circular O. Generally, but not essentially, the italic capitals and lower case also have a slight inclination to the right and are somewhat lighter in weight than the Roman. The same distinctions are obvious between the Roman lower case and the italic lower case, but in the case of the latter there are also certain changes of letter form which emphasize the distinction between the two alphabets. The round forms of *a*, *g*, *k* and *y*, and the flourished form of *f*, are typically italic forms derived from the Roman, as was the whole italic alphabet, for reasons of speed and economy in writing, an example of cursive writing modifying a formal alphabet and becoming itself, in time, a formal alphabet.

Two different italic lower case alphabets are shown, differing in a varying degree from the parent Roman. The second is a degree more formal than the first—we may, perhaps, classify this as 'sloped-Roman', in printer's terminology, to distinguish it from the first alphabet which is based on a 'true' italic. The italic has cursive arch-forms as well as the compression of proportions due to its being based on an oval O, slope (usually), and typical italic shapes of *a*, *f*, *g* and *k*. The 'sloped-Roman' is also a compressed alphabet based on an oval O. It also has slope and the typical italic letter forms, but it is distinguished from the italic by having the same kind of arch-forms as the Roman lower case alphabet (see Diagram 4). A further distinction might be made in giving the italic letters a simpler, more cursive hooked serif at the beginning

ABCDEFGHIJKLMNO

PQRSTUVWXYZ&?!;-"“

Fig. 26. *Italic Capitals*

abcdefghijklmnopq

rstuvwxyz

Fig. 27. *Italic Lower Case, i*

abcdefghijklmnopqrstu

vwxyz&

of vertical strokes whilst retaining the more formal, more 'Roman' beaked serif in the 'sloped-Roman'.

Although a slight slope (not more than about 15°) is usual in these alphabets, the result of the speed at which a cursive hand is usually written, it is not an essential. It helps to give a little more distinction to the italic hands when they are used together with Roman, but even then sufficient distinction may be obtained if the Roman and italic are both quite upright, but the italic has its compressed proportions and its peculiar letter forms. The Roman forms of *g* and *y* are often used with the italic in slightly compressed form to agree with the rest of the alphabet, but the rounded forms of *a*, *f*, *g*, *k* and *y* should never be used in a Roman alphabet even if made to agree with the circular O.

The more cursive italic arch-forms involve a pushing pen movement which is not found in the more formal alphabets, and this often involves some difficulty. Points to note in this connection are that the pen is commonly held at a slightly higher angle for the italic alphabet than for the Roman, and this helps the pushing upward movement which is largely in the direction of the 'thin' of the pen. It is especially important in this alphabet to avoid pressure of the pen on paper which prevents the pushing of the pen; the cursive arch-forms which occasion the push stroke must be written at a fair speed however slowly the remaining parts of the letters are written. This speed is the original cause of the adoption of an oval form for the italic type of letter—a speedy pen naturally tends to make this oval form of arch whereas a pen moving slowly will make a wider, more circular curve even against the will of the penman. The particular form of italic letters and the speed at which they are normally written tend to encourage longer ascenders and descenders (particularly the latter) and their flourishing. These flourished forms are not illustrated they are best left to the good sense of the scribe with a warning that they need plenty of room, whether flourished into a margin or between lines of writing, but particularly in the latter case when they are likely to confuse the strong left-to-right pattern of the line of writing and introduce an unpleasant vertical feature into the writing texture which will rather carry the eye vertically from one line to the next than horizontally along the line. If ascenders and descenders are extended, the proportion between height of capitals and 'x-height' of the letters should remain normal.

VII

The Design of Manuscript Books and Inscriptions

MANUSCRIPT BOOKS

Sir Edward Maunde Thompson in his *Greek and Latin Palaeography* says: 'Vellum books were designed upon an existing Roman model of two or more waxen tablets which were fastened together with rings acting as hinges.' This form of early book goes back to at least A.D. 100 and represents a transitional development between the ancient roll and the modern book. The lawyers of the time welcomed the use of skin prepared on both sides, arranged in the new way which was both convenient for reference and, as far as could be seen, permanent.

The earliest manuscripts on vellum are usually of the broad quarto size, in appearance almost square. The quires of which they are composed consist, in most instances, of eight leaves, that is, of four folded sheets quaterino (whence our word quire), and this number continued in general favour for all sizes of volumes throughout the middle ages. The sheets forming the quire were arranged so that hair side faced hair side and flesh or inner side faced flesh side, so that each book opening would be of the same colour and appearance.

At the period when most ecclesiastical manuscripts were on the decline a new set of books was being written in Italy which was to influence modern illuminators. These were the humanistic manuscripts of the fifteenth century, produced by scribes who wrote out the works of Petrarch. In designing these manuscripts they totally ignored Gothic text and the prevailing type of illuminating; instead they produced a script based on the Caroline Reformed hand and originated a new type of pattern for initials and decoration, based on twelfth-century work. This cannot be said to be a new phase in page design, yet it brought a new lightness of touch and a sense of delicacy quite unknown in the fifteenth century. This was later named white vine.

With the advent of printing, written books began to decline, leaving a mass of different types of letter form and ornament to be used by the typographer in so far as the new method would allow. By this time most of the problems confronting a book scribe had been worked out, including the page design of prose, poetry, music, calenders, and colophons together with headings and initial letters; but it fell to the lot of the typographer to design the title-page as we know it, which did not come into fashion until about 1480.

The design of the book page should be considered from the point of view of the book when it is open. The text space is

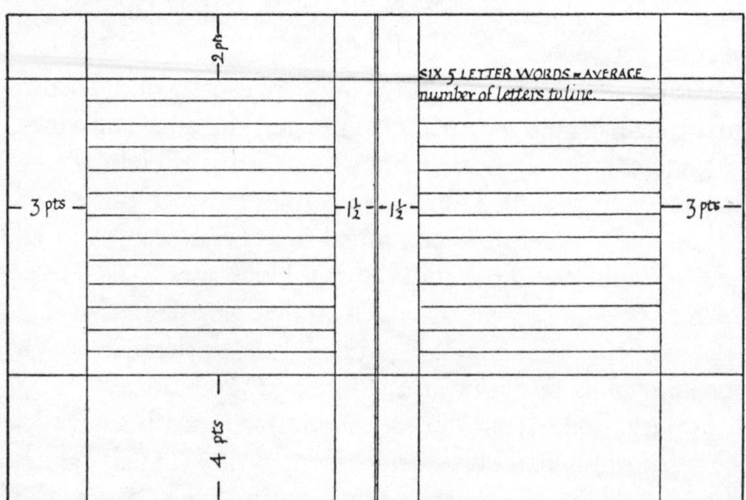

Fig. 29. Proportions of a Quarto Book Page

surrounded by three vertical margins and top and bottom margins. The vertical margins should be equal in width, the centre one being divided by the fold or spine of the book. The width of the top margin should be half that at the base, so that the text is lifted well up. To prepare paper or skin for a quarto book, take a piece 30 in. × 22 in., fold twice, and the result should be four pieces of the same proportion, size 15 in. × 11 in.

First divide the height of the page, which in the case of a large quarto will be 15 in., into eighteen equal parts and use these parts as shown in figure 29. Should the book be a thick one add a little to the inside margins to allow a certain amount

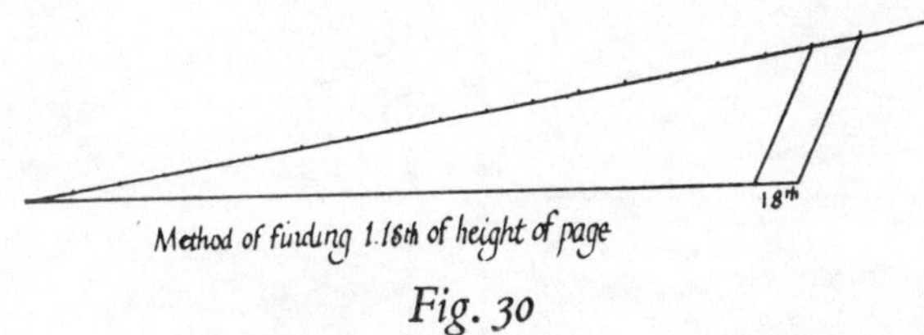

Fig. 30

to be taken up in binding. If the book is to be bound in the guarded manner it will not need any extra allowance. If, for any reason, you wish to have wider margins, divide the quarto height into sixteen or seventeen equal parts and proceed as above. A sixteenth unit will give equal margin area to the text; more margin than this would be out of proportion. To obtain satisfactory margins for a folio or octavo book, another method should be adopted as the proportion is different; the sheet is folded once for a folio size, three times for octavo, and twice for quarto. Experience in folding sheets of paper and arranging margins will be found useful when ordering cut sheets of vellum.

In arranging margins for folio and octavo sheets the following method is the best that can be devised although not as simple and convenient as that for the quarto. As it is impossible to reduce it to parts, the margins are arrived at the other way round, that is to say, from what is left when the proportion of the text is fixed. Take a similarly proportioned sheet of paper 9 in. × 7 in., fold once and make the following calcu-

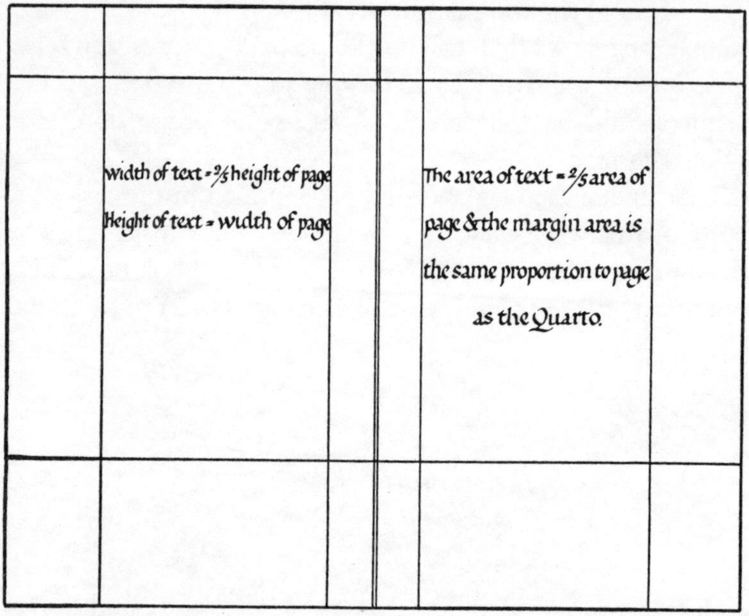

Fig. 31. Proportions of Folio and Octavo Book Page

lations. First measure the paper and draw the centre or spine line: the width of each of these leaves will be the height of the text column. Next divide the total height of the page into five

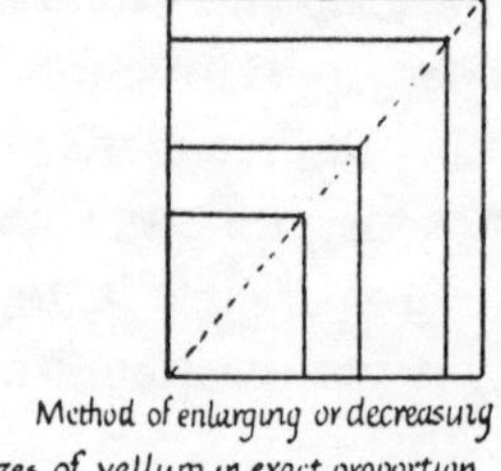

Fig. 32

parts, measure off two which gives the width of the text. When the proportion of text is obtained, arrange it within the page so as to give similar proportion of margins to that of quarto pages. Should it be necessary to enlarge or decrease a page of given proportion, draw the given shape, produce the diagonal and proceed as figures 31 and 32.

The octavo proportion is usually used for poetry.

In order to estimate the size of writing for a given line, write thirty to thirty-five letters in a line, or seven average words, between the margin lines of the page. If these fill the line the size of the writing will be, on the average, satisfactory and in good proportion to the page. Should the words need division to fit them into the lines more than two or three times, reduce the size slightly. This written trial is only a method of estimating the general writing size of the text of a book and is not applicable to larger writing when necessary for decoration or emphasis. Compressed hands such as italic or cursive would admit many more letters to the line, say forty-five; but for foundational hand in a quarto book thirty-five is a good average.

Lines with less than four average words of five letters each, or with more than nine, should be avoided as the first will become too large and the second too small; it is a question of scale one way or the other. Broadsheets will take rather more words to the line than book pages, probably because there is but one copy to read so the eye does not become weary, as it may do when reading a closely written book; they certainly take less if the matter is 'displayed' as in title-pages, etc.

Ruling is a very exacting part of the production of a manuscript book and should be approached with care and attention to detail. The equipment necessary is as follows: a good ebony-edged board and T-square, reliable screw dividers, a 6H pencil, and bone point or steel knitting needle. (See also page 94.)

It is difficult to lay down a rule regarding the style of writing to be used for any given subject or type of literature, but some suggestions can be made.

Broadly speaking, poetry looks better when written in italic or some free slightly sloping hand. Whilst prose generally is suited by an upright letter, such as what is now known by modern scribes as foundational, this being the hand modernized by Edward Johnston from English tenth-century manuscripts.

Where easy legibility is necessary, as in a memorial book, a well-spaced upright writing seems to be in keeping with its purpose; it can have notes in a narrow or informal hand for contrast and detail as well as for quotations.

Versals may be used for title-pages, headings, initials of ecclesiastical and memorial books when the main text, whether a list of names or prose, is in the foundational hand. The proportions should roughly follow those of a good Roman capital and be well spaced; there should be a certain amount of gothic feeling in the round strokes; the uprights should have a slight top-heavy appearance and be finished with fine swiftly made serifs.

As the title-page is the invention of the printer or typographer, it is no use looking back to see what the medieval writers did. It is a most interesting page and demands skill in both design and execution. The only rule seems to be that in a manuscript it shall be the first page, and be on the recto side, the letters being placed on the general ruling of the book, so it shall appear harmonious throughout. Apart from this and the general limit of the margins one can do almost anything that is in keeping with the tone of the work. It is the place for gilding and colour, sometimes with heraldry, symbolism or cypher. Ornament over and above this should serve the purpose of binding the whole composition into a satisfactory shape. Above all, it is the place for fine letters beautifully spaced, giving a sense of dignity with richness and reserve. Generally it should be written in capitals, but a shape made up of small letters if the title is long can look well. If it consists of one word, or a few, the title may be placed well above the centre of the page and generally be central between the margin lines. One word or decorative spot, such as a badge, can have the appearance of being too near the spine if placed centrally between the margin lines; in this case it is as well to move such a spot out a little towards the outer margin to prevent this. In placing lines of words in capital letters so that they look central, each line under the other, it is often difficult to find the exact centre of a word or line, as the optical centre depends on the outer shapes of the first and last letters. If a line begins and ends with letters such as N or H it can easily be found by obtaining the central point between the two outer strokes. But should the line begin with N or H and end with T or W the centre point between the two extremities will not be the optical centre, and the line so placed will not look central. Trial with various letter endings should be made to discover how to make odd-ending lines appear central. Speaking generally, round letters need pushing out from the centre and straight ones the reverse, so that a line beginning with O and ending with H would have to be moved to the left. The same adjustment has to be made when placing letters down a left-hand margin; the curved letters must be placed a little over the line and the uprights exactly on it.

The top left-hand corner of a written page is the traditional place for an initial or first letter, as can be seen in the fourth-century copy of the Georgics of Virgil. The letter is Roman in proportion, with geometric detail added to the thick strokes; it stands up into the top margin as high as three lines of the writing and is placed a little to the left of the text, as if to give additional emphasis to the letter. The design of this early example seems to have been improved upon, when in the eighth century initial letters, though rough, were sunk into the text whilst still emphasizing the corner. Early insular manuscripts show very childish attempts compared with the floriated letters employed in uncial manuscripts; whilst the superb Irish geometrical headings stand out with great brilliance only to be matched by later examples produced by the Norman illuminators.

Gradually the versal letter becomes the standard form and maintains its position right through until the end of the Gothic period. From small delicate beginnings it grew to enormous dimensions finally taking to itself nearly the whole of the page, reducing the text to three or four lines. During the course of its growth the initial letter became highly decorative and threw off illuminated pattern into the margins which finally crept round until it became a complete border. This motif of page decoration was taken over by the Italian printer, became torn from its parent, the initial, and became an excrescence completely overshadowing the text.

The initial letter should be larger and above the tops of the following letters, filling out the left-hand corner in such a way as to prevent it becoming rounded. It looks best when gilded and coloured in contrast to the text and can be enriched by a third colour with line ornament to lace into the page. The background can be solid as in the white vine type, or free as in arabesque. The ornament or symbol can cut through the letter or be confined to the counter of the form.

To design a new, simple, ornamental form in and about an initial letter has become a difficult matter seeing that so much has been done during the past eight centuries. One thing stands out clearly in the history of manuscript decoration, and that is, that a conventional treatment of ornament suits the letter forms of our alphabet much better than a naturalistic one, and that skilful play with a pen is often or generally better than modelling with a brush.

The size of an initial cannot be laid down without reference to the area of the text. For instance, when placing it on a page in a quarto book it can be from three to four lines deep, but in an octavo two or three are generally sufficient. It should be fitted snugly into the corner of the text throwing out springs of ornament which will knit it to the lettering. Versals which begin new paragraphs should be small in size so that there is no competition. Initial letters such as L, I, J and P, which invite one to bring the main strokes right down the side of the text, should be avoided; the parallels set up by this method produce a dull design seeing that the very nature of the letter form demands that it should be straight. Whatever interruptions are placed on it in its course down the page, it never seems to be a success. Contrasts in size, colour, weight, texture and direction are the mainsprings of good page design, but great experience is needed to know how much or how little to use.

INDENTING

Indenting is a method of creating interest and pattern on almost every page, and has been designed by typographers to give the reader's eye a rest at the end of a long sentence or paragraph. It is the simple device of beginning the new paragraph a little way in from the margin line and thus creating a white spot. The new sentence can begin with a coloured capital and can also be preceded by a paragraph mark to give the page a sparkle. Should it so happen that spots of colour occur at convenient places, say at one- or two-thirds down the page, it can impart a sense of simple design that is most effective, especially through a number of closely written pages, but in any case they add interest to a page. Similar decoration can be made by allowing the coloured capital of the new paragraph to project into the margin, with, if desired, a contrasting mark in front.

Notes written in the margin of a book, whether for explanation, direction or reference were primarily for use; and were first written in a free manner in the same hand, rather smaller than the general text. They were mostly used in liturgical books and were always in red as the name rubric implies. It is a simple way of giving slight decoration with a change of colour. They can be placed anywhere in the wide margin but if used only as a sub-title or chapter name, the most effective place is level with the top writing line, i.e. as a shoulder note. Rubrics give scale and a sense of decoration through contrast when no other decoration is thought necessary, but in order to keep the line structure running through the page they should be placed on the general writing lines extended into the margins. If several lines are required an additional line between the general ruling should be used which will cause the notes to be half the size of the text. Italics are frequently used to-day as they increase the contrast value and allow more words in the available space. Marginal notes should stop short of the edge of the page by at least a quarter of an inch, and be of good proportion to the total amount of margin.

Notes at irregular intervals can be decorative, whereas solid notes running half-way down, leaving the remainder free, will not give a sense of good proportion to the whole book page. If possible arrange notes in both wide margins to give balance.

There is a wide field in page design when names and details of a memorial book have to be set out. First there is the all-over pattern, when names and details are written the same size all down the page continuously as one would write prose. It is the simplest form giving a fine black page, but it has the defect of making it difficult to find a particular name. But with a rubric it can look extremely dignified and rich.

A second method is placing the names and details in two or three columns down the page when only initials of Christian names are required. First, surname and initials, second, rank and third, date of death. This method makes it easy to find particular names but does not make a satisfactory design. It lacks continuity in the horizontal line, so characteristic of the written page; moreover it cannot accommodate very long or

APOCALYPSIS xxi. 5–7.

Et dixit qui sedebat in throno:
Ecce nova facio omnia.
Et dixit mihi: Scribe, quia
haec verba fidelissima sunt,
et vera. Et dixit mihi:
Factum est: EGO SUM
A, et Ω:
initium, et finis.
Ego sitienti dabo de fonte
aquae vitae gratis. Qui
vicerit, possidebit haec, et ero
illi Deus, et ille erit mihi filius.

Profr A. B. Pite, F.R.I.B.A. with affectionate regards from E. Johnston.
20. July 1923. A.D.

Pl. 3. Quotation from the Apocalypse EDWARD JOHNSTON

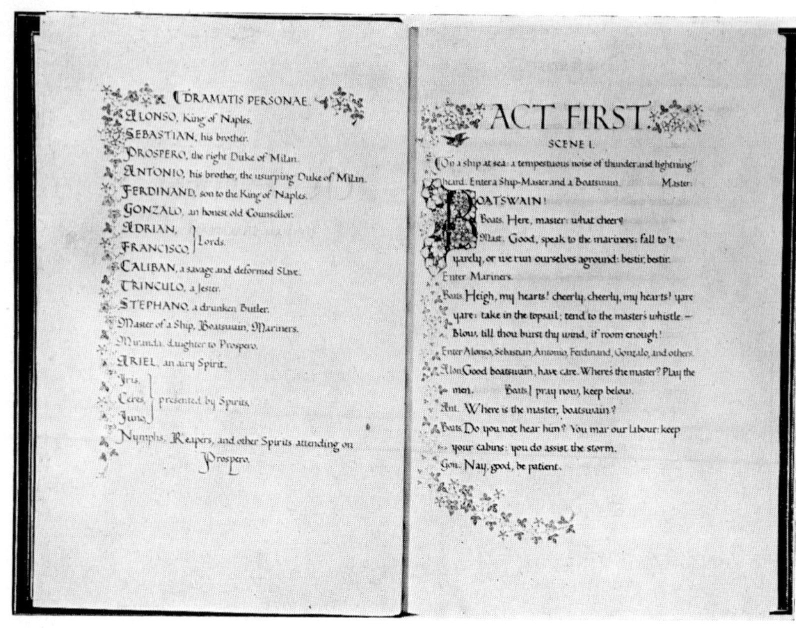

DRAMATIS PERSONAE.

ALONSO, King of Naples.
SEBASTIAN, his brother.
PROSPERO, the right Duke of Milan.
ANTONIO, his brother, the usurping Duke of Milan.
FERDINAND, son to the King of Naples.
GONZALO, an honest old Counsellor.
ADRIAN, }
FRANCISCO, } Lords.
CALIBAN, a savage and deformed Slave.
TRINCULO, a Jester.
STEPHANO, a drunken Butler.
Master of a Ship, Boatswain, Mariners.
Miranda, daughter to Prospero.
ARIEL, an airy Spirit.
Iris, }
Ceres, } presented by Spirits.
Juno, }
Nymphs, Reapers, and other Spirits attending on Prospero.

ACT FIRST.

SCENE I.

On a ship at sea: a tempestuous noise of thunder and lightning heard. Enter a Ship-Master and a Boatswain. Master.

BOATSWAIN!

Boats. Here, master: what cheer?

Mast. Good, speak to the mariners: fall to 't yarely, or we run ourselves aground: bestir, bestir.

Enter Mariners.

Boats. Heigh, my hearts! cheerly, cheerly, my hearts! yare, yare: take in the topsail; tend to the master's whistle.—Blow, till thou burst thy wind, if room enough!

Enter Alonso, Sebastian, Antonio, Ferdinand, Gonzalo, and others.

Alon. Good boatswain, have care. Where's the master? Play the men.

Boats. I pray now, keep below.

Ant. Where is the master, boatswain?

Boats. Do you not hear him? You mar our labour: keep your cabins: you do assist the storm.

Gon. Nay, good, be patient.

Pl. 4. 1st Act of the Tempest GRAILY HEWITT and IDA HENSTOCK
V & A Museum

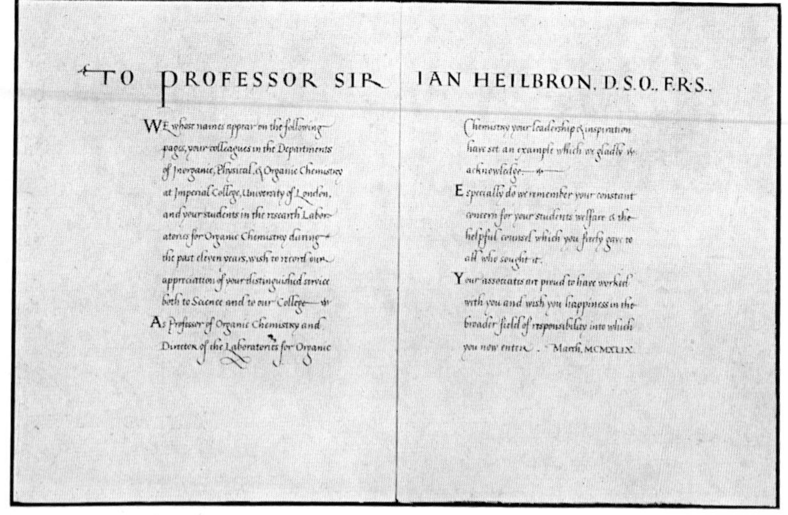

TO PROFESSOR SIR IAN HEILBRON, D.S.O., F.R.S.

WE whose names appear on the following pages, your colleagues in the Departments of Inorganic, Physical, & Organic Chemistry at Imperial College, University of London, and your students in the research Laboratories for Organic Chemistry during the past eleven years, wish to record our appreciation of your distinguished service both to Science and to our College.

As Professor of Organic Chemistry and Director of the Laboratories for Organic Chemistry your leadership & inspiration have set an example which we gladly acknowledge.

Especially do we remember your constant concern for your students' welfare & the helpful counsel which you freely gave to all who sought it.

Your associates are proud to have worked with you and wish you happiness in the broader field of responsibility into which you now enter. March, MCMXLIX.

Pl. 5. Address to Sir Ian Heilbron DOROTHY MAHONEY

+

INITIUM SANCTI EVANGELII
+ SECUNDUM JOANNEM +

IN PRINCIPIO ERAT VERBUM, ET VERBUM ERAT APUD DEUM, ET DEUS ERAT VERBUM. Hoc erat in principio apud Deum. Omnia per ipsum facta sunt: et sine ipso factum est nihil quod factum est: in ipso vita erat, et vita erat lux hominum; et lux in tenebris lucet, et tenebræ eam non comprehenderunt. Fuit homo missus a Deo, cui nomen erat Joannes. Hic venit in testimonium, ut testimonium perhiberet de lumine, ut omnes crederent per illum. Non erat ille lux, sed ut testimonium perhiberet de lumine. Erat lux vera, quæ illuminat omnem hominem venientem in hunc mundum. In mundo erat, et mundus per ipsum factus est, et mundus eum non cognovit. In propria venit, et sui eum non receperunt. Quotquot autem receperunt eum, dedit eis potestatem filios Dei fieri, his, qui credunt in nomine ejus: qui non ex sanguinibus, neque ex voluntate carnis, neque ex voluntate viri, sed ex Deo nati sunt. (Hic genuflectitur) ET VERBUM CARO FACTUM EST, et habitavit in nobis: et vidimus gloriam ejus, gloriam quasi Unigeniti a Patre, plenum gratiæ et veritatis. R. Deo gratias.

Pl. 6. The Last Gospel, Altar Card — Margaret Alexander

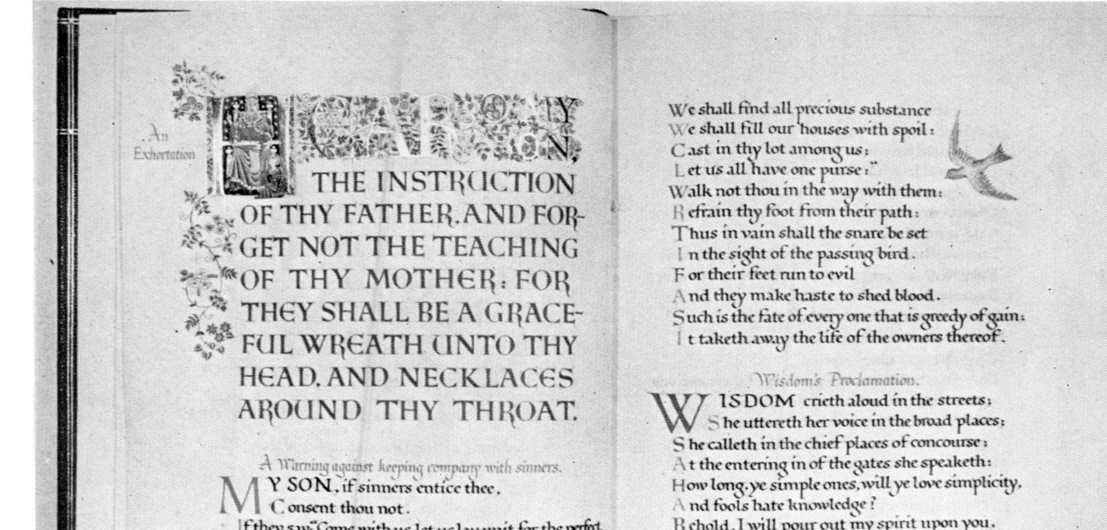

An Exhortation

HEAR, MY SON, THE INSTRUCTION OF THY FATHER, AND FORGET NOT THE TEACHING OF THY MOTHER: FOR THEY SHALL BE A GRACEFUL WREATH UNTO THY HEAD, AND NECKLACES AROUND THY THROAT.

A Warning against keeping company with sinners.

MY SON, if sinners entice thee,
Consent thou not.
If they say: "Come with us, let us lay wait for the perfect,
Let us swallow them up alive as Sheol:
And whole, as those who go down into the pit:

4

We shall find all precious substance
We shall fill our houses with spoil:
Cast in thy lot among us:
Let us all have one purse:"
Walk not thou in the way with them:
Refrain thy foot from their path:
Thus in vain shall the snare be set
In the sight of the passing bird.
For their feet run to evil
And they make haste to shed blood.
Such is the fate of every one that is greedy of gain:
It taketh away the life of the owners thereof.

Wisdom's Proclamation.

WISDOM crieth aloud in the streets;
She uttereth her voice in the broad places;
She calleth in the chief places of concourse:
At the entering in of the gates she speaketh:
How long, ye simple ones, will ye love simplicity,
And fools hate knowledge?
Behold, I will pour out my spirit upon you,
I will make known my words unto you,
Because I have called, and ye refused,

5

Pl. 7. Opening Page, Book of Proverbs for A. D. Power, Esq. MARGARET ALEXANDER hyphenated names without upsetting the rhythm of the column. If allowance is made for extra long names in this column method a great deal of space is wasted between columns and the page is thereby weakened. In contrast to these two methods there is a third which accommodates both those who wish to have a fairly full page with the horizontal line, and at the same time the full name plus a good deal of detail which can be easily read. The full name is written in black, or red, right across the page from margin to margin if it is long enough in a size which will allow an average of two Christian names, plus the surname. Names of extreme length can run into the margin, or the third Christian name can be indicated by the initial only. The details can then be written under in black if the names are in colour or vice versa; they look best if written in italic or some cursive hand, and can be indented half an inch or more from the margin. When these details are of about equal length, the page is orderly, the names running across both pages. But when both names and details are of unequal length the effect is still quite pleasing. This method, which fulfils a modern need in giving information, can also be used in writing a *Liber Benefactorum* which is in its very nature composed of unequal data.

The colophon or tailpiece was a note written at the end of the volume giving details of the making of the book, its author, and, from the early fifteenth century, the name of the scribe who often added a personal note of thanks for the completion of his task. It was a page allotted to him by the authority for whom he worked. In modern manuscripts the title and author appear on the first or title-page as arranged by early typographers, but the scribe's name is written as a colophon on the first plain page at the end of the book, often with the names of others who assisted in the work, including that of the binder. This information is usually written in a small italic hand, sometimes on a scroll, more often in small writing in colour, perhaps with some slight embellishment together with details of date and place of origin, and any information the scribe thinks fit to pass on to posterity.

A scribe who is approached by the organizers of a complimentary address is often asked about the various forms it can take. The following are the usual ones:

(1) The scroll laced with ribbon and presented in a cylindrical case.
(2) The framed broadside.
(3) The bound book.
(4) The bound folio or open page bound in leather with a leather edging showing when the folio is open.

The scroll is the simplest and quickest form to produce, as it can be completed entirely by the scribe while the case is being made by the book-binder. If thought fit, the scroll can be attached to a turned roller terminated at the ends with mouldings. This looks well in walnut or any other ebonized wood.

In designing a book of prose, such as a manuscript copy of a classic book or a record of a college, institution or society, a decision must be made regarding the general character of the writing. If it is to be strong, heavy and gothic in treatment it should not be more than four nib widths, and the space between the lines six to seven widths. But if, on the other hand, a light treatment is desirable, the width of the nib must be one-fifth or two-elevenths of the letter-height, and the space between up to as much as three times the height of the writing. This will produce a page similar to that which was written in the fifteenth century in Italy, and now known as humanistic. Notes in each case would have to be smaller and in italic for contrast. The initial capitals would be gothic in character, in the first instance, Roman or classic in the second.

Oliver Simon in his book *Introduction to Typography* gives valuable hints on spelling, punctuation and italicizing and recommends *Rules for Compositors and Readers*, published by the University Press, Oxford, 31st edition, 1938; also *Authors' and Printers' Dictionary* by F. Howard Collins, 8th edition, 1938.

'In descriptive matter numbers under one hundred should be in words, but figures should be used when the matter consists of stated quantities, numbers, ages etc. Spell out indefinite numbers, e.g. "has been a thousand times". Insert commas with four or more figures, 2,391. To represent an approximate date use the fewest figures possible. 1931–2 not 1931–32. Dates in descriptive matter should be written "on the 20th of January 1931" not "on January the 20th 1931".'[1]

The following order is normally used in a printed book and is of guidance when making a manuscript book:

Half-title (when included)
Title
Dedication
Table of Contents
List of Abbreviations (if any)
Preface
Introduction
Corrigenda or errata (if any)
Text of book
Appendix
Colophon, with date.

'Italic is used for emphasis and for the names of books, newspapers, plays and operas, appearing in the text; also for foreign words and phrases, and musical terms of expression; but extracts from foreign texts, however short, should be in the hand of the book.'

'Divide after a vowel, turning over the consonant. In present participles take over -ing, divid-ing, rest-ing. When two consonants come together put the hyphen between them, as haemor-rhage, forget-ting, trick-ling. The terminations, -tion, -cious, -cial, may be taken over entire, but must not

[1] Oliver Simon, *Introduction to Typography*, Faber & Faber, 1945.

themselves be divided. The part of a word at the end of a line should suggest the remainder of the word: starv-ation, not star-vation. A page should not end with part of a divided word. Words derived from Greek and Latin should be divided so that each component part retains its complete form. For example: philo-sophy, archaeo-logy, geo-graphy, manu-script, atmo-sphere.'[1] Edward Johnston's last words to the Society of Scribes and Illuminators were 'study your dictionaries'.

The writing of poetry is more complex than the writing of prose and any rules must allow for many exceptions. Poetry is read more slowly and deliberately than prose, which means that the writing may be more critically observed. 'The shape of a poem is not only pleasing to the eye, but a help to the mind in grasping the rhythmic character of the poem.' In writing out poems, indention plays a considerable part, and only a few general guides can be given. In lyrical verse and ballads when alternate lines rhyme, the second and fourth are indented, but in poems where the metrical scheme is produced by rhyming couplets, there is no indention. Sonnet arrangement varies according to period and poet: for instance medieval sonnets are arranged in two stanzas of four lines and two of three lines with space between the stanzas; but those of Italy are arranged in two stanzas of eight and six lines respectively. Shakespearian sonnets have a dropped initial with twelve lines, the last two only being indented. Keats indented lines 2, 3, 6, 7, 10, 12 and 14, while Wordsworth did not indent at all. No indention is used in blank verse or heroic couplets. Quatrains of alternate four and three stress lines should be indented. On the other hand some authorities have it that indention does not depend so much on rhyme, but on length of line and consequent appearance of the poem. When stanzas are short they are sometimes 'staggered' so that in a six-versed poem on a page, verses two, four and six are

[1] Oliver Simon, *Introduction to Typography*, Faber & Faber, 1945.

Pl. 8. Tribute to the Rt. Hon. Earl Lloyd George DOROTHY HUTTON
Fredericton University, New Brunswick

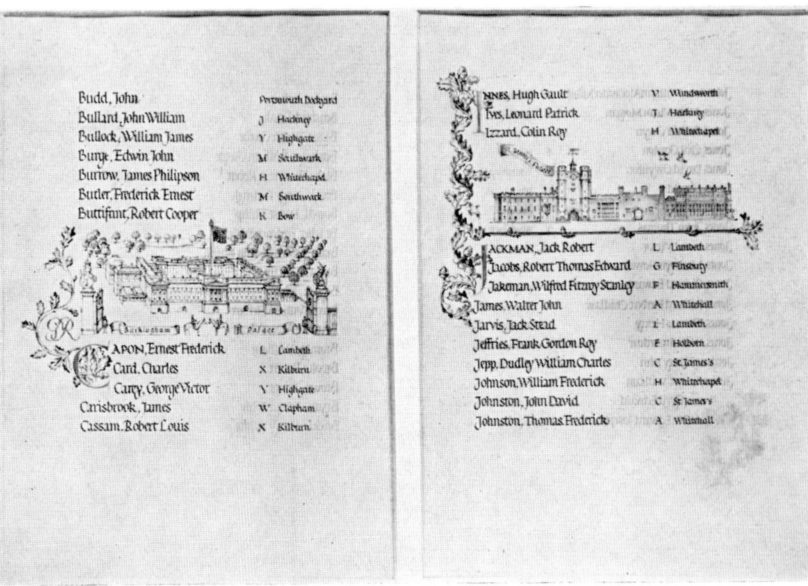

Pl. 9. Metropolitan Police Memorial, Westminster Abbey
DOROTHY HUTTON

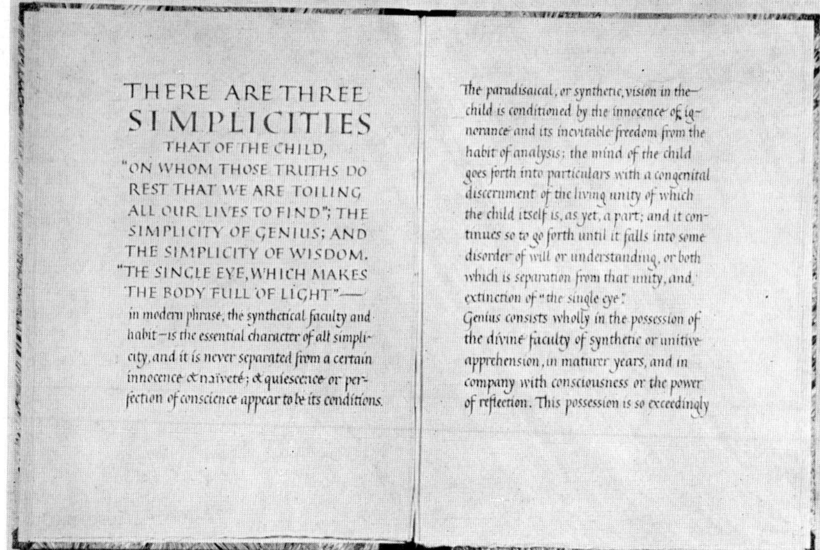

THERE ARE THREE SIMPLICITIES THAT OF THE CHILD, "ON WHOM THOSE TRUTHS DO REST THAT WE ARE TOILING ALL OUR LIVES TO FIND"; THE SIMPLICITY OF GENIUS; AND THE SIMPLICITY OF WISDOM. "THE SINGLE EYE, WHICH MAKES THE BODY FULL OF LIGHT"— in modern phrase, the synthetical faculty and habit—is the essential character of all simplicity, and it is never separated from a certain innocence & naïveté; & quiescence or perfection of conscience appear to be its conditions.

The paradisaical, or synthetic, vision in the child is conditioned by the innocence of ignorance and its inevitable freedom from the habit of analysis: the mind of the child goes forth into particulars with a congenital discernment of the living unity of which the child itself is, as yet, a part; and it continues so to go forth until it falls into some disorder of will or understanding, or both which is separation from that unity, and extinction of "the single eye."
Genius consists wholly in the possession of the divine faculty of synthetic or unitive apprehension, in maturer years, and in company with consciousness or the power of reflection. This possession is so exceedingly

Pl. 10. Essay by Coventry Patmore — IRENE WELLINGTON

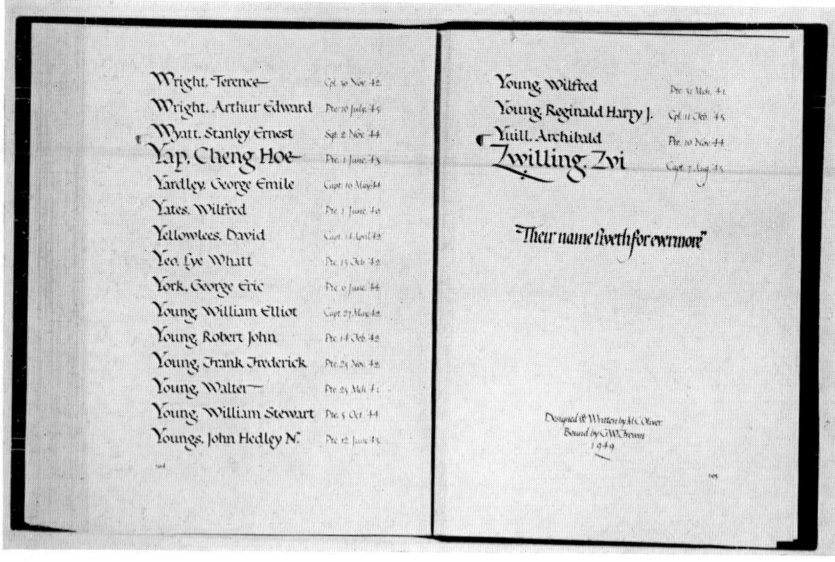

Wright, Terence—	Cpl. 30 Nov. 42
Wright, Arthur Edward	Pte. 10 July 45
Wyatt, Stanley Ernest	Sgt. 2 Nov. 44
Yap, Cheng Hoe—	Pte. 1 June 43
Yardley, George Emile	Capt. 10 May 44
Yates, Wilfred	Pte. 1 June 40
Yellowlees, David	Capt. 14 April 42
Yeo, Lye Whatt	Pte. 15 Feb. 42
York, George Eric	Pte. 6 June 44
Young, William Elliot	Capt. 27 May 42
Young, Robert John	Pte. 14 Feb. 42
Young, Frank Frederick	Pte. 25 Nov. 42
Young, Walter—	Pte. 25 Mch. 41
Young, William Stewart	Pte. 5 Oct. 44
Youngs, John Hedley N.	Pte. 12 June 43
Young, Wilfred	Pte. 31 Mch. 41
Young, Reginald Harry J.	Cpl. 11 Feb. 45
Yuill, Archibald	Pte. 10 Nov. 44
Zwilling, Zvi	Capt. 7 Aug. 45

"Their name liveth for evermore"

Designed & Written by M. C. Oliver
Bound by G. W. Brown
1949

Pl. 11. R.A.M.C. Memorial, Westminster Abbey — M. C. OLIVER

indented as a whole, as well as every other line in the verses themselves. Irregular verse should be dealt with from the point of view of satisfactory arrangement and balance, not having every line absolutely centred, but arranged on its optical centre. As far as possible lines should not be broken in poetry, especially in fine written examples, neither should verses be broken at the base of a page; it is better to carry over the first half to the next page and increase the margin of the last. But these hints on general arrangement do not affect the liberty of the scribe to play with or exaggerate the first line or lines, especially in the case of a framed poem when decoration is aimed at. Edward Johnston writes in his *Writing, Illuminating and Lettering*: 'Rational exaggeration usually amounts to the drawing out or flourishing of tails or free stems, or branches, very often to the magnifying of a characteristic part. It is a special form of decoration, and very effective if used discriminately.'

Formal writing should be evenly spaced throughout so that the whole page on broadside should present an area without dark or light patches. This can only be acquired by constant practice and attention to details of spacing, so that it becomes a habit to place each stroke in the right place. One general guide is that when two rounded letters as double OO occur together in a word they should nearly touch; but when two uprights occur, such as double ll, the space between the strokes should be about two nib widths for the foundational hand and one and a half for the compressed foundational and average italic, according to the density of the page. The general area of the space between letters is usually less than the area inside a letter such as O or H. The space between words in a well-packed page should be that taken up by a letter complete with its serif. If more is allowed, the space between will produce rivers of white down through the page giving it a ragged appearance.

In writing formal hands from large down to very small the

question of detail or simplification will arise. The serif that will suffice for an eighth of an inch letter will not be sufficient in detail for one of five-eighths. Very small scripts need scarcely any serifs whilst large written letters will not look well unless they are finely finished. So that in selecting hands for manuscripts, especially in italic, the pointed variety is not recommended for writing of less than five-sixteenths of an inch—a rounder hand will be found more suitable for this. On the other hand, a round italic will not have sufficient finished detail for writing of three-quarters of an inch. A design suitable for one particular size cannot be enlarged or reduced *ad lib.*

Sharp writing depends upon the right use of tools and materials. The quill must be really sharp-edged, and its cutting is a serious part of the preparation for writing. The split must be like a crack in glass, suitable in length to the quill's width; that is, about three times as long as the writing edge, according to the strength of the quill. A surgical scalpel or a gardener's budding knife will both be found suitable for quill cutting, providing that the underside of the blade is ground more than the top. A very smooth coin will be found convenient to cut upon. Use a magnifying-glass, or hold up to the light of a window after cutting. To ensure sharpness throughout a whole page, cut or scrape a little from the underside of the quill when two-thirds of the page is written; do not recut until the page is finished because the slight difference may show. The two materials used (ink and vellum or paper) also have to be considered in the light of sharpness. A Chinese stick of good quality may be found the best for black writing; it has the right amount of glaze when dry, and if properly rubbed down will give the finest possible thin strokes. The rubbing down is important in order to obtain the right density and to do this satisfactorily, a small deep dish roughened on the bottom by carborundum is necessary, or a Chinese writer's hollow stone. To test the density make a few marks on tracing paper, dry, and hold up to the light of a window. I prefer ordinary tap water for rubbing down the ink and not distilled water, because this somehow prevents the ink from becoming really black: stick ink rubbed down in this way can be kept many weeks by adding one drop of formalin. Waterproof inks will not give sharpness: there is too much gum in them. The best water-colours work well if a little parchment size and chinese white are added; some scribes add a very little glair to prevent a colour like vermilion from drying darker; but vermilions do not need the white as they have enough density of their own.

The third factor in sharpness is the skin or paper and it will be found that thin calf vellum is the best that can be used. The surface must be well prepared and a little sandarac rubbed on at the moment before writing. The flesh side is more difficult than the other which has a nap, and therefore needs more sandarac rubbed in, especially when the skin is whiter than usual. A good handmade paper will give sharpness with a pounce for work of an average size, but it is extremely difficult to find a paper that will be found satisfactory when very small writing is needed.

In addition to the use of the finest materials and tools, together with the correct adjustment of the writing board, the writer should possess an attitude of cautious dash which is so necessary for the production of fine writing.

FRAMED PANELS OF DECORATIVE WRITING

With the revival of interest in fine writing and lettering at the beginning of the twentieth century under the inspiration of William Morris, W. R. Lethaby, Sir Sidney Cockerell, Cobden Sanderson and Edward Johnston, written panels make their first appearance as wall decoration. At first these panels were of small size and the writing was on parchment. They were simply framed close up in narrow black and consisted of prayers, poems, hymns etc. The illuminating was generally of a floral nature, often simple leaf patterns to fill blank spaces, reminiscent of William Morris's decoration. The gilding was as yet in an experimental stage. After fifty years great developments have taken place; many halls, schools, colleges and churches have been enriched by framed panels of vellum on which touches of colour and gold enlivened lists of incumbents, benefactors, maps and memorials.

The framing developed as the size of the panel grew larger and became part of the wall decoration. The margins became wider and were often used for writing sub-titles and explanatory notes. The margins became influenced by those of books, the written matter being lifted well up, and the side margins made wider than the frame.

The layout of written matter at first was influenced by book design with its initial letter and subsidiary capitals down the left side. But during the course of time Edward Johnston realized that framed writing should have its own principles of design and that in the main it should be architectural; in other words a framed piece of writing should be designed as a central unit.

The open book with its equal columns of writing, together with its pieces of balanced decoration, gives a sense of complete design; but when one half is taken from it and framed, as is often the case in museums, the balance and completeness are destroyed, moreover a false value is put upon the design of an initial. That which is right for a book is therefore wrong for a framed panel and vice versa.

Interest and decoration can be obtained by various means, such as:

(1) Variation of the size and weight of the writing.
(2) Difference of tone and colour.
(3) Use of more than one style of letter form.
(4) Adding coloured decoration by means of heraldry, symbolism, drawings from natural objects, such as foliage, animals, birds, conventionalized by the tools used, and fine line ornament.

1. The simplest contrast of size and weight can be made by writing the first few lines with a larger pen putting emphasis on the top portion, thus producing a black and grey manuscript.

2. Bright colours, such as scarlet vermilion, venetian red, cerulean and real ultramarine blue or green greatly improve a simple black piece of writing. Care, however, has to be taken to obtain a good proportion between each. The bright spotting of capitals throughout a manuscript is a mistake.

3. The foundational hand is used for the main writing of prose, but for contrast and design versals and written capitals are introduced in headings; for the same reason small italic is used for notes and rubrics. For poetry italic is mainly used with flourished headings produced by rational exaggeration.

4. Heraldry from the simplest small shield to a full achievement will always make fine decoration and its use with writing seems to be fundamentally right. It brings with it dominating colour, historic interest, and a right use of gold. Care has to be taken, however, to get the correct sense of scale when setting out the general design. The colours of the field, charges and crest should first be put down, then all other necessary colours for mottoes, ribbons, mantling, etc. can be arranged to make contrasts and counterchange. Symbolism gives the manuscript designer a great chance for decoration and allows him the opportunity of endowing his work with hidden meaning so that it has a double interest for those who understand. Symbols that are used cover a wide range of subjects including religion, the Army, Navy and Air Force, astrology, freemasonry and astronomy. Each art, science, trade or business can be symbolized by the designer and so interest can be given almost to every piece of written matter that is to become a framed work.

Edward Johnston's experiments in ornament led him to declare that decoration should be written with a similar tool to that which had been employed to produce the writing; he ruled out the use of the brush. He advocated calligraphic ornament with a wide pen. He produced a written crest in a framed address to the National Galleries of Scotland which is illustrated in *Lettering of Today* to show that a unity can be attained by simply using the same kind of tool. The copying of nature and architectural ornament with a brush on the pages of Italian and Flemish manuscripts killed illumination in the sixteenth century.

The mounting of vellum needs a great deal of skill and experience and no large work should be undertaken without due trial and experiment. Small pieces of thin skin can be lined, damped and gum-stripped to the mounting board after a little practice, but thick vellum which needs to be stretched over a frame or panel of hardwood had better be prepared by an experienced framer or bookbinder. Should a panel warp before it can be put into its frame it can be straightened by pasting paper on the back to counteract the pull of the skin. It is advisable, therefore, to keep mounted manuscripts under pressure until they can be framed: once stretched properly and strongly framed with a fillet of wood to keep the vellum from the glass, a framed panel will last a very long time under reasonable conditions. The worst enemy of vellum, except fire or blast, is extreme dampness. First, it will destroy all gilding, not only taking away its burnish, but completely disintegrating the water size on which the gold leaf is placed, thus destroying the letter form, which will fall away. Then the water-colours, such as vermilion and cerulean, will probably run, and finally the non-waterproof ink will smudge at the slightest touch. Should the vellum not be damp enough at the moment of mounting it will not dry stretched as tight as a drum, but will cockle, and unless it is taken off and re-mounted it will remain so, especially if the wall on which it is placed is at all damp. Precaution should therefore be taken with an important piece of work to secure the back doubly by screwing a sheet of zinc completely over the whole, thus preventing any dampness from getting through to the manuscript. This should always be done before sending work abroad. Care should also be taken to see that framed manuscripts are not placed in any position near a radiator. This will not so much hurt the vellum as the frame; the joints will shrink, and if a lacquer paint is used, it will soon peel off.

As a last suggestion regarding framed panels, see that they are thoughtfully placed on the wall with an eye to a central position, or placed so that they will line up at the base with panels near by. If the site of the panel can be seen before any design is made or size agreed upon, it is advisable to consider the wall or background when settling the size of the frame. Should the space provided be a sunk panel in the wall see that the frame will be of such a size as will look well in it. Proportion of frame to wall space can be a vital factor in the complete success of the work; and frames of good section should be produced preferably made by a cabinetmaker.

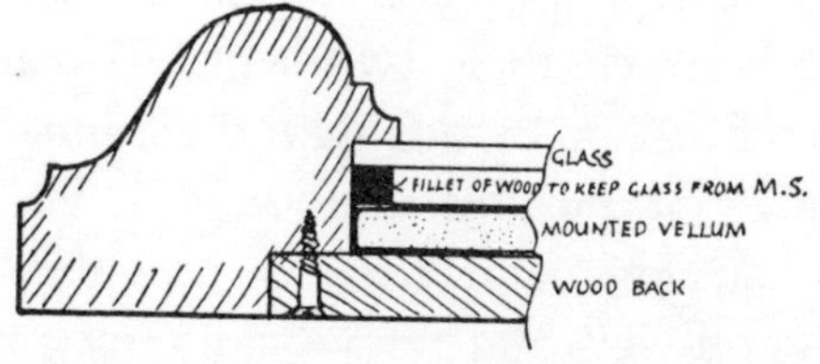

Fig. 33. Section of Handmade Frame

Figure 33 shows the section of a frame with a double rabbit to prevent dust from getting to the manuscript, the best method of fixing the back by screws and the slip of wood which prevents the glass touching the vellum.

The colour of a frame is very important; it may make or mar a fine piece of written work especially if the vellum is deep in tone or the manuscript of delicate colour. Frames of strong colour are not suitable for manuscript work, or for written panels which are to be sent to exhibitions of calligraphy. In exhibitions they compete one with another and often overpower a good piece of writing so that the manuscript appears lost. Many experiments in frames have been tried but, as the water-colour painters have found, nothing is so satisfactory as limed oak of good section, with perhaps a touch of gold leaf on the moulding: painted neutral tints such as grey or beige are useful and do not compete with the writing. For church work, such as altar cards or memorial panels, moulded gold frames look well, and are nearly always suitable. Black can also be used with success provided it does not overpower the work, but it is not a good plan to frame in black for exhibitions; the tone is usually too strong, and the frame is scratched before it is exhibited.

INSCRIPTIONS

The word inscription embraces a great variety of letter form from the roughest scratching on wax or metal to the finest stone-cut letters of imperial Rome of the first or second century. Yet between these two will be found numerous intermediate links. Side by side with the Roman letter, aiming at the greatest possible dignity, will be found other inscriptions of an ephemeral character, roughly executed with brush or stylus on walls and betraying no trace of pomposity. Between these two extremes there are many gradations, suiting the purpose for which they were cut. Chief among these second-rate types were the rustic, which were both written and carved in stone.

From the Roman capital, with the aid of writing, during the first seven centuries A.D. we get the small letter form and later the italic, both of which have enabled inscription designers to give greater variety to their work, and an interest to the text which was quite unknown to the ancients.

The intention in this chapter is to consider inscriptions solely for monumental and informative purposes. So that its first use is commemorative and the second decorative.

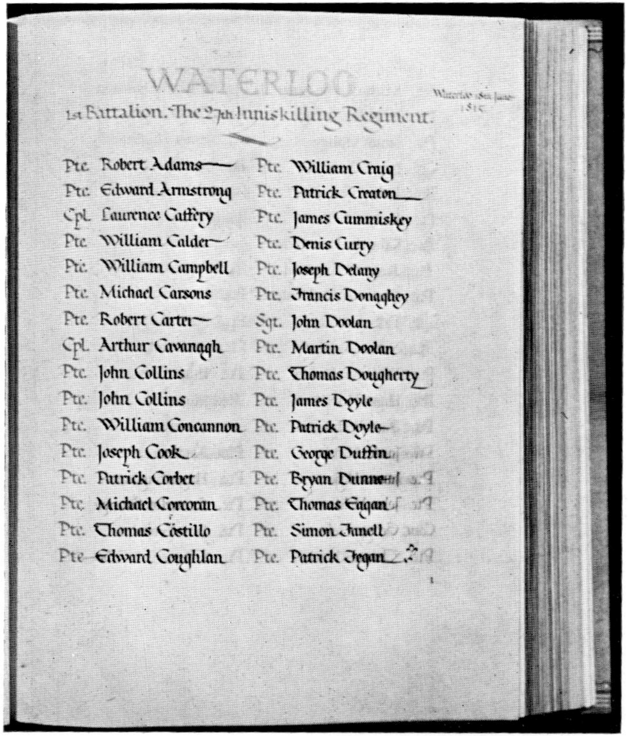

Pl. 12. Inniskilling Memorial M. C. Oliver

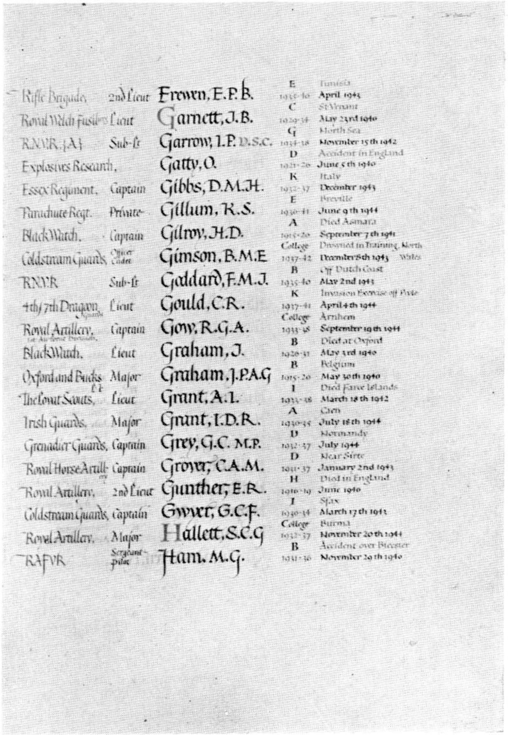

Pl. 13. The Roll of Wykehamists
Irene Wellington

To the Right Honourable Sir Rupert De la Bère M.P.
Alderman of the Ward of Tower.

ON your Election to the Office of Lord Mayor the Master, Wardens and Court of Assistants of the Skinners' Company offer to you and to Lady De la Bère their sincere congratulations & place on record their pleasure in the honour thus conferred upon the Company and their confidence that you will discharge the duties of your high office with wisdom and devotion maintaining the traditions of this illustrious city through an auspicious and historic year.

Master
Warden
Warden
Warden
Warden
Clerk

Pl. 14. Address to Sir Rupert De la Bère, M.P. M. C. OLIVER

Varying materials demand their own specific tools. Marble and stone, the chisel; wood and metal, the graver and gouge; painted wood the writer's brush with gold leaf and oil gold size. In all these materials, however, the Roman letter can be faithfully produced: it is the section of the cut letter that must vary according to the material and tools used.

The usual section for stone, marble, metal and wood is V cut at about 60°, but when this section is gilt on a memorial panel and lit from the side one half is in shadow and consequently looks thin. Therefore the section for gilding should be round cut, while for wood a hollow one is used. Again, if the V cut section is used on a wood panel and the only available position is in full or dull light, the letters should be painted. Large letters in relief need a heavy serif and the body of the letter carved concave. Details of stone sections are shown in A. E. R. Gill's chapter in Edward Johnston's book *Writing, Illuminating and Lettering*.

Edward Johnston's aim in life was to make fine letters and to space them: students and others have often forgotten the spacing—to the detriment of their work. This is a most important matter when considering permanent inscriptions. One or two large words beautifully and widely spaced can give a feeling of grandeur. But many widely spaced words are difficult to read and have a weakening effect. Not much help with spacing can be given to the letter draughtsman, but he can be told that the space between two curved letters is at the nearest point in general work, equal to the thick stroke; the space between one curved and one straight stroke, two widths, and between two upright strokes three widths or more. This gives the area of ground which must be allowed for between each letter. Again the amount of ground can be settled by placing a good Roman R next to an A as close as is convenient, adjusting the spacing to suit this area throughout the whole inscription. Crowding letters together for the purpose of getting each line the same length should be avoided.

Therefore unless even numbers of letters can be arranged to fill each line, it is better to centre conveniently phrased lines, and thus produce a well-shaped inscription as a whole within the rectangle. Should a circular tablet have to be designed it is best to fit the shape approximately.

When dealing with an inscription composed wholly of Roman letters the width between the lines should not be less than half the height of the letters: three-quarters of the letter height is, however, the most effective; more than this gives a weak look to the whole inscription. When dealing with small Romans with their ascenders and descenders, allow one and a half to twice the height of the body of the letter. This applies to numerals also, when the even numbers are taken above the line and the uneven ones below. When inserting numerals into a line of capitals keep them within the same height as the letters; i.e. no parts above or below the height line. The ascending and descending type should be used with lower case and italic.

The next consideration beyond a few well-spaced words is how to give emphasis and interest to an inscription containing important names and statements. The obvious answer is to enlarge the size of the important word or words making it stretch, if possible, to the whole width of the inscription and at the same time arrange that some of the lettering is made smaller and of a different type, say, Roman small letter or italic for contrast. Further interest can be attained by skilful use of gold and colour, guided by a sense of proportion in weight and placing.

A good plan when setting out an inscription is to begin making a rough with due consideration for the width of the letter and the spacing required, with pencil at arm's length. Scribbling rough letters is a waste of time: it provides no basis for calculation. Having settled the rough, take detail or tracing paper and trace through, correcting the letter form and spacing; and at the same time arrange that the whole inscription is placed centrally, the centre of each line, long or short, being placed on a vertical centre line. This at first may produce a poor shape as a whole; if so, retrace, making some lines shorter or longer so as to produce a pleasing shape.

In arranging a long inscription with more than six or eight words to the line, it is usually found that the lines of lettering fill out to the edge so that the total becomes a rectangle which only needs some tail finish to make it a good shape. But with a short inscription lines will not fill out to the edge, so that a shape must be somehow designed. Metal tablets need to be more completely covered with engraved matter than stone, wood or marble, as this material lacks the grain or texture that the others possess.

Colour can be of great assistance in designing inscriptions, especially when they are to be placed in churches, or other places where there is not enough, or too much, light. The tone of the colour can vary from bright to dull according to the position with regard to light; for instance, a portland stone or hopton wood tablet placed in a dark corner of a cloister would need cerulean blue, cream, or vermilion, while darker shades of the same colour would probably be more appropriate in a good light on the same materials. With regard to natural oak panels, when the lettering is carved in the traditional V cut section, it is essential that the letter be coloured as without it the text cannot be read except in a fairly strong side light. A natural oak tablet with ¾ in. letters V cut cannot be read from a greater distance than about two yards when strong light is directly on its face; but coloured grey blue or indian red it will carry up to about six yards. Other means are used in the case of brass or bronze plates, namely, black and red wax (which is not very durable) and black bronze stain, all three of which carry the inscription a good distance. Opaque enamel can be employed to-day since large enamelling stoves are available; hence heraldry can be used in memorial work on bronze with great effect.

Enamel, however, is mostly used in commercial name-plates of bronze which have taken the place of the old engraved brass plate with waxed lettering. The new method with flush enamel letters is a great improvement since it does not need to be touched except with a duster; although a brightly cleaned tablet with white enamel can look beautiful. Cream, red, and blue are the usual colours, but real white is too hard when the bronze is dark; it cannot be recommended.

Gilding also can greatly help to decorate inscriptions and to increase legibility. In this case the section of the letter must be adapted to this bright medium. For example, in relief lettering where the ground between the letters is cut away, a gilded ground will throw up the letters with great effect, as with grounds between ornament, such as can be seen in English illumination in the fifteenth century. In fact, gilded grounds were constantly used by medieval and Renaissance artists as the best method of employing gold. The gilded V cut letter is now regarded as a failure when produced on stone, metal or wood; the effect is poor and thin, as only one side catches the light for most of the day. The section for these materials should be cushion- or hollow-cut, as both these sections will give far more light on the letter.

From "The Dignitie of Man"

is the Fountaine

By Anthony Nixon 1612

of all vertue and duty.

From this Fountaine issue foure rivers—
Prudence, which knoweth what is profitable for itself & others & the common weale
Temperance, the Mistris of Modestie—Chastitie and Sobriety.
Fortitude, which maketh a man Constant, Patient and Couragious.
Justice, which is the bond and preservation of human society, by giving everyone that which belongeth to him, by keeping faith in things promised, by succouring willingly the afflicted, & by helping one as ability serveth.

Scripsit M. C. Oliver September 1937

The book from which this extract is taken is in the British Museum Library No. 8405.g.3 & is dedicated "To the worthy, learned, and judicious Gentleman William Redman of Great Shelford in the County of Cambridge, Esquire"

Pl. 15. Quotation from 'The Dignitie of Man' M. C. OLIVER

Richard le Scrope. Bishop. 1392
Gave Benefactions to the Vicars.

John de Moreton. 1381-1398
Prebendary. Gave Benefactions to the Vicars.

Robert de Stretton. Bishop. 1360-1385
Enlarged the Shrine of S. Chad.

Richard de Bermingham. 1369-1395
Canon. Gave various Benefactions.

John Burghill. Bishop. 1398-1414
Gave generous benefactions to all ranks of the Cathedral staff.

Walter Skirlaw. Bishop of Durham. 1406
Left large bequests to the Dean and Chapter, and to the Vicars.

George Radcliffe. Treasurer. 1436-1449
Gave various benefactions.

Thomas Chesterfield. 1425-1452
Canon. Gave a new copy of the Lichfield Chronicle. Contributed largely to the Vicars' Building Fund.

Thomas Heywood. Dean. 1457-1492
Gave many generous benefactions, including an Organ, Windows in the Chapter House, gifts to the Vicars, etc. Began to build the Library (pulled down in 1758)

John Halse. Bishop. 1459-1490
Built residentiary Houses.

Henry Ediall. Prebendary. 1480-
Built residentiary Houses.

George Strangeways. d. 1503
Canon. Built residentiary Houses.

Thomas Milley. Canon. 1488-1505
Built residentiary Houses & gave liberally to the Vicars' Common Fund.

Pl. 16. Litchfield Cathedral's Roll of Donors M. C. OLIVER

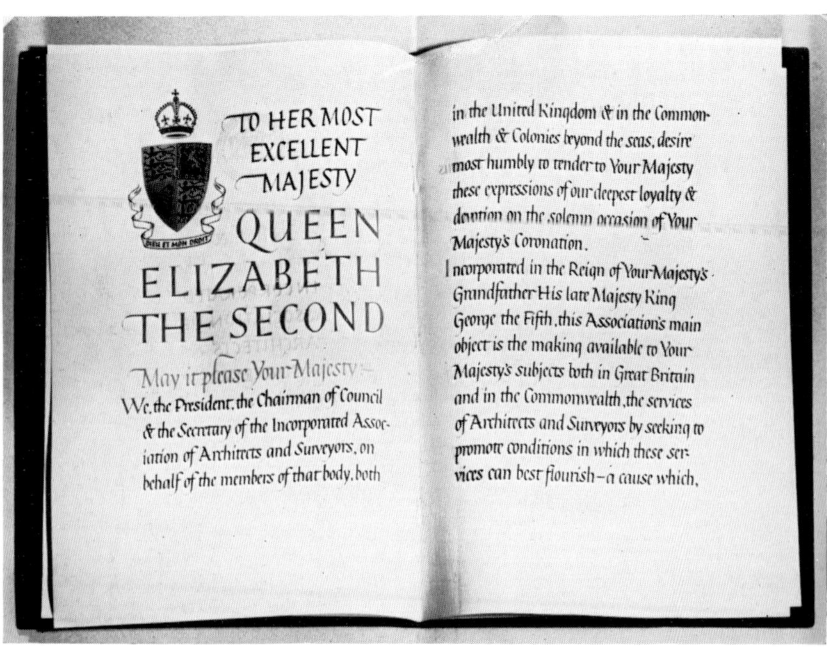

TO HER MOST EXCELLENT MAJESTY QUEEN ELIZABETH THE SECOND

May it please Your Majesty

We, the President, the Chairman of Council & the Secretary of the Incorporated Association of Architects and Surveyors, on behalf of the members of that body, both in the United Kingdom & in the Commonwealth & Colonies beyond the seas, desire most humbly to tender to Your Majesty these expressions of our deepest loyalty & devotion on the solemn occasion of Your Majesty's Coronation.

Incorporated in the Reign of Your Majesty's Grandfather His late Majesty King George the Fifth, this Association's main object is the making available to Your Majesty's subjects both in Great Britain and in the Commonwealth, the services of Architects and Surveyors by seeking to promote conditions in which these services can best flourish—a cause which,

Pl. 17. Address to H.M. The Queen JOAN PILSBURY

VIII

Heraldry in Illuminated Manuscripts

It might be fair to say that for most of us heraldry is no longer an everyday matter, whereas some five or six centuries ago the display of signs and symbols of a heraldic nature was commonplace. Very few industries and manufactures could ignore heraldry, which was then an accepted part of life. At tournament and festival, in church and courtroom, above workshop window, in library, and around the hearth, evidence was not wanting of a forthright pride in display and love of colour shared alike by all classes of society.

To illustrate the change of practice since those earlier times one need only notice the rarity of heraldic display upon the panels of the private motor vehicle in contrast with the frequent appearance of county or borough arms upon the sides of the public vehicles of our cities and towns. The cause is not far to seek, and the chances to-day of impressing one's neighbour in matters of descent, territory, wealth or temporal power are remote indeed. In default of individuals the heraldic lion is now principally maintained by the community, and it is to the corporation rather than to the person he must look for his keep.

In England one must approach the College of Arms for guidance in the devising of armorial bearings, and it should be understood that in the College, directed by the Earl

Marshal and headed by Garter King of Arms, is vested sole authority from the Crown to devise and issue new Grants of Arms and to confirm ancient ones.

Upon the establishment of the right to bear arms the owner is at liberty to display them in almost any way desired, certainly not least in the decoration of illuminated manuscripts and documents. It should be no surprise to find heraldry enlivening in this way a large proportion of the manuscripts of the last eight hundred years, reflecting faithfully all changes of style and mood throughout this period. A by no means exhaustive list would include the service books of the Church, private horae, charters, writs, treaty ratifications, petitions, addresses, diplomas, estate maps, rolls of honour and letters patent.

It should be remembered that an achievement of arms depicted in miniature in a book differs fundamentally little from its much larger counterpart carved or painted, say, over the gallery of an assembly hall. Each version must accord with the details of the blazon. The arrangement of component parts should not depart too far from traditional custom and usage, and the display should be legible in the prevailing conditions of lighting and distance. In the matter of scale there should be no visual strain either to take in the whole subject at a glance or to feel the need of magnification. If it is found necessary to peer too closely for comfort, time and effort may have been wasted on microscopic detail. While should one feel the need to move away in a restricted space in order to see the whole thing properly the craftsman may have been wasteful with materials. In the production of manuscript books the scale of treatment should differ between a book intended for a lectern and one meant to be held in the hand. In any case, whatever the intention, the work should reveal a thorough training in design—ideally from the hand of a specialist.

Heraldic illumination on vellum has often to stand up to

much handling and hard wear in use but may expect some protection from extremes of humidity and temperature. It is unusual for the contents of a bound, folded or rolled document to remain exposed to strong light for any length of time unless in an exhibition case or for a while accidentally in direct sunlight. Furthermore, in early medieval times exposure to light might perhaps amount to no more by day than through painted glass windows, and by night from oil lamp and candle, thus with scarcely any loss of brilliance of the pigment over lengthy periods of time. Books, moreover, were usually closed when not in use. Nowadays, however, larger windows, stronger artificial light and active chemical pollution of the air in urban areas may imply a somewhat shorter life for heraldic illumination, and are factors to be reckoned with both in the preservation of old manuscripts and in the production of new ones.

Heraldic illumination involves the application of gold leaf to vellum for fields and charges blazoned Or, while those blazoned Argent are customarily indicated by means of the pigment white. The metal silver will eventually darken through oxidization unless the air is excluded by a varnish, a process which in itself will change the surface quality.

Even though the craftsman may now have access to non-tarnishable white metal leaf—platinum, palladium and the less malleable aluminium—it is questionable whether in illuminating practice the yellow and white metals should be allowed to jostle each other, even when burnished, on the same page. On the whole, and for this we may examine heraldic illumination from the earliest times, gold leaf may well be allowed pride of place supported where so blazoned in the achievement by Argent of white pigment. Very frequently the vellum, parchment or other white material upon which the arms are rendered itself does duty for the blazon Argent (see supporters in plate 22).

Examples may be seen where Argent executed in silver leaf

has in the course of time entirely lost its original appearance and turned black. Instances also of the pigment vermilion turning black are not uncommon, and unless this is borne in mind confusion in blazon may result when examining old heraldic illumination.

With the materials and tools available the heraldic illuminator cannot afford to ignore entirely certain tricks of design in the production of that richness and legibility associated with heraldry. For instance, books seem best examined in a source of light coming from above and slightly to the reader's left, so that where an outline is used in depicting an achievement of arms it may with effect be heavier on the 'south east' side of the shield and all other component parts (plate 7).

It may be considered part of the illuminator's stock-in-trade that he should know something of the effect of work in relief or in the round, even if he is working in two dimensions only, though no such refinements are to be found in the earliest manuscript painting (plate 1).

The heraldic illuminator should understand at least something of anatomy. To bend a joint the wrong way is unpardonable and ignorance can find no excuse under the term 'heraldic licence'. Early examples evidence a fine regard for strength and movement in a severe conventional rendering (fig. 1). An illuminator will also need a sound general experience of pattern, contrast and colour and indeed the whole cut and thrust of composition. As much might be said for most other crafts. It cannot be claimed that the miniature scale of the work is arduous, the sight steering the work as a whole rather than observing every variation of every stroke. Confidence as to how brush and pen perform when used will come only from long practice in an evolved style of work.

In heraldic illumination it is rare to find a revolutionary departure from accepted methods and traditions. Probably the work of successive Herald Painters at the College of Arms forms one of the best examples of evolution in style—that of the Lyon Office in Edinburgh likewise. The official Herald Painter, with the work of predecessors at his elbow and the senior Officers of Arms looking over his shoulder, may be in no position to exercise violent experiments in style. Indeed we can be thankful that he figures rather as a steadying influence among all too many eddies in the main flow of design, and although the latest official work cannot but reflect the feeling of the day, 'isms' of all kinds are refreshingly absent and dignity is sustained.

Apart from the official depictions of arms, e.g. when letters patent are granted, their further display may be needful in various ways and, in company with carvers and engravers, it is in the adaptation of this 'authorized version' that the jobbing illuminator plays his part. Work of this kind has already been touched on above, and it will be appreciated that some is regularly and some only periodically in demand.

Two world wars in this century have set the task of inscribing and illuminating, often with heraldry, a considerable number of Books of Remembrance and Rolls of Honour containing the names of those fallen in battle, and members of the Society have given many of these manuscript volumes their care and thought. Addresses of welcome and appreciations for services rendered are constantly in demand, as often as not having the arms of the donor or recipient as a heading or tailpiece.

It will be understood that in certain work scribe and illuminator are one and the same. Sometimes, however, the task is too great for one person, and medieval practice is followed in the delegation of lettering, drawing, gilding and painting, in that order, to respective craftsmen (plates 32 and 33). Where heraldry and lettering are the work of more than one hand there should at least be a sympathy of ideals and workshop practice, all craftsmen concerned consulting together, and not least with the bookbinder, so that a finely-balanced product may be the more hoped for. When matching the visual weight of arms with its accompanying lettering on the page, we find that such a balance was not always thought necessary or even desirable (plate 18). However, examples in which a balance has been obtained tend to be the most satisfying in effect (plates 19, 21, 27 and 28).

At some risk of contradiction, one might wish for heraldry to-day a school of illumination more fully in step with the scribe as builder of the page, in which vigorous pen drawings were tinted with flat washes and with areas blazoned Or of unburnished gold—even of a quiet yellow pigment. The effect would not be too precious (though lively enough) and might well obtain for secular work (plates 18, 20 and 22).

In the depiction of arms it is of interest to consider where to stop in matters of detail. Reference has been made to a desirable knowledge of anatomy, but this does not mean we need delineate every hair on the lion's mane as may be seen in much heraldic work of the nineteenth century (plate 23). It might be supposed that omissions from the static rendering would run grave risk of notice; yet in heraldry among a welter of gold and colour, ramping of beast, rippling of scroll, and flourish of mantling, minor omissions may well succeed without any deviation from blazon. By visual means more may be implied than is actually present and a dozen or so distinct feathers on the griffin's breast (plate 34) prove entirely satisfactory where several times that number would be pointless and illegible. There exist certain heraldic yard-sticks of value in avoiding fantasy. For example, it may be mentioned that until 1953 the authorized pattern of the Imperial Crown allowed the placing of nine pearls upon each side arch and five pearls on the centre arch. Such 'rules' serve to check excesses in depiction. To be consistent nine pearls should be shown at the centre also, but as these would hide increasingly behind each other when nearing the orb at the top, a two-dimensional convention had been reached in which the relationship was nine to five whole pearls.

The early illuminators were closely bound in an apprenticeship which allowed only unhurried and steady development, yet gave scope for very many charming variations and mannerisms. Such an accumulation of experience has given the twentieth-century illuminator a splendid foundation upon which to build, to the exclusion of mere copyism. Moreover, the careful retrospection begun by such nineteenth-century artists and scholars as Stothard, Willement, Pugin, Boutell, Anselm and Nixon (see plates 24 and 25) has to a very great extent been responsible for the form of heraldic illumination to-day.

It is perhaps of interest to consider the illuminator's approach to some heraldic task. In dealing, for instance, with the shield of the United Kingdom (plate 26), the normal sequence of work would be:

(1) Re-designing the achievement (preferably a fresh interpretation from blazon) which would involve drawing, correction and modification to the limit of the artist's skill and taste.

(2) Transferring the result to the vellum in the form of a line drawing in which none of the previous struggles should be evident, care being taken to strike a satisfactory balance of colour and metal.

(3) Gilding those areas blazoned Or.

(4) Colouring the remaining areas also in accordance with blazon.

How then should we proceed with, say, one of the English quarters 'Gules three leopards Or' (plate 37)?

A. Gild the leopards accurately and fill in the field with red pigment?

B. Gild 'leopard-shapes' very broadly and trim up their edges carefully in the manner of the glass-painter by allowing the brush loaded with pigment to ride over these more generous edges of gold leaf?

C. Gild the whole quarter and superimpose a background of red pigment?

If the scale is very small the latter method may be found convenient, though the reluctance of *burnished* gold leaf to accept pigment is a factor to be borne in mind and overcome. Wherever the scale of the work allows, method A is recommended. In the English quarters there will be roughly equal amounts of red and gold to display. In the Scottish quarter (plate 26) the gold may predominate and method C will be found most suitable at smaller scales. The labour involved in gilding and painting the details of the Scottish 'double tressure flory counter flory' is considerable (plate 35).

At this point the factor of halation may be mentioned. Light reflected from a small polished flat surface appears to spread and therefore to diminish the size of adjacent pigmented areas—at times to the point of compromising legibility. Applying this factor to the Scottish quarter, for instance, and presupposing the flat area of burnished gold is reflecting a strong source of light directly to the observer's eye, the red tressure and lion painted upon it may appear unduly thin—whereas conversely this same mirror-like gold surface, when reflecting darkness instead, may present the illusion of tressure and lion much fatter than intended. Upon slightly wavy vellum there may be partial halation only (plate 36), and in the turning of the page this can be a charming characteristic of illumination. A good deal might be said in favour of the glow and colour of unburnished gold and the consequent reduction of halation to a minimum.

A workable extension of method C may be suggested for the courageous. The areas of gold leaf for conversion to red may be scratched away from the assize (see chapter V) using the sharp point of a knife, and if the gilding has been well and truly done only a small thickness of the assize will be removed bringing with it the adhering gold leaf. Red pigment is then applied to these areas (dryly, for if too wet the assize may mix with it) thus holding down the edges of the remaining gold leaf. Remember that tracing down upon burnished

18. St. Albans Scriptorium. c. 1250

Pl. 19. Furness Abbey Scriptorium. 1412

Pl. 20. College of Arms. c. 1510

Pl. 21. Amiens. 1527

Pl. 22
College of Arms.
c. 1620

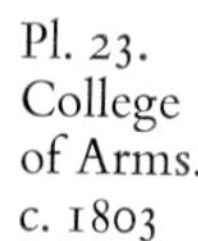

Pl. 23.
College
of Arms.
c. 1803

Pl. 24.
Left: Fr. Anselm
Published 1880

Pl. 25.
Right: J. Forbes Nixon
Published 1880

1948: in the Twelfth year of Our Reign

Pl. 26. College of Arms. 1948

Sir Pyers George Joseph Mostyn 11th Baronet

M.C., of Talacre, county Flint, J.P., capt. late Royal Welch Fusiliers, served in the Great War 1914, despatches, wounded, military cross, 2nd class order of St Anne of Russia b. 28th August 1893; succeeded his cousin 1917; m. 22 Nov 1927 Margery only daughter of the late Alfred Stanley Marks of Sydney N.S. Wales, and has issue Pyers Edward b. 12 July 1928, Margaret Claire b. 9th Sept 1931.

Written out by Norman Ball, and was complete on the 19th October 1937.

Pl. 27. N. Ball. 1937

Pl. 28. T. Wrigley. 1939

Pl. 29. N. Ball. 1948

Pl. 30. W. M. Gardner. 1950

Pl. 31. T. Swindlehurst. 1935

gold leaf is also hazardous, so there must be no doubt in the mind as to exactly where the knife may attack the gold surface.

So far we have obtained a red silhouette of the Scottish lion and the counter-flowered double tressure. The detailed line work of head, mane, and other attributes may now be expressed, using a small water-colour brush with powdered gold suspended in some suitable medium. This when dry will tell its story legibly enough and with care may be given a limited burnish.

Though pigments are dealt with more specifically in another chapter, mention must be made of the colours used in heraldic illumination. It may be pointed out that artists' colour-manufacturers supply 'heraldic tinctures' in jars ready for use. One may buy Gules, Azure, Vert, Purpure and Sable as well as Argent and Or, but since Ermine and Vair do not figure in the list of reach-me-down tinctures the omission may serve to suggest that at least a proportion of practising illuminators dispense for themselves in all such matters. In painted heraldry both of the past and present, reds may be seen to vary from pink to darkest plum and blues from sky to navy. Even allowing for fading or darkening we know that the earlier illuminators were personally responsible for the visual effect of pigments used in their own scriptoria or workshops. Questions to put to oneself to-day, as then, might well include, 'Is it a distinct colour?' 'Is it a stable and good quality pigment?' 'Does it look well when applied in its intended setting?' It is solely a matter for the painter whether to make use of a warm blue or a cold one, a yellowish or a bluish green, and considerations (conscious or otherwise) of legibility, harmony etc. will govern what he feels to be a good and suitable colour—also the lengths to which variation may be carried. In heraldic display there must at least be distinction between red-purple-blue, and blue-green.

Some thought should now be given to the manner of rendering component parts of an achievement of arms.

THE SHIELD

The merits of a very wide choice of shield shapes cannot here be fully discussed, but a few suggestions may be made as to suitability. The shield with the surcoat originally offered convenient space for the display of armorial bearings in war and at the tournament. On the whole a squarish and not a pointed base of shield may best be used in the display of quartered arms (plate 22). A tall single charge such as the golden lion of Harold with its forked tail will look happiest within a fairly tall shield (plate 18), whereas a wider shield is more appropriate for Hulson's leopard (plate 34).

The scribe and typesetter will vary their choice of script and fount to suit the subject matter of the text, and likewise the illuminator of heraldry will vary the shape of shield with the demands of the charges thereon and with the mood of the occasion. Gaiety may be out of place in a book of remembrance, but a sober outline of shield might be thought to do less than justice to the opportunities afforded by an illuminated address of welcome or a festival proclamation (plate 21).

The shape of the shield should be decided. It may be placed upright (plate 27), or tilted (couché) (plate 33), either so little as to be hardly out of the vertical (plate 24), or practically resting on its side (plate 28). There is no symbolism or hidden meaning attached to any particular angle, and free deviations of this kind may be studied in the Garter Stall Plates at St. George's Chapel, Windsor, and in the many spirited renderings of arms in Foster's *Peerage and Baronetage, 1880–81*.

It is best for a beginner to tread gently. Experienced craftsmen, however, may perhaps be allowed a degree of exuberance and abandonment on occasions with entire satisfaction to all; and in the shape and positioning of shields a remarkable amount of variation is in fact possible without compromising blazon.

THE HELMET

In England we are settled with a legacy of sealed-pattern helmets of rank upon which to display the crest, and hardly any latitude is now authorized. Such distinctions date from the times of James I and may be studied in detail in the contemporary first edition of Guillim's *Display of Heraldrie* dated 1611. These conventional patterns of helmet undoubtedly assist in the recognition of degree. The thoughtful designer, however, might wish to be excused too frequent a rendering of the open-visored and front-facing Knight Baronet's helmet of rank with its quilted red cloth lining, and in one instance, the Badge of Ulster has done duty by itself, allowing the artist a happier time with the Esquire's helm (plate 27)—a distinct liberty, but one taken deliberately. In the heyday of practical armory the helmet design was always a matter of battle and tournament usage, and rank was made known mainly by the charges displayed on shield and surcoat and by the crest.

An important factor in the illumination of an achievement of arms is the relationship in size between shield and helm, largely a matter of practicability. The question is whether the wearer of such a helm could carry and use a shield of such and such a size—the correct relationship being thus fairly easily decided.

Reference here is only to shields displaying few charges and the issue is at once confused in the case of a shield bearing, say, over one hundred quarterings, where it becomes almost impossible to reconcile legibility with the scale of shield and helmet. (Although the marshalling of so many quarters on one shield may correctly show descent, few would seriously attempt to bear them all, and the Heralds may see fit to grant a reversion to the arms in the first quarter, or at any rate to an earlier quartering sufficient to establish the paternal line.) It is to be regretted that armorial helmets frequently bear little resemblance to any form of wearable armour—a fault which only slight research would cure.

THE CREST

There is also a scale relationship between crest and helm as between shield and helm, the guiding principle being again one of usage. Originally of light-weight material, such as pressed and moulded leather, or thin metal built upon a frame, the size of these splendidly gilded and painted objects was limited only by the demands of mobility and comfort.

In depicting the crest in an illuminated achievement of arms the craftsman should avoid being niggardly, and though crests are still to be found drawn unduly small, following the general practice of the nineteenth century, we can with advantage revert to a happier proportion. As a suggested working rule the area occupied by helm and crest together may equal that of the shield itself (plate 29), or all three items may be of similar size (plate 28). Wherever possible crests should appear firmly attached to the helm (plate 27) and not merely poised at one point.

THE CREST WREATH

This is the least item in the achievement and shows a twist of the colours (i.e. those tinctures first blazoned, a metal and a colour) resting upon the brow of the helmet in such a way as to display six distinct pieces alternately of metal and colour (plates 22, 27, 28 and 34), metal appearing first to the Dexter, with the last twist therefore of colour to the Sinister—though this was by no means a hard and fast rule in earlier times. In heraldry the term Dexter implies the right hand of the wearer of a surcoat of arms and therefore is to the left as we look at it, conversely for the term Sinister.

A crest wreath looks its best when pressing firmly down upon the mantled helm in fulfilment of its function of keeping the mantling in place. Thus at times the top of the mantled helm may show (plate 27). A charmingly adventurous use for the crest wreath is shown in plate 20. Here it is arranged as a decorative surround to the shield, and it is to be hoped that similar excursions may be enjoyed in modern heraldry.

THE MANTLING

It is primarily in the design of mantling that the skill of the artist may be assessed and especial attention must be given to it. What may at times pass satisfactorily as a black and white line drawing can become entirely out of balance when coloured and thus seen as a series of twists and turns alternately of coloured cloth and metal lining. To quote Boutell: 'The Mantling is painted of the first-mentioned colour and is lined with the metal first mentioned.' No such rule, however, checked the medieval illuminator's powers of invention.

The problem of balancing these alternations of coloured cloth and metal lining is particularly noteworthy in the case of an esquire's achievement of arms, in which a Dexter-facing helmet tends to display the exterior of the mantling to the Sinister while allowing a view of its lining to the Dexter (plate 27). This point is entirely ignored in plate 22, the mantling apparently bursting upon us from the right cheek of the helmet. Following a good start it is desirable to obtain an eventual balance of colour and metal within the sum total of its twistings and convolutions around the shield. (See plates 28 and 29 for answers to this problem.)

A further important factor is the 'flow' of cloth. This is most convincing when an apparently heavy stuff, pendant from the helmet initially, gathers momentum in turning, to flourish into the space available (plates 27 and 29). Mantling which would appear to have been starched, arranged and then ironed stiffly into position is rarely convincing, and the study of acanthus decoration from the best classical sources and the carved heraldry of the Renaissance in England should bring out the point.

In relief and in the round, the carver is forced to make the mantling function or he fails in his task. For the illuminator working only in two dimensions his depiction will be the better if also feasible in three. This of course does not imply that the painting need appear to stand out from the vellum page or cast a shadow.

The amount of mantling to display will depend upon the general disposition of the whole achievement and the space remaining available. One might avoid an undue amount of mantling by considering to what extent the wearer would be inconvenienced.

THE SUPPORTERS

These human, beast, bird and fish forms should by their very classification uphold the shield in its chosen position (plate 24) and not lounge upon it as is only too often seen, though certain exceptions may be tolerated in retrospect. The nineteenth century produced many delightful versions of arms in which supporters are shown squatting or lying down comfortably on either side of the shield, or emerging placidly from behind it and the lack of such a pleasant Alice-in-Wonderland conception of heraldry to-day must be set as a loss against gains in other directions.

Though this is not the place to examine the evolution in design of the arms of the United Kingdom, much may be learned from the various interpretations of the Royal Supporters to be seen on the packs and containers of proprietary articles 'By Appointment', and more especially perhaps from the carvings and enamelled plates happily still to be seen affixed to Royal Warrant holders' places of business. In the former the reduction in scale is at times so severe as to require the omission of items blazoned, yet a glance will show what is intended—as it were, heraldry by implication.

In the illuminated manuscript, however, there can be little excuse for anything but full and correct interpretation of blazon while maintaining the maximum vitality of treatment.

THE MOTTO AND SCROLL

In England the motto or war cry is not usually included in a grant of arms by letters patent but appears by custom upon a scroll flourished beneath the shield (plates 22 and 23). The scroll may offer something for the supporters to stand on (plate 22) and usually marks the lower boundary of an achievement. In Scottish practice the motto is part of the grant and is to be found upon its scroll above the shield, flourished about the crest. If more than one crest is displayed each may be accompanied by a scroll and motto.

Heraldry does not need to be borne on a shield to qualify as such, nor does a motto cease to be one in the absence of a scroll—a fact which the scribe may take advantage of on occasions.

Ideally the scroll, like the mantling, should be rendered carefully enough to stand a three-dimensional test without difficulty. Its folds and flourishes may be assembled to accord with the length of individual words or groups of words (plates 27 and 28) or may be disposed at will, even treating the words of the motto by syllables (plate 22) or in any other way convenient (plate 21).

The style of lettering used for mottoes is on the whole most satisfactory when in sympathy with lettering elsewhere in the same manuscript.

The illustrations which follow have been chosen to

exemplify points raised and to represent the growth of the illuminators' technique. For twentieth-century examples of illumination it is appropriate that the majority shown are the work of members of the Society of Scribes and Illuminators, and acknowledgement has been made to these and to other sources at the end of this chapter.

In general it may be said that heraldic illumination moves always with the main stream of design but, by reason of having strong traditions as yet unbroken, is also shyer of innovations than are many other branches of the useful crafts.

Personal expression has remained largely subordinate to tradition, and probably for this reason little is known about the identity of heraldic illuminators of the past. It would seem that few, excepting Matthew Paris, may be named much earlier than the nineteenth century.

In conclusion it cannot be too often stated that illuminators of many ages have interpreted the same written blazons into the idiom of their own times and their own particular style of work, so that in comparing a leopard from the Royal Arms of 1750 with one from those of 1950, or indeed with a royal leopard of 1250 as drawn by Matthew Paris, it is not possible to say which is correct and which incorrect—all express the same blazon in different ways, and all are to that extent correct.

This factor is frequently forgotten by both parties when an illumination of arms is commissioned. By all means let some existing version of the arms be shown to the artist, but beware of any cramping of style which such influence may bring about. It is the blazon in words, which matters initially, from which a new and lively interpretation is required.

COMMENTARY ON THE ILLUSTRATIONS

(*The work of members of the Society is indicated thus* *)

Plate 18. (The Minor) 'Historia Anglorum' by Matthew

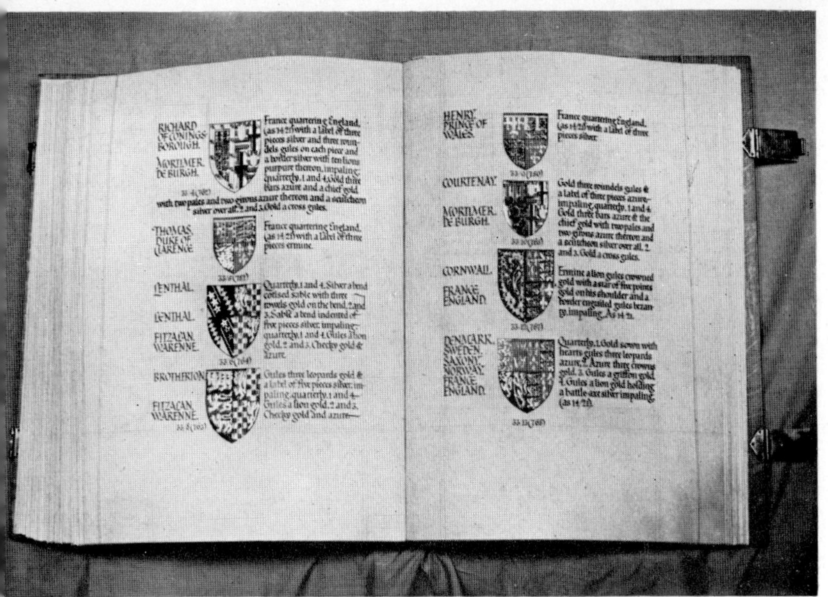

Pl. 32. W. M. Gardner, N. Ball & T. Wrigley. Completed 1939

Pl. 33 (*below*). Detail of title page

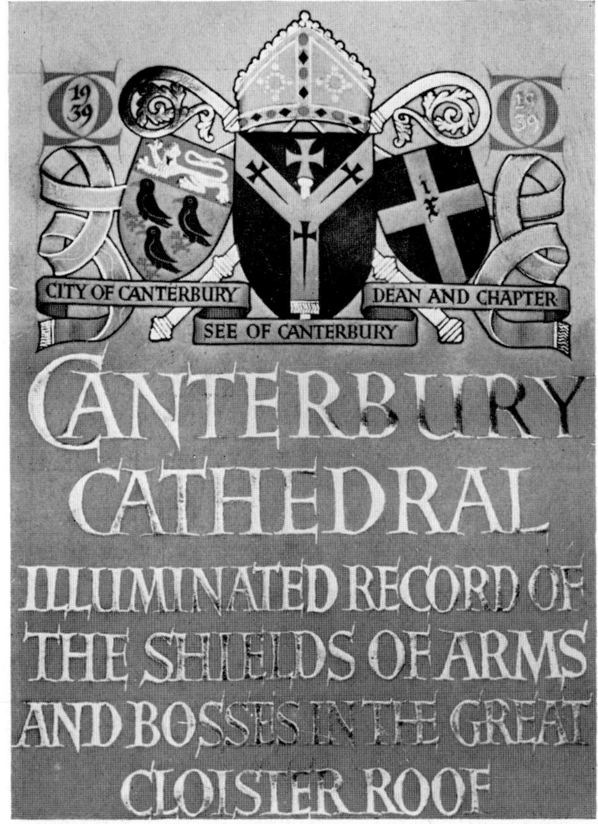

Pl. 34. College of Arms. c. 1510

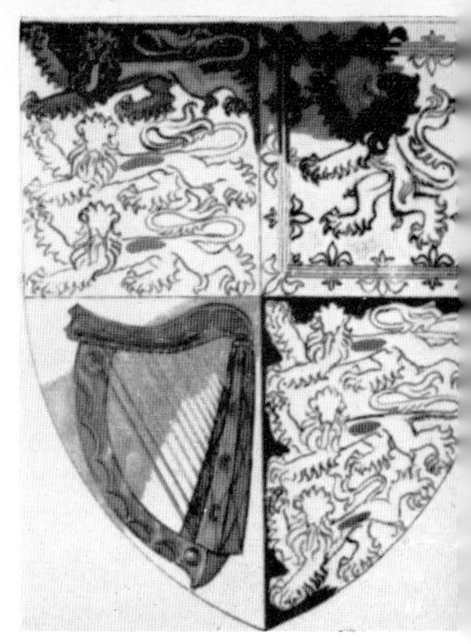

Pl. 35. Gerald Cobb. 1938

Pl. 36. N. Ball. 1948

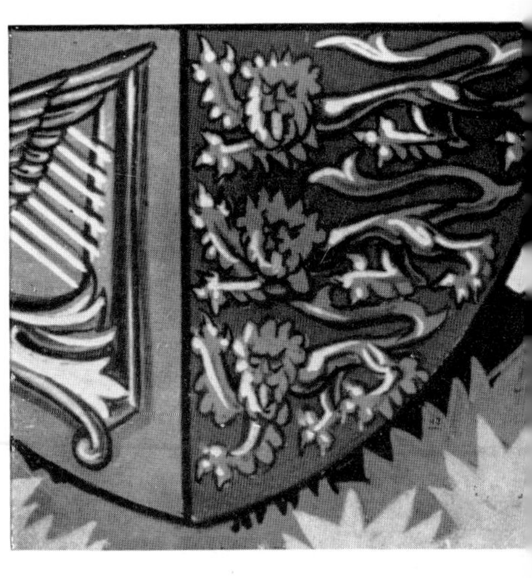

Pl. 37. College of Arms. 1948

Pl. 38. Edward Johnston. 1930

Pl. 39. W. M. Gardner. 1950

Paris, written *c.* 1250 (Folio 2A of B.M. Royal MS. 14c. VII). Sir Frederick Madden has described the shield assigned by later heralds to Harold as 'Azure a lion rampant double quevé Or', introduced between the columns of text, but reversed in token of his death.

A modest crown symbolical of kingship tumbles from a shield closely resembling in form that of a contemporary stone carving in the third bay of the N. Aisle wall arcading of Westminster Abbey nave (Simon de Montford).

The drawing shows a shield of usable and handy proportions while the painted charge upon it is both vigorous and legible. The scale of the painting is ideal for this manuscript volume and there are no unnecessary embellishments to confuse the representation of a royal downfall.

In the original manuscript the line work of crown and shield is drawn in ink with a quill pen, the field is subsequently filled in with blue pigment and the lion with a gummy yellow, upon vellum typical of the period and now polished with use. There is at once a most happy and spontaneous balance between respective areas of blue and gold. Complete confidence on the part of the draughtsman is evident.

Matthew Paris considered it appropriate to show arms throughout this manuscript inverted where their owners are mourned, and upright when acceding to the throne or other high office.

Plate 19. Furness Cartulary. Illuminated vellum Register in Latin of the Charters and Writings of the Monastery of St. Mary Furness. Compiled by Abbot William Dalton in 1412 (Public Record Office Museum).

Some one hundred and sixty years later than (The Minor) 'Historia Anglorum' a marked change of style and treatment may be noticed. Here upon a burnished gold background and suspended upon a guige or strap within the h of Henricus may be seen a shield conforming in shape to its counterpart in battle.

Though perhaps with less precise balance between the areas of field and charges than appears in plate 18 and with somewhat attenuated beasts upon a wider shield, the effect of gilding with colour is stimulating and there can be no question as to legibility, scale or economy of detail.

No less than five of these illuminated shields of England (Gules three leopards Or) enrich the exhibited opening of this manuscript.

Plate 20. Tudor Armorial Manuscript, Folio, on Vellum. Probably made *c.* 1510 for Sir Thomas Wriothesley, Garter King of Arms 1505–34. (College of Arms Library pressmark L.9.)

Upon the lower half of folio 1 *b.* appear two wreath-encircled impalements displaying Wriothesley's marriage firstly with Joan Hall of Salisbury and secondly with Anne, widow of Richard Goldborough and Robert Warcop and daughter of Sir William Ingleby of Ripley, Kt.

As an exercise in blazon (College of Arms): 'Quarterly 1. and 4. Azure a Cross Or between four Doves Argent (WRIOTHESLEY) 2. Argent a Fret Gules within a Bordure engrailed Sable on a Canton of the second a Lion passant Or (DUNSTAVILL. Sir Thomas's mother was Barbara, daughter and heir of Henry Dunstavill of Castlecombe). 3. Argent a Pale Fusilly Gules within a Bordure Azure Bezantée (probably LUSHILL of Co. Wilts.).'

On the left these arms are shown impaling those of Hall comprising 'Argent on a Chevron Sable between three Columbines slipped proper an Estoile Or'; and on the right impaling the arms of INGLEBY—'1. and 4. Sable an Estoile Argent with two other quarterings not identified.'

Encircling each of these shields appear crest-wreaths of the colours garnished in both cases with green foliage to Dexter. Charmingly worked into the garniture are

Columbine buds for HALL and six pointed stars for INGLEBY respectively.

These two shields with the two Gartered and Imperially Crowned Royal shields above them (not here shown) together comprise one of the most carefree and vigorous expressions of heraldic illumination in an altogether splendid Armorial (see also plate 34).

Plate 21. Duplicate of the Ratification by Francis I of a Treaty of Perpetual Peace with England. In Latin upon vellum. Dated at Amiens, 18 August 1527. Signed 'Francoys', Countersigned 'Robertat' (Public Record Office Museum).

This illumination is included to confirm, by comparison with plate 20, how far the development of style upon the continent is in advance of that of England. Wriothesley's Armorial holds strongly to the medieval idiom while the French illumination already embraces the greater liberties of the Renaissance.

The Royal Shields exhibit a gaiety of outline superficially apt for the occasion, but belied by Anglo-French wars within a decade. They are set off respectively by the lilies for France and the red and white roses of Lancaster and York for England.

The circlet of the crown of France bears fleurs-de-lis; that of England fleurs-de-lis alternately with crosses, still its form to-day.

The third lion in the third quarter of England is delightfully independent of the shield outline.

The background of the panel appears to be of powdered gold setting off the blue, red and green detail. A brownish ink script.

Plate 22. Vellum manuscript (*c.* 1620). 'Arms and Descents of the Nobility.' (College of Arms Library pressmark E. 16.)

On folio 34 *b*. The arms of William Lord Knowles may be blazoned 'Azure crusilly a Cross Moline voided Or quartering Gules on a Chevron Argent three Roses of the

Field barbed and seeded Proper. Crest: An Elephant statant Argent. Supporters: On either side an Heraldic Antelope Argent armed crined and unguled Or the shield surrounded by the Garter and surmounted by a Viscount's coronet of rank'.

In this interesting painting may be seen the bridge between two worlds of illuminating style. The rendering is distinctly of the Renaissance in England thence to proceed on the whole with increasing somnolence (though with the most charming passages) until the second half of the nineteenth century, while at the same time are echoed strong traditional modes of expression of a century earlier. (See plate 20.) This 'explosive' manner of mantling is to be found a feature during the subsequent hundred and fifty years.

In the depiction, Argent is expressed by the surface of the vellum itself shaded with grey—a deep warm blue for the Garter, with crest wreath and mantling of a colder blue. The scroll is shaded with pale pink and is made to serve as a platform for the supporters. The helmet of rank is that of a peer of the realm. The viscount's coronet carries a greater total of pearls than the sixteen authorized to-day, of which nine usually appear on the forward rim of the circlet.

Plate 23. 'A Vellum book, sumptuously emblazoned in gold and colours and bound in brass and velvet, of the Genealogy of the Sovereigns of the Most Honourable Military Order of the Bath—prepared in 1803 at a cost of upwards of £2,000 for King George III, Sovereign of the Order, by George Nayler, Genealogist and Blanc Coursier Herald of the Order, afterwards Garter King of Arms (1822–1831), but never being paid for was retained by him and in 1864 was given by his daughter, Miss Francis Nayler, to the College.' (College of Arms Library pressmark No. 133.)

This is indeed a sumptuously illuminated manuscript, the illustration here being of the arms then borne by His Most Excellent Majesty, part of the volume's title page.

Such meticulous care and painstaking skill might be said to represent the very limits of heraldic illumination, giving place before the century is out to a fresh approach. Upon superb vellum, the polished gold leaf is over-painted where necessary with detailed line work of brown. The foliage accompanying the scroll is of a very bluish green; the garter of a purplish blue; the cap of estate crimson. Argent is of the vellum itself shaded a bluish grey.

The Royal Arms at this time carries an Escutcheon of Pretence for His Majesty's Hanoverian Dominions, ensigned with the Electoral bonnet, and containing an escutcheon bearing the Crown of Charlemagne (as arch-treasurer to the Holy Roman Emperor).

Even at this comparatively late date the name of the illuminator (if not Nayler himself) remains unknown.

Plate 24. No excuse is needed in illustrating woodcuts from the drawings of Fr. Anselm and J. Forbes Nixon which have influenced the development of heraldic design, and therefore of illumination, so decisively.

Among many enthusiastic press reviews upon Mr. Joseph Foster's production of *The Peerage, Baronetage, and Knightage of the British Empire* in 1880, *The Athenæum* is provoked into admitting—'An attractive feature of this work and one which seems likely to commend itself to the public is its engravings, and the armorial designs which accompany each article are of more artistic merit than those usually supplied in works of the kind.' It would seem from this modest statement that Fr. Anselm and his co-illustrator were seen to be reviving heraldic design to very good effect, with the help of the engraver's burin.

Designed by Fr. Anselm, plate 24 shows an admirable command of proportion between Baron Sudeley's crests, helmet, shield and supporters.

The slight tilt of the shield prevents any impression of stiffness, while the Falcon supporters vary between them their grasp of the shield and hold up the baron's coronet of rank in their beaks.

THE BLAZON (Foster): 'Quarterly 1st and 4th Or an escallop in the chief point Sa. (Sable) between two bendlets Gu. (Gules) TRACEY. 2nd and 3rd Or a bend engrailed Vert cottised Sa. HANBURY. Crests: 1. On a chapeau Gu. turned up Erm. (Ermine) an escallop Sa. between two wings Or, TRACY. 2. Out of a mural crown Sa. a demi-lion Or holding a battle axe Sa. HANBURY. Supporters: Two falcons Ppr. (Proper) belled Or.' Motto: 'Memoria pii aeterna.'

Plate 25. J. Forbes Nixon reminds us that there are ways of displaying armorial bearings other than upon supported shields of stereotyped form (see plate 27 also).

THE BLAZON comprises (Foster) 'Quarterly 1st and 4th Gu. a cross Arg. in each quarter five plates in saltire WELLESLEY. 2nd and 3rd Or a lion rampant Gu. ducally gorged Or, COLLEY, and for augmentation in chief an escutcheon charged with the Union (being the badge of Great Britain and Ireland, viz. the crosses of St. George, St. Andrew and St. Patrick conjoined). Crest: out of a ducal coronet Or a demi-lion Gu. holding a forked pennon of the last per pale Arg. charged with the cross of St. George. Supporters: Two lions Gu. each gorged with an Eastern Crown and chained Or'. Motto: 'Virtutis fortuna comes.'

Where only one supporter is shown thus, both are alike. Where supporters differ they may appear facing each other, holding the staff between them and with the banner centrally above.

Plate 26. Manuscript record of the armorial bearings of H.R.H. Prince Edward George Nicholas Paul Patrick, Duke of Kent. (College of Arms Library pressmark I. 81. 210.)

Of recent date (1948) this illustration is representative of the current style of College of Arms work.

Upon pale violet-blue paper, ruled red, the achievement (helmet and mantling taken for granted) is in colour only, the metal of the blazon being skilfully expressed by brush work (see plate 37 also). The painting and blazon together may be said to constitute the College of Arms 'reference copy' of this Grant.

BLAZON (College of Arms): 'The Royal Arms surmounted by a coronet composed of Crosses and Strawberry leaves and differenced by a label of five points Argent the centre point and the two outer points charged with an anchor Azure and the two inner points with a St. George's cross. Royal crest and supporters differenced with a like coronet and label.'

The whole painting is strikingly outlined in a dark red, and the unicorn (of the colour of the paper) is shaded with a pinkish grey. The grassy mount below is rendered in diminishing tones of green, setting off the red of the English quarters and the cap of estate.

*Plate 27.** A panel of lettering with illuminated arms, by N. Ball, Esq. Such a departure from the normal arrangement of arms, assisted in this case by a secondary motto with its scroll, is refreshing.

The golden lion upon the shield supports with its Dexter paw an inescutcheon of Ulster, signifying the status of Baronet in addition to a mention of this degree in the words of the heading. In place of the knight baronet's helmet of rank appears a fine rendering of the tilting helm—compare the painted high lights upon the helm with those of the burnished gold leaf itself. The play of light upon a pattern of impressed dots enlivens the golden lining of the mantling.

The lettering in support of the achievement is of red and black upon goatskin of a delightful texture, and among present day illumination it would be difficult to find a more vigorous heraldic panel.

*Plate 28.** Illumination upon goatskin by T. Wrigley, Esq. The Arms of the Borough of Oldham, County Palatinate of Lancaster (Granted 1894).

BLAZON (Fox Davies): 'Sable a chevron invected plain

cottised Or between three owls Argent, on a chief engrailed of the second a rose Gules barbed and seeded Proper between two annulets also Gules.'

The red first line of heading, roses of crest, rose and annulets in chief, and the red doubling of the scroll set off the black and burnished gold achievement to excellent effect, while there is a fine balance between arms and lettering.

*Plate 29.** Illumination upon vellum by N. Ball, Esq. The achievement, supported by red and black lettering, of FOWLER. A happy disposition of charges within the shield and most restful mantling. BLAZON (Burke—an example of abbreviation in blazon) 'Per pale Gu. and Sa. on a chev. Or betw. three lions pass. guard. Erm. crowned Or as many quatrefoils Vert. Crest: A stork Arg. membered Gu. holding in the bill a cross fitchy formy Or'.

The display of red, black, Ermine, green and burnished gold is particularly satisfying.

*Plate 30.** Illuminated Document, Wye College, Kent. By W. M. Gardner, Esq. upon calfskin vellum. The Arms of Cardinal Archbishop Kempe, founder of the College, with supporting lettering of red and black.

BLAZON (Burke): 'Gu. three garbs within a bordure engr. (engrailed) Or.'

*Plate 31.** Section of a large Panel 'Arms and Badges of the Sovereigns of England'. Illuminated upon vellum by T. Swindlehurst, Esq. showing how successfully heraldry and lettering may be woven together. Much the same considerations arise in the assembling and setting out of illuminated genealogies.

*Plate 32.** Completed in 1939. A manuscript inventory of some 860 stone shields of arms carved circa A.D. 1400 in the ceiling vault of the Great Cloister, Canterbury Cathedral. The gift of the Friends of the Cathedral and the co-operative work of three members of the Society, W. M. Gardner, N. Ball and T. Wrigley.

Upon vellum leaves $13\frac{1}{2}$ in. wide × 19 in. high, the arms are illuminated in burnished gold and colour with each shield named and blazoned. Bound by Douglas Cockerell and Son, in oak boards with pigskin spine and silver clasps.

The structure of the page allows no gilded surface to close against gilding opposite, and this arrangement also avoids an accumulation of thickness in any one place when the volume is shut. (Dean and Chapter Library, Canterbury Cathedral.)

*Plate 33.** Upper part of Title-page to the manuscript last described. Cream coloured mitre and infulae, with burnished gold lettering, pastoral staves etc., and white pigment for the silver.

BLAZONS (Messenger): 'Silver three beckets in their proper colours and a chief Gules with a leopard gold thereon.' (CITY OF CANTERBURY) 'Azure a cross-staff gold with its cross silver and overall a pall silver charged with three crosses formy fitchy Sable.' (SEE OF CANTERBURY) 'Azure a cross silver with the text letter X surmounted by the text letter i Sable on the cross.' (PRIORY OF CHRIST CHURCH, CANTERBURY.)

Plate 34. From folio 27a. of the Tudor Armorial Manuscript at the College of Arms (plate 20), being one of twelve coats to the page.

BLAZON (College of Arms): 'Azure a lion passant guardant Argent between three Suns in Splendour Or. Crest: A demi-Griffin Or holding the Rudder of a Ship Sable the Tiller and Pintles Gold' (ascribed to Hulson).

The blue is of a dark tone; the red of orange-vermilion and all charges blazoned 'Or' of a bright mustardy yellow pigment. The shield, charges and crest are outlined with black—and the whole is at once legible, vigorous, colourful and straightforward.

Plate 35. Coloured drawing by Gerald Cobb, Esq. of the College of Arms, showing the charges of the shield of the United Kingdom assembled in their respective quarters. The dovetailing into place of the English Leopards, particularly that of the third leopard in the fourth quarter, is noteworthy. (Compare plates 21, 36 and 37.) The colouring is indicated only, and was done originally as guidance for a very much larger painting.

*Plate 36.** Shield of Arms of John of Gaunt. Illuminated upon vellum with colour and burnished gold. Detail from a manuscript page by N. Ball, Esq.

It will be noticed that the slight natural waviness of vellum is at times an advantage with gilding in producing an interesting play of light. (See also plate 33.)

BLAZON. Quarterly 1. and 4. Azure semée of fleurs-de-lis Or (FRANCE ANCIENT) 2. and 3. Gules three leopards Or (ENGLAND) with a label of three points Ermine.

Plate 37. Enlarged Detail from plate 26, fourth Quarter (q.v.) with skilful brushwork suggestive of gilding. 'Gules three leopards Or' (ENGLAND). The semblance of a glitter is obtained by shading yellow with brown and touching in the high lights with yellowish white.

Plate 38. A freely rendered quill pen drawing upon vellum by the late Edward Johnston of a lion upon a crest wreath, being a detail from an Illuminated Address presented by the National Galleries of Scotland to Sir James L. Caw. (1930.)

The drawing might be described as a 'Heraldic finial' to the decorative heading of the document and is spontaneously done with the same pen—an example of the 'square-cut' pen seeking expression in heraldry.

*Plate 39.** Enlarged detail of gold mantling doubled Ermine from an illuminated translation of the Royal Arms upon vellum, by W. M. Gardner. Compare present day tendencies with mantling in plate 23, and earlier in plate 22.

William Gardner

ACKNOWLEDGEMENTS

No attempt is made here to explain the Grammar of Heraldry, already clearly set out in the works of Sir W. H. St. John Hope and other accepted authorities.

Familiarity with the more common heraldic terms is assumed—to be supplemented where necessary by reference to dictionary or encyclopædia. It may be found helpful, however, to link a display of arms with the blazon, and as far as possible this has been done in the commentary upon the illustrations. Similarly the illustrations include at least something of the script which accompanies the originals.

Most grateful acknowledgement is made to Her Majesty the Queen for gracious permission to reproduce (plate 23); H.R.H. The Duke of Kent (plates 26 and 37); The Keeper of Manuscripts, British Museum (plate 18); The Deputy Keeper of Records, Public Record Office (plates 19 and 21); The Dean and Chapter of Canterbury Cathedral (plates 32 and 33); The Trust of Insurance Shares Ltd. (plate 31); The Chairman of the Governing Body, Wye College, Kent (plate 30); The National Galleries of Scotland (plate 38); Gerald Cobb, Esq. (plate 35); to Garter King of Arms and especially to Colonel J. R. B. Walker, Lancaster Herald, for plates 20, 22, 23, 26, 34 and 37.

Assistance very much valued was given by the late Professor E. W. Tristram, D.Litt., F.S.A., in reading and commenting upon this article in manuscript.

IX

Cursive Handwriting

This book is primarily concerned to help those who desire to make works of artistic craftsmanship by means of formal penmanship. Information is given concerning the best tools, materials, and methods, and the principles of design. It is not out of place, however, to offer advice as to the writing of a cursive hand, since the only significant factors that divide the formal from the cursive hand are speed of performance and purpose.

The letters and words written by the calligrapher, giving pattern, form, and grace to inscriptions, are made with slow pace to allow precision of construction, for the appearance of the writing is more important than the speed of execution. A calligrapher, when writing his formal script, will naturally be intent on making satisfactory progress but yet will proceed with no faster movements than are appropriate to the careful formation of the strokes which, when fitted together, will make good letters. It is inconceivable that a contemporary calligrapher who has spent much time preparing a precious vellum sheet will hurry his quill with undue urgency along the writing lines. But a calligrapher's alphabetical interest may not be wholly confined to formal usages and he may wish, when writing his correspondence with proper speed, to maintain quality belonging to a penman's script. Being a calligrapher he will not mind if the hand he writes shows some writing-consciousness and control, so long as it is legible and speedy enough for his purpose; indeed it might be expected of a calligrapher (though it would not apply necessarily) that his everyday handwriting would give some indication of his calligraphical skill and that whilst writing quickly he would have half-an-eye on appearance. The need, therefore, of the student of formal calligraphy who wishes his cursive handwriting to be related to his formal penmanship, although without close propinquity, is to know what examples, past and present, he should look at, what sort of pen to use, how to hold the pen, and what to do about joining letters. When he has arrived at his principles he will find that his hand and arm, being different things from his head, will not be entirely compliant; and that handwriting implies a compromise between head, hand, and pen, as well as a reconciliation of freedom and control; and so an expression of individuality emerges.

Undoubtedly the most promising hands for the calligrapher to study in order to gain an appreciation of good cursive handwriting are the humanistic cursive hands of the fifteenth and sixteenth centuries, developed as a result of the revived use of the Caroline minuscule. Scholars of the Italian Renaissance in their study of the classic authors came upon and were attracted by the Caroline scripts of the ninth to twelfth centuries. Through the adoption of these antique hands by the 'humanists' for their own use, we may see in fifteenth-century manuscript books two sorts of humanistic hands, namely those we should recognize as related in form either to the Roman or to the italic types of to-day. The italic is the freer letter, cursive in character, and having an oval *o*. Models of italic are often to be seen in the books of the writing masters of the sixteenth century. Sometimes these models are of a 'set' cursive tending to return in the direction of the formal, i.e. they may incorporate certain formal characteristics, such as letter forms that require too many pen-lifts or too much attention to be truly cursive in character.

The sixteenth-century writing books which may offer the

greatest help are those of Ludovico Arrighi (Vicentino), G. A. Tagliente, Gerard Mercator, and Francisco Lucas, but there are examples of writing of the period not intended as models which can serve for study and are reproduced in various contemporary publications. The masters of the copperplate tradition of the seventeenth and eighteenth centuries (Lucas Materot, Jan Van den Velde, Louis Barbedor, Ambrosius Perlingh, Edward Cocker, Colonel John Ayres, Charles Snell, etc.) have given place with the associated copperplate tradition in the estimation of amateurs of calligraphy to the masters of the preceding era, some of whom are named above.

William Morris in 1876 was practising an italic hand derived from the sixteenth century and possibly from a copy of Arrighi's manual in his possession. In 1898 Mrs. M. M. Bridges, wife of the late Poet Laureate, showed in *A New Handwriting for Teachers* models related to 'Italianized Gothic of the sixteenth century'. In 1906 the late Edward Johnston published his classic book *Writing, Illuminating and Lettering* and in pages 317 to 323 he illustrated and described a sixteenth-century Italian hand (also to be seen in plate 40) which he considered might conveniently be termed *semi-formal*. He noted the good shapes of the letters and their great uniformity and that the hand combined great rapidity and freedom with beauty and legibility and he concluded that it 'suggests possibilities for an improvement in the ordinary present-day handwriting—a thing much to be desired, and one of the most practical benefits of the study of calligraphy'. Perhaps in describing it as *semi-formal* Johnston diverted some attention from its cursive characteristics. Be that as it may, it did not excite as much interest amongst Johnston's early pupils as his models of formal hands. It is not quite a pure hand: indeed it might well be called a cursive hand with some formal characteristics. A word such as *nunc* may be written without lifting the pen and yet the small letter *d* is made with three separate strokes fitted together with great skill. The mixture of opposed factors is well hidden, however, by the general easy uniformity and patterned rhythm of the script and in spite of its slight impurities it constitutes a remarkable and valuable example for study.

At one time Edward Johnston was of the opinion that the *ideal* method of teaching children handwriting was to go through the evolutionary phases. In giving a tribute to Edward Johnston at a Memorial Meeting of the Society of Scribes and Illuminators held on 10th November 1945 the author read the following extract:

'The Board of Education pamphlet *Print-script* states that: "At the annual Conference of Teachers held under the auspices of the London County Council in January 1913, Mr. Edward Johnston of the Royal College of Art, gave an address on Penmanship, in which he suggested that, in the early stages of teaching children to write, the Roman alphabet, as used in the manuscripts of the ninth and tenth centuries, with its italic development of later date, might with advantage be used as a model. Before the end of the year two London Schools were experimenting on these lines."

'On 13th November 1932, when I was preparing to read a paper to the Royal Society of Arts on the teaching of handwriting, Edward Johnston sent me the following comment:

' "To quote from my address of 2nd January 1913 (p. 19 of Report): 'It is the broad nib that gives the pen its constructive and educational value. It is essentially the letter-making tool. . . . It may therefore be relied on largely to determine questions of form in letters. . . . In fact a broad-nibbed pen actually controls the hand of the writer and will create alphabets out of their skeletons, giving harmony and proportion and character to the different letters.'

' "I went on to suggest an ideal course in which children might begin with:

Roman capitals and their origins;

let them trace with stylus and wax tablets the passage of the Capital into the skeleton small letter;

followed by the practice of a half-uncial book hand;

followed by the practice of a *Caroline* book hand (such as the tenth century 'Foundational hand');

followed by the development of the Foundational hand into the italic.

I believe that this (F.H.)[1] would make a good model and that in practice it would develop into a fluent hand.

' "I should not wish to be thought that I was *directly* responsible for the *form of print-script characters.* I was not consulted in the experiments and have not even become 'familiar' with the P.-S. characters. My impression is that they are *rather formless skeletons of roman l.c.*? It is difficult to *give* or *preserve* form in letter *skeletons* except by skill and knowledge. I advocated the broad nib and the study of the book hands for the giving and preserving of Form. Recently, however, I have been given evidence that very young elementary school children (at 5–7, I *think*) found the broad nib a difficult tool to manipulate, which seems quite to justify the use by such children of (carefully planned) skeleton forms and 'pointed' or stylus-like tools. But, of course, as soon as they were able, they should be given the broad-nib and a broad-pen Book-hand (or a modification of B.H.) as a foundation for their future handwriting."

'In reading this comment I have wanted to make it clear to what extent Johnston was responsible for the reform of print-script.'

A modification of Johnston's views is to be noted in 'An Appreciation of the Dudley Writing Cards' (included in Sets A and 1 of the *Dudley Writing Cards* by Marion Richardson), for in April 1928 Johnston states:

'I still believe that some of the formal "bookhands" (to be

[1] By F. H., Johnston meant 'foundational hand'.

P. Victoris de Notis Antiquis.

ſt etiam Cura circa praeſcribendas, uel paucio-
ribus lr̃is annotandas uoceſ ſtudium necesſa-
rium. quod partim pro uoluntate cuiusq. fit,
partim uſu proprio: et obſeruatione communis;
nanq. apud ueteres. cum usus notarum nullus
esſet pp ſcribendi facultatem maxime in Senatu
qui aderant in ſcribendo: ut celeriter dicta com-
prehenderent quaedam uerba, atque nomina
ex communi conſensu primis lr̃is notabantur
& singulę literę quid significabant ut i prom-
ptu erant. quod in nominibus pronominibus
legibus publicis: pontificumq. monumentis:
iurisq. Ciuilis libris etiam nunc manet. Ad
quas notationes publicas accedit ſtudiorum uo-
luntas: et unusquisque familiares notas pro
uoluntate signaret, quas comprehendere infinitu
est. publicę ſane tenendę ſunt, quae in monume-
tis plurimis, et historiarum libris, sacrisque publicis reperiuntur. ut Sequitur.

Pl. 40. Italian manuscript book, a catalogue of early Roman inscriptions
the possession of Mr. James Wardrop (Late fifteenth or early sixteenth century)

Pl. 41
Binding of House Commons Book Remembrance. Wh alumed morocco w gold and blind toolir Size 15″ × 11″

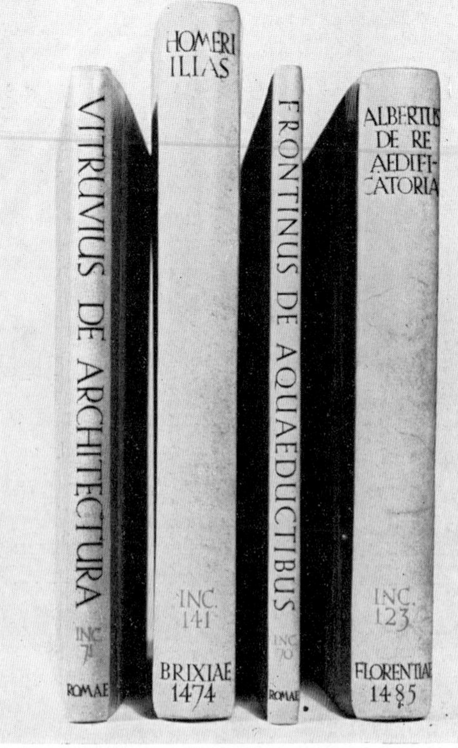

Pl. 42
Bindings of Incunabula: vellum spines: black ink lettering. Reproduced by kind permission of the National Library of Scotland

found in MS. Books, etc., from the third to the sixteenth century) offer the best models and the best training for the various purposes of penmanship—where time is not of first importance. But I fear that their use as models for speed writing is impracticable: for though they are capable of being written with considerable speed, and even of being modified into Approximate Running Hands, they cannot—without radical changes—produce the great speed required in the modern penman, because they consist of essentially static forms, while that great speed is compatible only with essentially Running Forms.'

In 1916 the publishing of Mr. Graily Hewitt's model in a booklet *Handwriting: Everyman's Handicraft* coincided with the reading of papers at a meeting of the Child Study Society on experiments with print-script in the two London schools. Neither Mr. Hewitt's early model nor print-script have running forms, for at that time it was thought by the reformers that joins offered no advantage. Mr. Hewitt's fine italic script involves the use of an edged pen but its beauty depends also on the good formation and spacing of letters: there are no joins in his model and therefore there is no rhythmic flow. Print-script is a letter related to Roman, made up simply of straight strokes, circles and parts of circles, and it is said to help children to learn to read, but its circular motions, its static quality, its lack of any hint as to how letters may be joined, and its independence of penmanship, make it seem but a poor expedient. Doubtless it has contributed (with other factors) to the decay in the nation's handwriting. The late Dr. P. B. Ballard remarked that there was 'one matter in connection with the print-writing movement developing into a cursive hand which violated a pedagogical maxim, namely, that one should begin with what one meant to go on with'.

Two tracts of the Society for Pure English on *English Handwriting*, edited by Robert Bridges, appeared in 1926 and

1927, and contained numerous illustrations of the hands of contemporary scholars, calligraphers, and artists, and these could be contrasted with sixteenth-century Italian scripts. Other collections have since been reproduced in *Lettering of To-day*, *Written by Hand*, *Sweet Roman Hand* and *Italic Handwriting*, but the examples are principally in the italic tradition. The two tracts were soon followed by the first model offered by the late Marion Richardson, an alphabet with joins written with edged steel pens and owing much to italic sources, namely *The Dudley Writing Cards*. Miss Richardson's *Writing and Writing Patterns* shows a development of the art of teaching handwriting by the making of patterns related to the letters of the alphabet and simple writing rhythms but her later models are lacking in distinction or promise.

Following the publication of the author's book *A Handwriting Manual* and *Woodside Writing Cards* in 1932 and through the interest of the then Director of Education of Barking, Mr. Joseph Compton, a further set of cards was produced in 1935 for use in Barking schools, later titled the *Dryad Writing Cards*.

In recent years so much interest has been shown in italic handwriting that, in November 1952, the Society of Scribes and Illuminators inaugurated successfully a new Society: the Society for Italic Handwriting.

At this stage it is convenient to consider, in greater detail, what we should regard as a cursive hand. Cursive is the writing for ordinary usage, and it is so related to an individual that it has a special value to him, and his friends, and in business transactions, as an expression of personality, and this quite apart from its function as a means of communicating, recording, and remembering. A person may write a cursive hand with different standards of care and speed so that his writing ranges from something that all can read to a scribble which he himself finds illegible; yet his varying handwriting could always be identified as his own. When the writing master executes a model for the teaching of cursive penmanship, that model may be regarded as a *set* cursive. The *free* cursive is what the pupil develops in time. The set cursive of a writing master's model, of, say, the eighteenth century, engraved on copper, may be executed with an astonishing skill but having little about it to suggest that a fallible human has used a pen. He may conceivably have written his script with much greater control than a contemporary calligrapher employs when executing a book hand. The slow and exact writing of a model is not only to show a high standard but to make intentions clear. The writing master says in effect: 'This model represents an ideal of legibility and pattern, but I admit that when I write quickly the writing is different. Even when making a copy slowly your writing will be different because it is yours and not mine. Regard the model, therefore, not as an impossible standard but as a guide to economical method and to form. The faster you write the more easily will your handwriting be seen as belonging exclusively to you. But bear in mind that legibility should come before speed and that no two persons can write alike.'

Fast writing necessitates economy—labour-saving devices and time-saving expedients. In a formal hand the pen is often lifted from the vellum: for example, there may be eight or more pen-lifts in writing the word 'and'. Pen-lifting when too frequent expends time and energy and must therefore be reduced in cursive writing. One must not assume, however, that this argues that all letters should be joined. There must be some joins, both oblique and horizontal, brought into use as the hand quickly decides. Some fast writers may naturally connect up most if not all letters of a word, even joining, say, *g* to an *h*, but the author holds that a moderate use of pen-lifts aids the moving of the hand and reduces fatigue and is advantageous both to legibility and appearance. The principle then is not to join every letter nor, on the other hand, to separate every letter, but to do what is expedient.

The diagonal join, so frequently a significant feature of the humanistic cursives of the Renaissance, is not suitable for the pointed pen of the copperplate tradition, and so was forgotten. The stiffish edged pen is held and used differently from the pointed pen in making up-strokes. The author learned the character and importance of the diagonal join in studying a model in Tagliente's manual and he recommends calligraphers to consider its function as an aid to speed and good spacing and its dominating influence on the rhythm of writing and therefore on the form of letters. In designing a set cursive hand one might begin with the letters *u* and *n* (opposed counter-clockwise and clockwise movements) and the join that connects them. The rising interior stroke of both letters should be but slightly different from the diagonal join. The appropriate but slight deviation from the join will ensure *n* and *u* being recognizable particularly if they are curved and not pointed sharply. Once the shape of the two letters has been decided on little difficulty should be experienced in devising more than half the alphabet (conforming to the principle of family relationship of letters of the alphabet and the contrasting principle of individual distinctiveness of letters) and when that is accomplished, calligraphers will find that, with the Renaissance examples as guides, the whole alphabet will occur to them, and unity is achieved. Then to the alphabet the other common join can be added, namely the horizontal join, which would, say, join *f* to a succeeding letter and which is demonstrated by Arrighi (fig. 34).

The classic Roman capitals at their finest are letters cut in stone. Through the use of the pen, uncials, half uncials, and minuscules were developed. But if the minuscule *o* is to be oval, as in italic, whereas it was circular in the earlier scripts, there is an argument that the capital O should be oval too. The calligrapher has, therefore, to decide whether capitals and lower case letters are to conform generally in this respect or whether capitals may still be considered as something quite different from minuscules, as they were regarded at the time of the Renaissance, and be in the classic tradition. A third factor is that many writers, including children only ten years of age, like to flourish some of their capitals, and the swash capitals of the Italian writing masters are indicated for study.

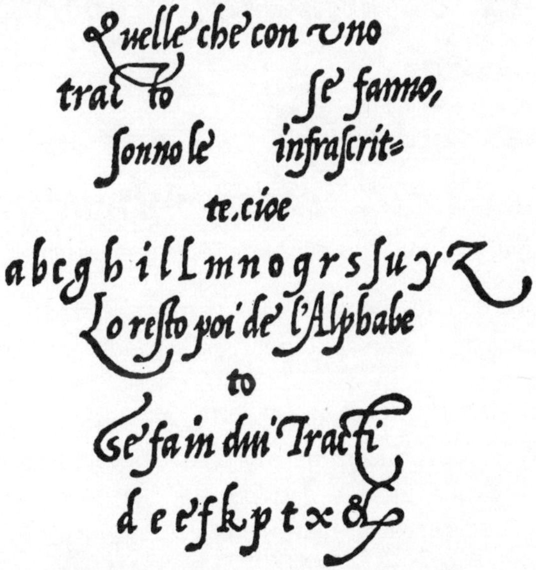

Quelle che con uno
tratto ſe fanno,
ſonno le infraſcrit=
te. cioe
a b c g h i l l m n o g r s ſ u y z
Lo reſto poi de l'Alphabe
to
Se fain dui Tratti
d e e f k p t x &

Fig. 34. Part of page from Arrighi

The pens used by the Renaissance writers were quills, sometimes sharply cut, sometimes quite blunt. We, to-day, do not write to our friends with a quill: we use a dip-pen or fountain pen. A straight-edged metal stub called the 'Flight Commander', which was made by Geo. W. Hughes at the suggestion of the author and is obtainable in four breadths, is recommended both for adults and children. This pen is straight-edged because being so it will allow the diagonal join to ascend at an angle of about 45° to the horizontal if the pen is held with the shaft pointing in the general direction of the elbow: an excellent join and a comfortable position for holding the pen. There are, of course, other suitable nibs (cf. chapter I). Fountain pens can be obtained which give a contrast of thick and thin strokes, and of these the Swan 'Calligraph' fountain pen is now well known. For the left-handed, an oblique-edged stub with the longer part of the nib on the right side, is recommended, whilst for those who are right-

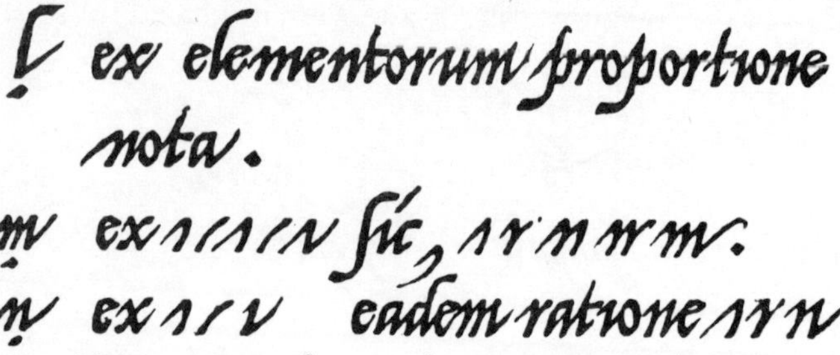

ex elementorum proportione nota.

m ex ı ı ı ı ı ı sic, ı r n w m.

n ex ı ı ı eadem ratione ı r n

Fig. 35. Part of a page from Mercator's Manual

handed but extend the elbow far from the side of the body the oblique-edged stub should have the longer part of the nib on the left side.

A reference has been made to Lucas and a page from his book is reproduced in my *Handwriting Manual*. The exquisite forms of his letters are an inspiration. The words move forward with elegant dignity; and legibility and beauty are served splendidly. We cannot hope, however, to write quickly with the precision of this set cursive. Discipline will give way to freedom (but freedom does not mean one is to be completely free of discipline). Fine letter shapes will always delight the eye, but the fashioning of each letter must yield something to the inherent rhythm of the words and motions as well as to the urgencies of the scurrying hours. The calligrapher, however, has two opportunities in the writing of italic: he can write a set italic with quill on vellum and employ all the means by which a manuscript is made a work of art, and he can dash down by rhythmical movements the thoughts he wishes to communicate pleasingly by visible words.

X

The Binding of Manuscripts

The purpose of binding a book is to hold the leaves together so that it can be opened for reading and closed for protection. The book should open easily, the leaves lying in a gentle curve. When closed the manuscript should be well protected with the leaves held flat between the boards of the binding. Basically, binding is a matter of mechanics and strength of materials, as is the case with the building of a house or of a boat.

Binding is only a part of book production and if the final whole is to be a satisfactory unit there must be co-operation between the craftsmen concerned: the vellum-maker, the scribe and the binder. It is not sufficient for the scribe to write and illustrate a manuscript, and when it is finished to send it to the binder with a note that it is to be bound and must open flat.

The now usual Codex form of book (fig. 36) as opposed to the scroll is made up of one or more sections of folded leaves of vellum, parchment or paper (Codex comes from the word *caudex*—tree trunk—as the books were bound between wooden boards). This form of book, made up of folded leaves of papyrus, came in about 200 A.D. By 400 A.D. vellum was being used for the leaves of codices, the vellum withstanding the folding better than the papyrus.

The section of a book (fig. 37) is the binder's unit and may consist of a single sheet folded in the middle (folio) making two leaves, or several folio leaves placed one inside the other; thus two folio leaves together would be called quarto, making four leaves of eight pages; four folios together would make an octavo section. Folded leaves are used because it is convenient to sew through the folds in order to attach the leaves together and hold them to the binding.

If the book is of a few leaves it may be bound as a single

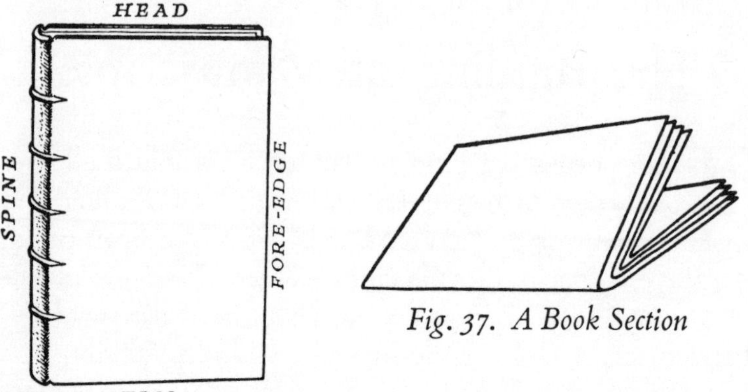

Fig. 36. Codex Form of Book

Fig. 37. A Book Section

section, the leaves being sewn together with thread or silk (fig. 38). This will keep the leaves in order but they will need

Fig. 38. A Single Section Book

some further protection if they are not to become dirty and dog-eared. Therefore stiff cards (boards) are attached to the outside. These boards are cut slightly larger than the book so that they will project beyond the edges of the leaves; these projections are called the 'squares'. In order that the boards may be firmly attached, two or three folios of strong paper are folded round the section and sewn into position together with a strip of thin linen for additional strength. The outside papers are pasted and the boards stuck in place, a space being left between the back edge of the boards and the spine of the book. This space enables the boards to open freely.

The covering materials may be leather, cloth, or a combination of these such as a leather spine with paper sides; the paper sides may be plain or patterned. The four outside corners of the boards can have vellum tips—these are very hard and durable and do not interfere with the rectangular shape of the book as leather corners do. The title of the book can be lettered in gold on the leather up the side of the spine; or the book may be covered wholly in leather and lettered and tooled with a pattern. Alternatively the cover may be made separately from the manuscript, and the manuscript attached to the cover by means of a leather joint sewn to the manuscript with a suitable number of blank paper or vellum leaves.

The number of leaves that can be bound as a single section depends on their thickness and size; as an approximate guide I would say that not more than six thin vellum or ten thin paper leaves should be bound as a single section. With a larger number of leaves the book is not likely to open well or handle nicely as a single section, and should be arranged and bound as a multi-section book. For this the individual sections must be held together and also attached to each other (fig. 39). This is achieved by sewing down the centre of each

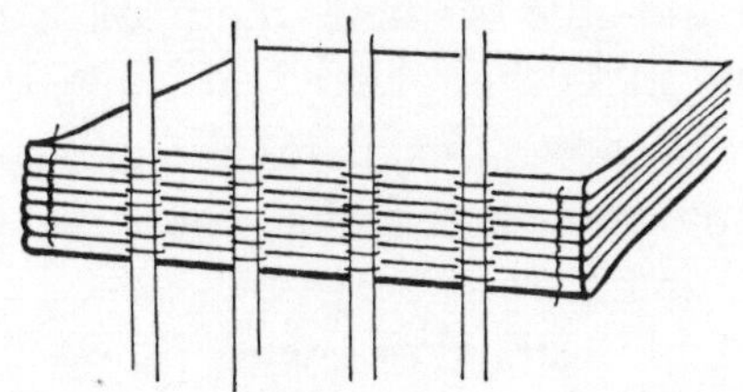

Fig. 39. Sections Sewn Together

section over tapes or cords stretched at right angles to the spine of the sections. The thread is taken in near the end of the first section, along inside the central folio, out and over the first tape or round the first cord, and back into the section, out for the next tape or cord and finally out near the end of the section and up into the second section and so on until the book is sewn.

The thread is looped together at the head and tail of the sections, so joining them together at these points (kettle stitch). A section of end papers is sewn on at each end of the book; these end papers may be of paper for a paper book or vellum for a vellum one, with linen or leather hinges (joints).

The ends of the cords or tapes to which the book is sewn are left projecting on each side of the spine; these projections are called slips and are very important as they form the main attachment for the boards. After the book is sewn the spine is given a thin coat of glue, well brushed in between the sections; the glue is to hold the sections in position so that the book will keep its shape. It is only the glue between the sections that serves any useful purpose.

For some time now when binding manuscripts on vellum I have been sewing a narrow guard of handmade paper round the back of each section because I have noticed from the bindings of early manuscripts that when glue has been used on the spine it is liable to break away from the backs of the sections, leaving an ugly dark space between them when the book is opened; or, if the glue has held, the book is liable to open stiffly. The glue sticks the folded guards together and leaves the vellum free to move; the guards also prevent the hot glue from coming into contact with the vellum and this avoids the liability of cockling it.

A sewn book has a strand of sewing thread at the centre of each section and the sum of these strands of thread cause the spine of the book to be thicker than the fore-edge. This swelling of the spine as it is called, enables the closed book to be rounded and results in a convex spine and concave fore-edge (fig. 40). The amount of swelling is controlled by the thickness of the sewing thread in relation to the size and number of sections in the book, and the choice of the right thickness of thread needs careful judgment as too much or too little swelling can spoil the shape of the book.

The rounding is done after the glue has been applied and

Fig. 40. Rounded Book *41. Backed Book*

before it sets; the book is gently tapped into shape with a hammer, causing the first section to slide slightly forward over the second, the second over the third, the third over the fourth and so on from each end of the book. When the glue sets, the sections are held in this position.

After rounding, the book is put into a lying press between wedge-shaped backing boards and the backs of the sections are carefully fanned out so as to form ridges on each side of the book equal to the thickness of the boards (fig. 41).

The boards are cut to size, allowing for suitable squares, and attached to the book by means of the slips. When the book is sewn on tapes, the boards are made up of a thick and thin card stuck together (split boards) (fig. 42), the ends of the

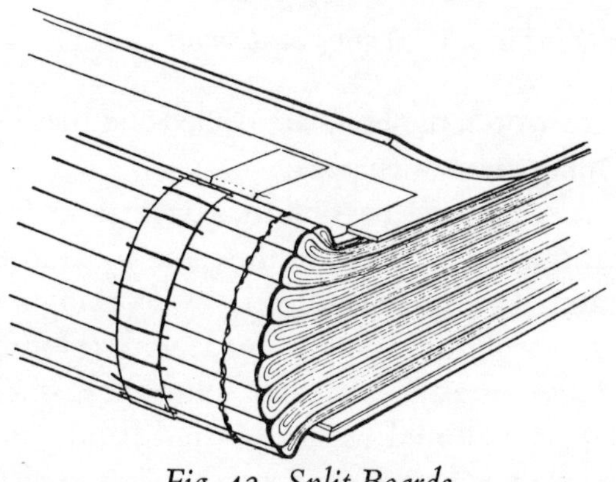

Fig. 42. Split Boards

tapes being inserted between the thick and thin cards and stuck in position. If the book has been sewn on cords these are laced into the boards; (fig. 43) sewing on single raised

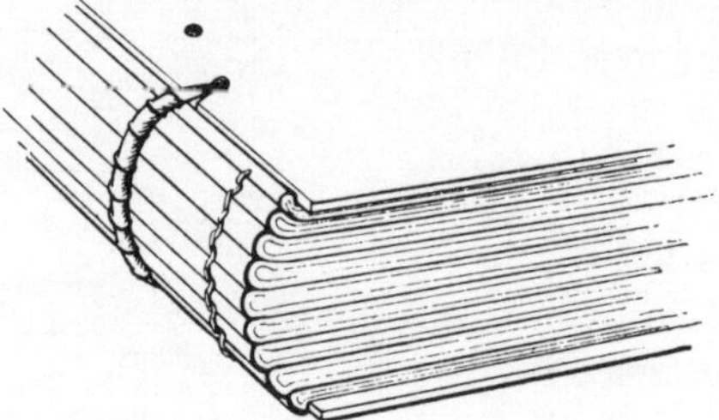

Fig. 43. Sewing on Single Cords

cords; (fig. 44) sewing on double cords; two holes are punched in the boards for each cord, the slips are threaded through the holes and the burrs round the holes hammered flat. If the

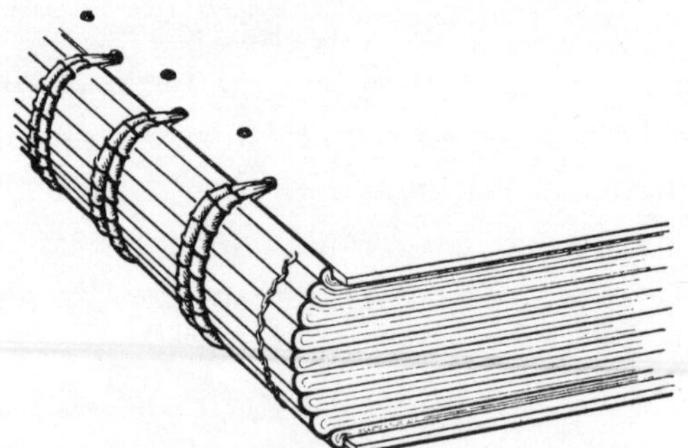

Fig. 44. Sewing on Double Cords

boards are of wood, the holes are drilled and the slips held in place by gluing in wooden pegs.

As the boards project beyond the edges of the leaves there is a space at the head and tail of the spine equal to the height of the squares. This space is filled in by working a headband over a strip of vellum; it may be made with coloured silks or thread and gives the appearance of buttonhole stitching. It is important that it should be flexible and firmly attached by frequent tie downs below the kettle stitches so as to form a firm foundation for the head and tail caps of the covered book. The headbands are a constructional feature that can be decorative.

The book may be covered wholly with leather, or with a leather spine and cloth or paper sides. The leather is cut to size and carefully pared along the joints for flexibility and neatness where it will be turned in at the head and tail and over the boards. The leather is pasted with flour paste brushed well into the leather; the moisture in the paste softens the leather which enables it to be moulded to the shape of the book. A well-covered book should look as if the cover has grown on it.

Leather joints are then pasted down, and the turn in of the leather is trimmed out on the inside of the boards, the space being filled in with thick paper or thin card. The cover is polished, lettered and tooled and the board papers are pasted down.

This, briefly, is the principle of binding. There are, of course, numerous variations.

To be specific:

1. The leaves of the book must bend if the book is to open.[1] The binder cannot make a book of playing cards open except by drastic methods.

2. The sections must be of a suitable size for if they are too large, with too many leaves to the section, the book will tend to open in chunks and it may have a very flat spine owing to insufficient swelling. If, on the other hand, the book is of too many folio sections it will tend to have too much swelling in the spine, and will be floppy and wedge-shaped. Therefore it is important to plan the size of the sections before beginning to write the book and it will always be a wise precaution for the scribe to send particulars to the binder before beginning on the writing; a sample of the vellum or paper that is going to be used, a sketch of the layout, number of leaves, etc. are

[1] See Edward Johnston's *Writing, Illuminating and Lettering*, p. 99.

important, so that the binder may advise on the size of the sections and comment if necessary on the inside margins and the position of raised gold. If the manuscript is to be on vellum the sections may be folio or quarto; if paper is being used they must be at least quarto sections as it is not safe to sew through a single thickness of paper.

If the scribe should have the misfortune to spoil a page that is part of a folio leaf the whole folio need not be scrapped provided that the faulty leaf be cut from the folio so as to leave a fold of vellum along the back margin, in order that the binder may have something to sew through. The same applies should it be necessary to insert a single leaf in the manuscript. The sheet must have a fold along the back margin and not be cut to the dead width of the page; otherwise it will have to be guarded in and the guard will show.

The back spine margins must not be too small and flourishes must be kept within limits, particularly on the inside margins as a book does not open flat like a double page on a drawing board but in a curve from the spine to the fore edge. The illustration of the Wilton Psalter (pl. 45) (Royal College of Physicians) shows that the tails of the initials on the recto page tend to be obscured in the spine in spite of the book opening well (pl. 44).

This is an instance of the repair and binding of an old illuminated manuscript. It was because of the flourishes going too far into the back margins that the book had to be thrown out on guards. These guards are sewn on through the centre of each section so that the sections still have their original makeup. It is the method that was used for the rebinding of the *Codex Sinaiticus* and is particularly suitable for some early manuscripts as it enables the book to be examined right to the back of the sections. It is not the same as the guarding of single leaves where the vellum is too thick for folding.

The Wilton Psalter was resewn on double cords laced into English oak boards; white alumed morocco was used for the spine with joints of the same leather; it was tooled in gold and blind with a simple pattern similar to the patterns in the manuscript, and fitted with silver clasps with leather cross-overs; the size of the book is 11¾ in. × 8½ in. (pl. 43 and pl. 45).

Unfortunately a good deal of the present manuscript vellum is very thick and stiff and in some cases this means that the book must be written on single leaves and each leaf swung on a linen guard. I dislike having to do this, particularly when I see the beautiful, supple, opaque vellum of the early manuscripts that come in for repair. However, I have had to guard a number of contemporary manuscripts in order that they may open. The method I found most satisfactory is to rub down the back of each vellum leaf to about half its thickness and sew on a guard of linen and handmade paper with a sewing machine in such a way that the handmade paper covers the stitches of the sewing (fig. 45). If this

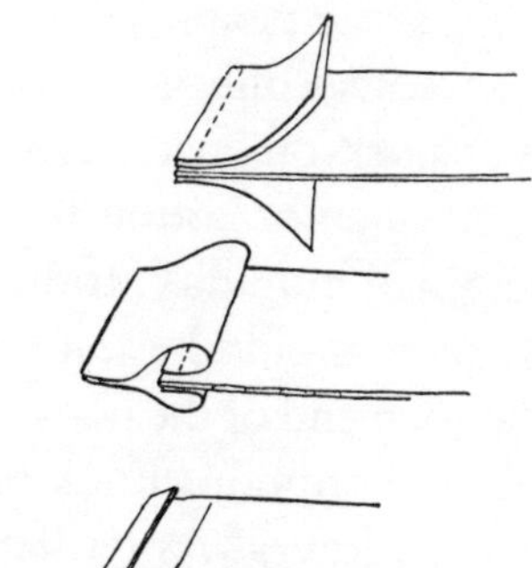

Fig. 45. Guarding a Vellum Leaf

operation can be done before the vellum is written on it saves some handling of the finished leaves.

The Metropolitan Police Roll of Honour in Westminster Abbey, written by Miss Hutton with gilding by Miss Law, was done in this way; it was bound in blue morocco with gold and blind tooling, rhodium-plated silver nails and tooled leather doublures; the size of the book is 16 in. × 12 in.; also the Somerset Roll of Honour, written by

Miss Base, had to be guarded. The book is in Wells Cathedral. The binding is in dark red Levant morocco with gold and blind tooling and silver gilt corners; the size of the book is 21 in. × 14 in. The Coastal Command Roll of Honour, written by Miss Hutton with gilding by Miss Base, is a book with the guards sewn on by hand; it was bound by Roger Powell in blue Levant morocco with gold tooling, built up letters and silver gilt nails and clasps. The size of the book is 16 in. × 11½ in. It is important that the guards be as narrow and inconspicuous as possible; I think they should be sewn on rather than relying on adhesives only because, from evidence in old manuscripts, guards and large patches stuck on to vellum tend to come unstuck in time, due I think to the two pieces of vellum expanding and contracting a different amount with changes in humidity, thus fracturing the adhesive. In fairness I must say that there are two schools of thought about this and some people are of the opinion that it is safe to rely on adhesives only for guards. I think there will be more chance of stuck-on guards staying in place when the guards are made of linen or cotton that will move with the vellum with changes of humidity. If the book must be of single leaves the title page should be folio, unguarded, with a folio of end leaves at each end of the book. Plate 41 is of the binding of the House of Commons Book of Remembrance. The manuscript of folded leaves was written by William M. Gardner with gilding by Norman Ball. The binding is white alumed morocco with gold and blind tooling; the size of the book is 15 in. × 11 in.

Parchment. A book of parchment leaves is not so satisfactory to bind as one of vellum leaves as the parchment is slippery and it may be difficult to get the book to keep a good shape. Nevertheless, parchment certainly has the advantage over some of the present manuscript vellum in that it is much more flexible and enables the book to be bound without having to resort to guarding.

Pl. 43. Binding of the Wilton Psalter. White alumed morocco: gold and blind tooling: English oakboards: silver clasps: size 12″ × 8½″. Reproduced by kind permission of the Royal College of Physicians

Pl. 44. The Wilton Psalter showing opening and guards

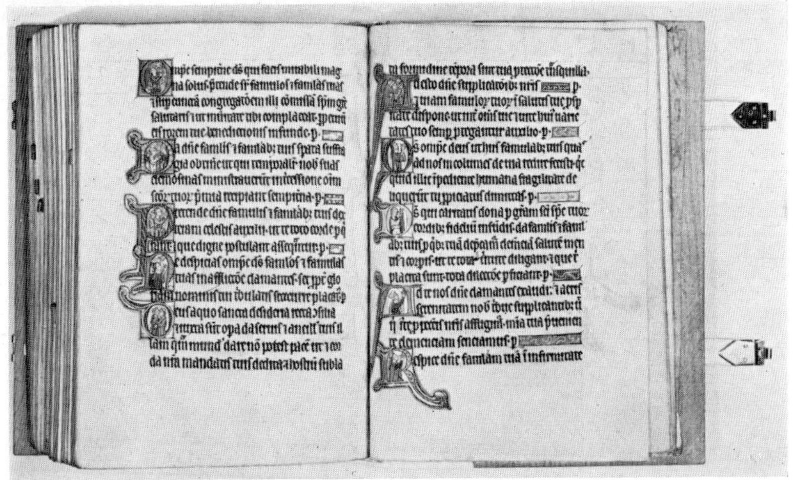

Pl. 45. The Wilton Psalter showing flourishes on recto pages

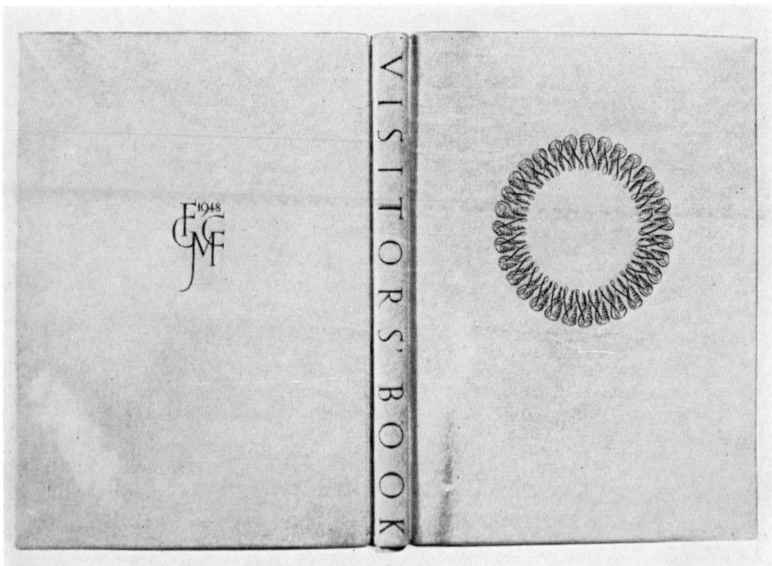

Pl. 46. Natural toned vellum binding with black ink lettering and decoration combined with gold tooling. Reproduced by kind permission of Roy M. Hyslop, M.V.O.

Raised gold. This causes a local thickening of the leaf; the book can assume ungainly proportions where, for example, an illuminated shield is in the same position on each page, because the aggregate of all the shields can make a serious lump in one part of the book. This unevenness will prevent the book from closing properly and will tend to make the pages cockle. It will mean that the pressure of the closed book will be on the gold; for instance, if the book has sixty-four leaves and there is an initial of raised gold one sixty-fourth of an inch high at the head of each recto page, the additional thickness caused by the raised gold through the whole book would be an inch—an impossible lump to deal with. It is, of course, an exaggerated instance, but it illustrates the point and can very easily happen in modified form. Therefore if there are to be a number of initials or shields of raised gold they should be staggered so as to even up the thickness as far as possible. Incidentally, this can make for interesting variations in layout. Gold on recto and verso pages should be arranged so as not to touch when the book is closed.

Title-pages. From a binding point of view it is better to have the title-page on the inside recto of a folio leaf with a blank leaf before the title (fig. 46), rather than have the

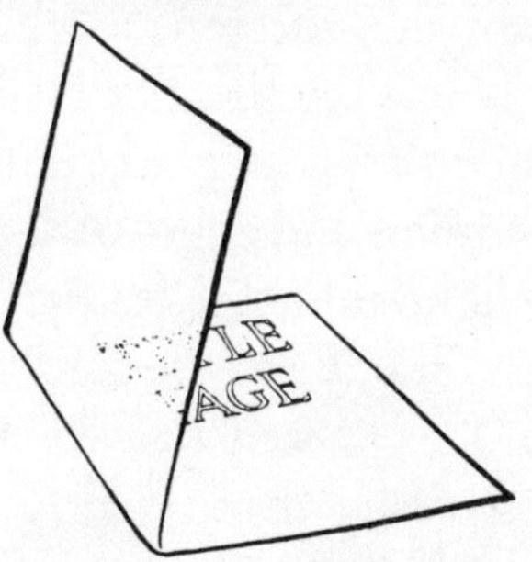

Fig. 46. A Title Page

title on the outside recto page of the folio. The reason for this is that end leaves will be necessary to connect the manuscript with the binding, as well as leather joints, which will be folded round the end leaves. This causes a ridge at the spine that looks unsightly when it has to come next to the title-page. The edge of the leaves of a manuscript must at least be square at the head and square with the spine margin, before the book can be bound so that the writing may be in register through the book.

Binders will cut vellum leaves square and to size before they are written on and this is a better plan than trimming them after they are written on as it saves some handling of the manuscript. If the binder is required to trim the finished manuscript it is a help if the marginal guide lines can be left as it provides something to work from. Otherwise a fine gold title-page without marginal lines can be a frightening thing to square up.

End papers. For manuscripts on vellum a blank folio of toned vellum, hair side out, slightly darker than the book at each end, helps to lead one from the dark exterior of the binding to the relatively light interior of the book.

Board papers. On the inside of the boards there will be the turn in of the cover which, with the leather joints, will form a leather frame and this must be filled in with paper, vellum or leather.

There is no doubt that the toned vellum doublure looks well with a toned fly leaf but there is the difficulty of making sure that the vellum will stay in place; in time it is very liable to come up at the corners and edges of the boards. The alternative is to use a light-coloured leather doublure and tool some simple pattern on it, or to use a good handmade paper, plain or patterned. I have seen both used satisfactorily and have myself used specially made lightly patterned marbled paper and tooled doublures. On several occasions recently I have used vellum board papers stuck down with a plastic adhesive and am waiting to see how long they will stay in position. I am doubtful of plastic adhesives as we do not know what their durability will be but as a board vellum can be easily replaced it is an opportunity to try the plastic adhesives where I have found the more usual glue and paste to fail.

If the manuscript is of paper, handmade paper ends will be in place, a toned paper being preferable to a dead white one. Alternatively the board paper and first fly-leaf may be of a suitably patterned paper.

Tooled leather fly-leaves have been used with tooled leather doublures, particularly by the French binders, but I do not care for the feel of the leather leaf. Roger Powell has used simply tooled vellum fly-leaves with similarly tooled vellum doublures, and this is much more satisfactory than the leather fly-leaves. Silk board linings and fly-leaves have been used but on the whole they are unsatisfactory.

3. The spine of the book must be flexible and bend if the book is to open (fig. 47). Therefore it is most important that

Fig. 47. A Flexible Spine

the minimum amount of material be stuck to the backs of the sections. The spine of the book should be convex when the book is shut and concave when the book is open.

4. Leather is used for binding because it is flexible and also because it is malleable when damp and can be nicely shaped.

If the book is sewn on raised cords these will show as bands on the spine (generally five or more in number). If it is sewn on tapes it will normally have a smooth spine though in some cases the tapes may show through the cover and can be emphasized by tooling. There is no excuse whatever for dummy raised bands on a book sewn on tapes or on a book with a hollow back.

Whether the book should be sewn on tapes or cords depends on a number of factors—the size of the book, the material it is made of, the make-up of the sections, the use the book is to be put to and how it is to be lettered and decorated. There is also the cost factor as it takes more time to sew and bind a book with raised cords than one with tapes; also more judgment is needed for the paring of the cover and the covering of the book.

When the book is sewn on tapes with split boards it is usual to have a french joint, a space which is left between the back edge of the boards and the joint of the book, thus forming a groove (fig. 48). This groove enables the covering

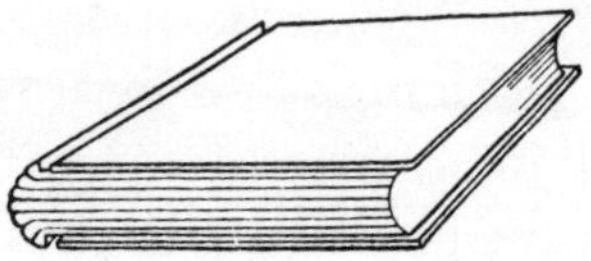

Fig. 48. A French Joint

material to be thicker at the joints than is the case with a cord book as the boards hinge on a relatively wide area. It is a sound constructional feature as it is at the joints of the boards that the binding is liable to give way.

When it comes to decorating and tooling the binding, the french joint has to be taken into account, and calls for rather different treatment from the book that is sewn on cords with the boards right up against the spine and the cover running smoothly off the spine on to the boards.

Leather. Morocco (goatskin) is mainly used for binding because the goat has a hard, close skin that is not excessively thick. One of the nicest of these leathers is the native tanned and dyed red niger morocco. It is very strong, easy to work, of a good colour and has a long durability record. Quantities of partly tanned niger goatskins are imported to this country and retanned and dyed in various colours for binding. The trade name for some of the best of these is Oasis. A goatskin with a heavier grain comes from South Africa and is known as Cape Levant morocco and is suitable for large books. Calfskin has been used a good deal and if properly prepared can be satisfactory for large books, bearing in mind that it is the soft thick skin of an immature beast and therefore not suitable for small books as it means excessive paring which destroys the strength of the skin. I am doubtful about tanned pigskin as a binding material, particularly when it is dyed. Sheepskin is not as a rule satisfactory for binding as it is too soft and apt to split in its thickness, the surface coming away.

Alumed skins. These are pickled in salt and alum instead of being tanned. They are very strong and apparently one of the most durable binding materials that the world has produced. They do not rot like some tanned leathers have done and are unaffected by our industrial atmospheres. The disadvantage with them is that they are dead white though they do go a good ivory colour in about fifty years or so. The usual alumed skins are pig and morocco.

Vellum. Is a very strong and durable binding material provided that the construction of the book is suitable. The book must be bound with a hollow back and french joints. The hollow back is made from a paper tube and allows the spine of the binding to remain convex while the spine of the open book is concave (fig. 49). This is necessary for a vellum bind-

Fig. 49. A Hollow Back

ing because the vellum used for covering is a relatively stiff, obstinate material that is not satisfactory when stuck direct to the spine of the book; the spine of the book is usually lined with linen or leather under the hollow. Vellum bindings are very satisfactory and durable as the hard surface resists damage and like the alumed leather is not destroyed by the sulphur dioxide of our city atmospheres, though it is sensitive to sudden changes in humidity which causes vellum-covered boards of a closed book to warp. This is due to the outside only of the boards being subjected to a change in humidity. This is sometimes noticeable in an exhibition when a closed book is shown. Under more normal conditions the boards will usually straighten out again when the insides of the boards have become conditioned to the atmosphere. Most materials swell with moisture and shrink with dryness. The shape of the book boards is a matter of balance between the covering material and the lining. Therefore if one side only is exposed to a change in humidity the boards will tend to warp until the other side is equally conditioned. I have stressed humidity rather than temperature for although changes of temperature are likely to cause changes in humidity a still, cold atmosphere will usually be dryer than a still, warm one. For this reason it is most important that strong rooms for the storing of books be well ventilated and not over-heated. Limp vellum covers offer little protection to the book and are very liable to cockle.

Cloth. If cloth is used for the sides it should be one of the waterproof, fadeless ones like Sundour book cloth. The colours are good, fast to light, and do not come off with moisture.

Paper. Handmade paper has the important characteristic of swelling evenly in every direction when damped, and correspondingly shrinking and pulling evenly when dry. This is of importance to the binder as it means that end papers and the paper of blank books can be cut from either way of the sheet.

Machine-made paper has a definite grain as, like weeds in a river, the fibres are drawn out on their way through the machine more or less according to the speed of the flow. This means that the paper swells with moisture and shrinks when dry very much more across the grain than with it and bends more easily with the grain than across it. Therefore with a book of machine-made paper leaves the grain of the paper should run from head to tail of the book if the book is to open. Machine-made paper can be strong and durable if well made of good materials. It is as a rule easier to write on than handmade paper.

Mould-made paper is made in single sheets on a slow running machine and has a definite grain though not so emphasized as the grain of paper from a fast running machine making paper in a continuous web.

To find out which way the grain is running hold a sheet of paper so that it bends and note which way it bends most easily; or cut out a 3 in. square of the paper and damp one side only. It will tend to curl into a cylinder, the grain running down its length. The same applies to machine-made card used for book boards, and it is important that the grain runs from head to tail of the book and that any thin lining card or paper used for the making of the book boards should run the same way. If a book board is made of card and lining papers with the grain running in different directions the boards will tend to warp and wind and it will be practically impossible to get them to stay flat.

Marbled paper. The patterns can be quite unlike marble or account books and can have a calligraphic quality of sharp, clean lines. For the sides and end papers of books it is important that it be on a strong paper.

Lettering and Tooling. As the finished book will be a co-operative production the scribe should let the binder know what he has in mind for the decoration of the binding, and the final pattern for the tooling should be arrived at by the binder in consultation with the scribe.

The tooling of a binding is done with hot brass finishing tools that are put down by hand, making impressions on the leather. These can be left blind of a darker colour than the surrounding leather or may be in gold. For this the impressions are painted with white of egg, the gold leaf is laid in position and the hot tool put down again, which fries the egg and holds the gold in place.

Lettering. This is usually done with brass handle letters, each letter being put down separately. The letters are hand cut or cast and the faces available are very limited as the demand for good binder's letters is not sufficient to warrant them being made in quantities. Individual sets can be made but are very expensive. Alternatively large letters can be built up by the use of lines and gouges.

When designing for the tooling of a binding there is much to be taken into account: the book itself, its size and how it is going to be used, whether it will be held in the hand or placed on a lectern, or start its life in a glass-sided case like a Roll of Honour. If these things have been considered from the beginning of the making of the book it is likely that the actual decoration of the binding will fall into place, for the design of a binding starts from the first stitch of the sewing and is influenced from the time that the first word of the manuscript is written.

Tooling on leather has a quality of its own and designing for it is not the same as designing for black on white because, besides the shapes and the spaces of the tooled areas, the quality and texture of the tooling have to be remembered. A binding is not just a flat surface for decoration but a three-dimensional object with a function, and number one rule is that the decoration must not interfere with the working parts. For instance, gold lines and tools will not be satisfactory if put down on the joint of the boards, because when the boards are opened the leather will crease on the joint and the gold tend to break and come away. Neither will heavy gold tools be satisfactory on the tight spine of a book where the leather is stuck direct to the backs of the sections, because here again the leather will crease when the book is opened and the gold will tend to crack. If there should be heavy gold tooling on the spine a hollow back must be used, as this does not bend when the book is opened.

There is an unfortunate method used to get over the

difficulty of gold tooling cracking on the spine of a binding, and this is to line the book up so heavily that the spine will not bend; the closed book keeps a good shape and it may look smart in the library shelves and have what is termed a 'full gilt spine', but it will be impossible to open a book of this kind, except by brute force.

The three usual textures of a binding are leather, blind tooling and gold tooling. The book may be entirely blind tooled or tooled entirely in gold or a combination of the two. If the book is a small one that will be held in the hand there is the feel of the tooling to be considered besides the look of it. I think the feel of a book is important. Some books come to hand very sweetly and are pleasant to hold. Colours can be applied to a binding by means of inlays. It is called inlay though it is usually leather that has been pared very thin and stuck in place on top of the leather of the binding. Alternatively oil or water colour may be painted on. This has been most successful for coats of arms. If possible the coloured surfaces should be below the general level of the leather so as not to be subjected to rubbing.

Coats of arms. These are sometimes required on bindings and have been used a great deal in the past. For these it is usual to have a block made and to strike the arms in a blocking press. The result is different from hand tooling as the gold impression will be all on one plane and of an even depth. If the arms are simple they can be hand tooled though it may mean getting special tools cut. Hand-tooled arms are likely to be brighter than blocked ones, and although they may take longer to do than the actual striking of the block, the total time and expense may not be more than blocking, as apart from the cost of the block the actual adjustment in the press to get the block just in the right place, straight and even, can take a long time. The portcullis in plate 41 is blocked.

For the making of a block a drawing of the arms must be

made in black on white, as simply and boldly as possible without fine lines or small spaces, as leather is soft material that does not take the impressions of fine lines readily, and small spaces tend to fill in. The best blocks are cut in brass by skilled engravers and they are the nicest to use. A cheaper method is to use a binder's zinco, a special kind of etched line block produced photographically. They have the advantage of being accurate to the drawing and the disadvantage of being shallowly cut and soft. A zinco is more difficult to use than a brass block but a reasonable method where the block is only to be used once.

Metal work. If the book is a heavy one it may be advisable to fit metal corners and possibly nails with raised heads or bosses for the book to ride on. Silver is used and may be fire gilt (fire gilding is more permanent than electro-plating), or if a silver colour is required the metal work may be rhodium plated, as silver of course will tarnish. The metal work may be engraved with a suitable pattern and may be pierced to show the leather of the binding or another coloured leather through the piercing. Bosses may be of metal or ivory with piqué. Whichever is used in the way of metal work it must be smooth, free from sharp corners and unobtrusive. It must be securely attached to the book by riveting through wooden boards and all nails must be clinched on the inside of the boards.

Clasps. Clasps are to keep the boards of the binding shut and the vellum leaves flat and in good order. I have made a number of books with clasps but on the whole, except in certain cases, I am inclined to think that they are more trouble than they are worth as they are seldom done up properly. It is usual to have two clasps at the fore-edge with two metal pieces securely attached to each board and two crossover pieces hinged to the back board. The crossover pieces may be of metal or a stiff vellum strip covered with leather (plate 44). It needs careful adjustment to make a clasp close with a firm snap and yet not be too hard to open. This depends on the spring of the book which is caused by undulations in the leaves; therefore it is very difficult to make satisfactory clasps for a thin book with few leaves. If a vellum book is left open the leaves are likely to form undulations that may not fit into each other when the book is closed and this may make it difficult to do up the clasps. What is needed is an adjustable clasp with a crossover with some give in it. Various attempts have been made but so far I have not seen a satisfactory one. Crossovers made of vellum strips covered with leather have more yield in them than metal ones, also the clasps are easier to adjust should this be necessary, and less vulnerable to damage when they are open.

Finishing vellum bindings. Tooling on vellum is not as durable as on leather because impressions on vellum tend to pull out in time. Blind tooling hardly shows as the warm tool does not change the colour of vellum as it does leather. Gold tooling can look very brilliant on white vellum and a white vellum binding can look very pure. Natural-toned vellum has more character and is more practical than white, though gold tooling does not show up so brightly on it. I like to have vellum bindings lettered by a scribe in black ink as this shows up very well on library shelves (plate 42). Interesting results can also be obtained with black ink decoration combined with gold tooling (plate 46). Joan Rix Tebbutt was the scribe for these bindings. Vellum bindings have been lettered with ink for some time, but I had not seen the drawn decoration combined with gold tooling. I arrived at this idea from a photograph of a white leather binding on a papyrus manuscript of about A.D. 700. This binding had been decorated with a pattern freely drawn with a pigment. The criticism that has been made about ink lettering and decoration on vellum bindings is that it may not wear well. However, the evidence to date seems to be that it will probably wear as long as tooling on vellum and is therefore a legitimate method.

Scrolls. I have had little to do with scrolls apart from repairing a few old ones, and little to add to Edward Johnston's notes on them in his book.[1] If large and made up of several joined skins I think the joins should be sewn together as it is not safe to rely on adhesives only. The stitches of the sewing may well be included in the decoration. Scrolls are best framed or kept in a scroll case, a round box made by pasting layers of paper round a former and covering with leather which may be left plain or elaborately tooled by a binder. They are difficult things to house as although they were suitable for the Alexandrian Library in 200 B.C. they do not fit in to our present day book cases. I suggest that normally an address will be more acceptable in a codex form as it will be easier to keep and look at than a scroll.

Rolls of honour. These books often start their life open in a glass case with a leaf turned over every day or so which is beneficial for the manuscript, but may not be so good for the binding if it is not closed from time to time. If the book is left open for a long time it may fail to close altogether, or even break if it be suddenly closed. Therefore, if the binding is to fulfil its purpose of protecting the manuscript, it should be closed for a night once a week, and sometimes picked up and handled. For some rolls of honour that I have had to deal with I have arranged for this to be done.

Slip cases. Can be made for bindings which protect them in transit and make a nice finish when a book is presented. They can be elaborate, covered with leather and lined with a soft material or they may be simply covered with cloth or paper. Their use certainly protects the binding from getting scratched and marked. With a normal slip case the spine of the book will show but if the spine is to be protected then an inner folder has to be made to fit the book and the book and

[1] Edward Johnston, *Writing, Illuminating and Lettering*.

folder fitted to the slip case; in this case the spine will not show and it is usual to letter the back of the folder. I feel the slip case, and boxes for bindings, tend to be over elaborated as after all the binding is made to protect the manuscript, and it should not be necessary to have to make an elaborate protection for the binding.

Show cases. The case may be of wood or metal with glass sides and a glass top. The base board that the book rests on should be slightly sloping and have a narrow ridge to keep the book straight. The glass top should also slope and be parallel with the base. The case should not be deeper than necessary and arrangements must be made for adequate ventilation. If the case should be mounted on a stone pillar there must be an air space between the bottom of the case and the stone to allow for condensation. If artificial light is necessary it must be very carefully arranged to avoid heat being reflected on to the book.

Repair and flattening of vellum. When vellum is made it is allowed to dry under considerable tension in a frame. Should it get damp at a later date it will tend to curl and cockle and go back to the shape of the animal. In order to flatten it out again it must be damped and allowed to dry under tension and even the cockled leaves of a twelfth-century manuscript can be flattened in this way. If new vellum has become creased and cockled it can be damped and pinned out on a board to dry. If it is a written page, or the page of an old manuscript, it must still be damped if it is to be flattened. It can be held in tension by means of bulldog clips which should be lined with paper or cloth to prevent staining. The clips can be put in place all round the leaf and pinned down on a board with thick needles in wooden handles or the clips may be held in tension by being attached to strings with a weight of about one pound on the end, and weights being allowed to hang down over the edge of the table or frame. A modification of this that avoids swinging weights is to use a frame with piano wrest pins in it and to tune the vellum up the required tension. Of course, great care must be taken with old manuscripts should they be fragile or have bad tears in them. Where the vellum cannot be damped direct it may be put between damp blankets, arranged so as not to touch the surface. However the vellum is damped it must be allowed to dry under tension.

Tears. If they are small ones they may be mended by sticking on small vellum patches with paste. The area round the tear must be scraped and roughened slightly with a knife or sandpaper, the patch cut to size, the edges pared and surface roughened. If the tear or cut is a serious one it should be sewn up with silk or fine linen thread as the old scribes used to do. If there is a large part missing the patch should be stuck and sewn into place.

Adhesives. With recent developments, some of the polyvinal acetate adhesives are apparently more efficient for the repairing of vellum than flour paste.

Bindings of old manuscripts. There is not very much fundamental change in the methods used for the binding of the early illuminated manuscripts and those in use to-day. The books were then sewn on leather thongs whereas now we use hemp cords as they are more flexible and appear to be more durable. The old books had wooden boards and were unbacked as we know it though a form of backing was achieved by lacing the boards on tightly, thus pulling the backs of the sections round when the boards were closed. Headbands were laced into the boards; it is not usually done now as it means cutting or making a hole in the leather of the cover at a very vital spot. Thin metal work was often nailed on in a rather haphazard manner and liable to come loose and be very scratchy. Some book boards were covered entirely with metal and mounted with semi-precious stones; elaborately carved ivory was also used and there have been some sumptuously embroidered bindings. Few, if any, embroidered bindings are being made at the moment, nor are books being covered with plates of metal which is more in the province of the silversmith than the binder, and more suitable for a box than a book.

From a binder's point of view, it is difficult to make a nice book out of a few magnificent leaves of a large area, one reason being that the thickness of the book boards has to be increased as the area is increased in order to be stiff enough to protect the manuscript; so that with a few leaves of a large area the manuscript will be thin but the boards clumsy and out of proportion. It will also be difficult to make the binding a good shape as there will not be sufficient swelling in the spine to accommodate the thickness of the boards. In some cases large leaves may be better framed than bound.

With a manuscript of a number of thin vellum leaves of small area it is possible to make a well-proportioned book that will open and close sweetly, a book that will be pleasant to handle, easy to read and look at, a book that can be loved.

Leather. I should mention that a great deal of research on the durability of binding leather has been done by Mr. Farraday Innes, F.R.I.C., for the Leather Manufacturers' Association.

As a result of this research, only leather that will stand the P.I.R.A. test should be used for binding.

Old bindings show us that leather can be a very durable material; but to be durable it must be properly prepared, free from sulphuric acid in manufacture and protected against absorption of sulphuric dioxide from our city atmospheres. If sulphur dioxide is absorbed it eventually turns to sulphuric acid and destroys the leather.

Leather can be protected against this by the addition of potassium lactate, or a similar salt, and such leather is stamped 'Protected to withstand the P.I.R.A. Test'. For further information on this subject, see the British Museum pamphlet *The Preservation of Leather Bindings*.

APPENDIX A

The Development of Illuminating

At first sight it would seem that the three great books of the Anglo-Irish school of illuminating of the eighth century, namely the *Book of Durrow*, the *Lindisfarne Gospels*, and the *Book of Kells*, were the earliest examples of decoration on vellum with formal handwriting.

But if a search is made a little deeper into the past it is found that as early as the third century a Roman emperor had a handwritten poem of Homer given him which was written in uncials on purple vellum; and that Greek painting on skin with early Christian symbolic ornament was known to the church as early as the fourth century. These examples, together with portraits of the Evangelists in psalters, prove that the ancient world had developed this art earlier than the Anglo-Irish.

The finest work of almost every age has been preserved by being carefully cared for, consequently the steps by which masterpieces were developed have become lost. It seems therefore that Anglo-Irish ornament, Roman gold writing and Greek portraiture became the three main sources from which medieval illuminating emerged.

St. Patrick, the English missionary in the fourth century, must have taken some written matter, perhaps decorated, into Ireland and have set his converts to work copying the Gospel story and decorating the initials. Thus there was about three hundred years for the Irish to produce their insular writing together with their type of decoration so well known.

This is seen not only on vellum but also on their gold and silver work used in the service of the church as well as for personal adornment. The units of this adornment were composed of simple patterns such as all early races possessed, namely zigzags, frets, whorls, dots, spirals, interlacing and other geometric arrangements. These elementary details when massed together produced the full-page illuminations and the large initial letters seen in all the remaining examples of Anglo-Irish work. The missions to Iona and Lindisfarne greatly increased the output of illuminated books, building up the schools into something formidable by the year A.D. 700 when the *Book of Kells* was written. The missionary zeal of the Irish did not let them stay at Lindisfarne. Instead, we find them somewhat later in France, Italy and Switzerland, building monasteries and thus producing in time schools of writing such as Luxeuil and Bobbio founded by St. Columba and St. Gall, a follower of St. Columba, to say nothing of Tours which under Alcuin of York became the famous home of the Caroline script.

England was linked with the Irish traditional ornament from the first when Aidan came to Northumbria, and thus the queer capitals which seem to be influenced by decorative Greek letters and headings set an example or basis for subsequent illuminating. These letters are part of a large movement in the eighth century to set up a capital pen letter for use in headings and initials. They are now known as versals, a word not used before the twentieth-century revival by Edward Johnston, who is said to have coined it. Versals came to perfection during the eleventh and twelfth centuries and can be seen in the Winchester Gospels.

During the twelfth century, manuscript ornament became a mixture of conventional leaf forms and Celtic interlacing. The leaf work seems to have grown from examples of early continental initials sometimes in the shape of fish; probably owing to the fact that the fish was an early Christian symbol.

This rough leaf work was also the type of ornament then being carved on Romanesque churches, and we have yet to discover whether the carvers had manuscript details to guide them, or the illuminators were able to copy their ornament from carvings. Both these manifestations of taste in ornament occurred at the same time, namely when Charlemagne was Emperor of the west. From that time on illuminated pattern arose from the use of the pen which develops as the era of Gothic approaches. The Romanesque scroll pattern, together with Celtic interlacing, was still used in the twelfth century by the Netherland scribes and illuminators: in this period were blue backgrounds inside the initial letters, together with a plain shape of gold with hollow sides. The points of these sides provided springing places for sprigs of delicate penwork in later days, when the Italian humanistic artists in the late fifteenth century produced what is now called white vine ornament. This style was patronized by the Dukes of Urbino until after 1500 when it seems to have died out, giving way to the extravagant styles used at the time of the late Italian Renaissance. The use of the brush now became paramount, relegating in Italy the penwork to a system of dots between forms that are completely alien to all earlier manuscript decoration, thus ultimately causing the decline and degradation of the illuminated page. It was now about a hundred years since writing and illuminating had been transferred from the monasteries to craft-guilds and thus when printing took over, most of the bookwork came into the hands of tradesmen. 'By 1350 France had absorbed all the antecedent varieties of illumination. From France', says John W. Bradley in his book on illuminated manuscripts, 'therefore spring all the succeeding styles now considered national.'

Illuminators, like other craftsmen, travelled from city to city. Princes employed men who resided at their patrons' palaces and who had learned their art in other countries. So style became mixed in the centre of fashion, and it was some time before each of the principal countries had produced a recognizable style of its own. France developed the vertical structure from which grew the lovely ivy-leaf pattern together with the miniature group on diapered ground in gold and colour and its developed versal and black script, such as one can see in the Harleian manuscript 2897 in the British Museum. England also adopted the vertical line which held the illuminating together against the writing from which, instead of ivy-leaf, came conventional leaf-like forms in two or more colours undulating in groups at the extreme of the vertical line, while sprigs of tiny detail spread out to fill a zone of space in the margins of the writing. The initial occupies a space of about one-fifth of the height of the writing and both letters and background are ornamented with gold and colour which is picked out with fine white lines.

The Netherlands work of the late fifteenth century is influenced by contemporary French work. The miniatures are beautifully executed and occupy sometimes one-third of the height of the page. The vertical line is retained but now only as a barrier between the writing and a slab of scroll ivy-leaf with patches of bright groups of floral ornament treated in a naturalistic way, a new conception, probably copied from Italian brushwork, that was later to strangle the conventional penwork of earlier days. These slabs of ornament look almost as if they had been drawn by the yard, cut off and placed on without thought of growth or attachment to an initial or to any part of the writing. Later Netherlandish work degenerated into pages of spiky writing with enormous leafy initials filled with figures surrounded by borders of naturalistic flowers, shells and insects, without growth or connection, on a washy ground.

Of the twelfth-century work of Germany examples are exceedingly numerous; towards the middle of the century the Romanesque style arose of which many examples are to be found in continental libraries. It is not easy to select the most typical example but one good and typical manuscript is found in a Gospel book at Carlsruhe, which contains some fine miniatures of this most thoroughly German style.

In Italy, the Lombardic section of the country seems to have produced the finest work before the Renaissance; after that the Italians lost taste in illuminating, but the splendid rotunda hand was still retained. By 1530 the decoration developed into a complete hard border, consisting of panels depicting scenes between Renaissance ornament, influenced by architectural carved work. These manuscripts are executed with great skill and knowledge of the materials and tools, but their effect on one who has lately looked through the masterpieces of earlier generations is that of disgust. Unfortunately this was the style which was to influence ornamental printers for generations to come.

During the seventeenth century in England, ornament on manuscripts took the form of involved pen strokes made with a quill using the thick and thin strokes crossing one another in a decorative way. Later when the influence of the metal engraver became strong it lost its semi-Gothic quality and became weak and scroll-like, poor in composition, full of mannerisms, but adapted to the new italic writing.

William Morris during the latter part of the nineteenth century worked and wrote to show how degraded the design of everyday things had become; and writing and printing with its stale ornament did not escape his eye. He influenced architects and art workers to study past work and experiment in new ways of expression. W. R. Lethaby, a disciple of Morris, encouraged Edward Johnston to produce finer formal writing, who in turn induced Cobden Sanderson and St. John Hornby to print books equal to those of the fifteenth century. It was also W. R. Lethaby and Edward Johnston who at the Central School of Arts and Crafts aroused such interest as to induce Graily Hewitt to leave the study of the law and devote the whole of his long life to revive the study and practice of illuminating, as well as the art of gilding as known during the middle ages. This he succeeded in doing after many years of patient study and experiment, passing it on to students who in their turn added their knowledge to the subject as can be seen in another part of this volume.

At first Edward Johnston experimented in the traditional types of illuminating, but as time went on his work in penmanship led him to forsake the brush entirely and to look to the broad pen to furnish the decoration he needed to complete his manuscripts. He relied largely upon red and black writing with contrasting sizes and finely written notes. His decorative headings and initials were swiftly written needing nothing around them to enhance their quality except some strong decorative strokes by way of interesting exaggeration. This became his ornament and to see it was thrilling: it was used sparingly and was direct and simple in conception, strong in line and always seemed to be in the right place.

Graily Hewitt on the other hand took two elements from tradition; one the vertical line against the writing, and the other the white vine ornament of the Italian humanistic illuminators and, modernizing it to present day needs, produced a satisfactory style to suit his writing. He used a blue background, beautifully gilded versals, together with flatly drawn leaves and flowers, which he grouped into shapes with filigree at selected places on the page as was done in the best French work of the fourteenth century. He made this choice of style and kept to it right to the end of his career; his standard of execution was high and his output considerable. His finest work is in the Chapter House, Westminster, where he and five assistants show a manuscript book known as the Royal Army Medical Corps Roll of Remembrance for the years 1914–18.

These two men, as different from one another as possible, set styles of decoration which have been followed more or less by others who have been attracted to the craft. Both used heraldry in a limited way; Graily Hewitt used shields in colour and gold; Edward Johnston experimented at times with a full achievement having a theory that heraldic drawing could be 'written' with a wide pen so that ornament and writing would be of the same character. But this has not been found very successful by later illuminators, except for simple symbols, and has for the most part been abandoned.

Heraldry has proved to be of the utmost value to the modern illuminator who has been trained to draw and design. It gives an opportunity for bright colour, burnished gold, and fine drawing; and given artistic ability plus good materials, together with finely written text on vellum, bound and tooled, it should produce works of art equal to anything made during the past half century. Illuminators of to-day have sometimes been urged to design in a more modern way. They have been told to be up-to-date, while at the same time continuing to use the scripts that have been thoroughly developed and purified.

But the illuminator has found himself in a difficult position. He must not make his work like an illustration; that is a separate art: he dare not draw anything of everyday use for that would look like commercial art, and he has to conform in scale and dignity with his script. Others have urged that manuscript ornament should be naturalistic as medieval books show, but these have developed into herbals, etc., and can no longer look in keeping with written text. Printing has become the vehicle that combines them all. Surely, therefore, writing should continue to use pen-drawn ornament which took so long to develop and, if well designed, is so characteristic.

At the time when great books were produced by hand, the church had wealth and power. There was no competitive press and so the service books of the church could be ordered and paid for with comparative ease, especially as the labour needed was cheap. With regard to to-day the situation is very different; there are now very few private patrons, the manuscripts that are commissioned are of necessity much plainer, therefore the emergence of a school of illuminating as in the past is improbable. If fine writing, plus gilding and a restricted amount of ornament, is kept at its present level, the second half of the twentieth century will have an opportunity to maintain the standard it has already attained, through the efforts of the late revival.

APPENDIX B

Illumination and Decoration

The aim of illumination and decoration is to tell the story and to enrich the page. Provided that certain conditions are observed there is no one technique which is right to the exclusion of others. The descriptive calligraphic outline drawings of the eleventh and twelfth century Winchester School of illuminators differ in treatment from the richly-coloured and gilded French manuscripts of the fourteenth and fifteenth centuries, yet both serve their purpose and remain marvels of beauty and workmanship. Behind each lie the same principles of approach; candid expression from which springs a sense of vitality and life, realization of a balanced design within the limits of a page, and, pervading all, an enjoyment in execution.

Within these principles which still persist to-day the scope is limitless both in treatment and subject matter. For some illuminators the pen is the chosen tool, for others the brush; some prefer the formal approach, others the naturalistic. But, however dexterous the work, if vitality is lacking, the result is a sad dull statement, and when it is present, however faulty the technique, the illumination may charm and delight.

Practice differs considerably; the approach is largely personal. Once the subject of the book has been decided it is of considerable assistance to look at a few fine manuscripts at the British Museum or elsewhere. If this is not possible a close perusal of reproductions may help. The purpose of this step is to set a standard, to observe how the masters of illumination worked. Gradually the mind begins to visualize a scheme and becomes saturated with ideas. A book is conceived as a whole, with text and spaces for decoration left at appropriate intervals. The plan and colour of the decoration should be largely uniform throughout the book. A dummy book may be useful; by this means difficulties are avoided, otherwise it may be found too late that a full-page illumination appears on the 'flesh' or smooth side of the vellum or that the text terminates on the bottom line, leaving no space for a decorated finial. This preliminary planning may take many days but it is time well spent. The mood of the subject matter or the occasion or person for whom the manuscript is intended probably dictates the theme.

The text of the manuscript should be written to its conclusion before any illuminations are added. Blank spaces are left, however, in the text as arranged in the dummy book, and in these faint pencil indications of the subject matter can be drawn as a reminder of what is planned to fill them. Meanwhile material for working drawings can be collected. This collecting of material is frequently a considerable undertaking and may involve visits to museums, the making of studies from life and objects of many kinds, requiring more drawings than may be finally used. Results will be worth the effort, for, unless intelligent studies are to hand there may be gaps in knowledge which will become distressingly apparent when making the final drawing. The idea that artists draw 'out of their heads' is largely a fallacy; the idea may come from their heads but studies are necessary to make the idea convincing when set down on paper or vellum. No details should be neglected, for instance, careful drawings of beaks and claws of birds, drapery, attachment of leaves, windows and cornices of buildings; these give the character. The decorative qualities of objects should be observed as, for instance, how one leaf answers another on a stem in rhythmic balance. Such details give freedom of expression in the final work.

Having obtained sufficient studies for the subject the drawing can be composed referring to these studies as required. The act of drawing has to be 'lived'; this is an alert, not a gentle action. The essential 'movement' of the object is important with accent on structural details. The relative proportions of beasts and men and flowers and houses are immaterial, nor need the colours be rendered literally. In view of the fact that an illumination is within the convention of a book containing calligraphic symbols and not that of a framed picture, a formal treatment appears to agree better with the text than a naturalistic one. Even in this there can be no fixed rule, though whichever manner of expression is adopted the statement should be clear and precise.

The amazing marginal decorations in the Luttrell Psalter[1] illustrate the points mentioned: the precision of 'movement', the structural details such as the attachment of the reins to the horses' collars and the nails on their shoes, the lack of proportion between the driver's head and his feet, and the unexpected blue tint of one of the horses. Yet the subject of a 'Harvest cart going uphill' has been convincingly and graphically described in a lively candid statement (plate 48).

Unless the artist is very skilled it is as well to make a tracing of the finished drawing and to transfer this on to the blank space left for it in the manuscript. Lead carbon paper should be used (never typewriting carbon paper which is indelible). The outline is traced with a fine point, the tracing on the vellum is then freely redrawn with a hard pencil using a light touch.

By now the subject matter of the drawing should be clearly understood which is as well for the test is now to come. A duck quill pen is taken, one of its prongs is cut shorter than the other and this makes an excellent drawing pen. If a brush

[1] Brit. Mus. Add. MS. 42130 written about 1340, English.

Pl. 47. A free calligraphic pen line. XIth Century, English School
fr. Aurelius Prudentius, Psychomachia. Brit. Mus. Cotton MS. Cleopatra cviii f 15

Pl. 48. A simple statement, emphasis on the decorative element of detail (e.g. collars, reins, etc.) Colour added as design, XIIth Century, English School
The Luttrell Psalter. Brit. Mus. Add. MS. 42130 *f* 173 *b*

Pl. 49
Full colour work, arranged within a formalized architectural setting, remote from naturalism. XVth Century, French School

Book of Hours of John Duke of Bedford

Brit. Mus. Add. MS. 18850 *f* 257 *b*

Elthaureo albergho
collaurora inanzi
Siracto usciual sol
cinto diraggi. Che
dicto arestu ilsi col
cho piu dianzi.
Alzato unpoco come fanno isaggi
Guardossi intorno a se stesso disse
Che pensi omai conuien che piu cura aggi
Ecco sion che famoso interra uissi
De la sua fama per morir non esce
Che sara della legge che el ciel fisse

Pl. 50
An interesting example of unfinished decoration, showing preliminary lay-in of the main lines of the design in pen and pencil. XVth Century, Italian School

Petrarch, Trionfi

Bodleian Library. MS. Can. Ital. 83 *f* 44 *v*

is preferred with which to draw, a sable size 'o' or 'oo' is useful. Chinese ink is rubbed down with distilled water as this produces a paler shade of black than tap water. The pen outline should in no way compete in strength or colour with the script or the illumination will overpower the text instead of making an harmonious balance. A fine pale ink line is freely drawn, structural details being accentuated or even enlarged, never slurred. When the ink drawing is completed the pencil marks are removed with a soft india-rubber and the waste rubber wiped off with a silk cloth. Pumice powder is sometimes used instead of rubber to remove pencil marks but this is liable to pull up the vellum surface thus attracting dust and dirt in future handling. Should gold be included in the design this is the time to gild. It may be noted here that the introduction of raised burnished gold if used sparingly has the power to formalize a design and remove from it any naturalistic tendency.

The illumination is now ready to be coloured. A hurried impulse to paint has ruined many a promising beginning and it is now that restraint is necessary. Colour can be swiftly laid on but not so swiftly removed and with alteration the spontaneous brilliancy is impaired. The colour plan of the entire manuscript should be remembered for, when the first decoration is completed, the scheme is irrevocably set for the whole book. With this in mind it is sometimes a useful plan to begin with a small decoration within the text rather than a full scale first-page illumination before confidence of execution has been gained.

The manner of treating the colouring is a personal matter which may have been gained by trial and error. One illuminator may prefer merely an ink outline with the addition of a few touches of local colour introduced as a pattern, whilst another may favour a fully toned and lively colour scheme obliterating the ink outline. The choice of the medium for the colour may control the technique. Liquid paint used as a wash may cockle the skin, therefore paint is better applied in a dryish consistency, possibly stippling with a fine brush. One method of application is to lay a foundation tone on the design; then the lighter and darker tones are modelled when this foundation is dry. Another method is to lay a coat of white; the colours are then applied on top of this coat, thus giving solidity and brilliance. This technique is, however, not possible if a gum medium is used, as the white underpainting will 'move' and make a muddy mixture with the superimposed colour. Yet another method is to model the drawing with *terre verte* or other neutral shade; on top of this modelling when dry, a semi-opaque coat of colour is lightly washed. This method was frequently used in figure subjects by the medieval illuminators.

It is through constant and courageous attempts that some satisfactory results may be achieved. There is a vast field of enjoyment open to all. However simple the theme, if the decoration is descriptive, lively, fearless and sincere, it will be of interest and will enrich the text.

APPENDIX C

A Note on Simple Binding

Calligraphy and book binding require two separate courses of training. However, certain handwritten books do not need the bookbinder's skill but can be bound simply and competently by the scribe himself. The piece of occasional writing, a poem or congratulatory letter for instance, can even better retain that lightness of touch in a simple flexible cover. If desired a slipcase or box can be made afterwards by a professional bookbinder.

The style of binding now to be described does not require glueing at the back nor anything in the way of tools except a knife, a paste pot and a needle and thread. If the book consists only of one section the sewing is quite simple. It is advisable to add a few leaves of blank paper wrapped round the outside of the manuscript to act as endpapers. Next the cover paper, which should be much stronger than that used for endpapers and text, is cut sufficiently large to overlap the book by about one eighth of an inch at head, fore-edge and tail. This extending part of the cover is known as the square.

The book now consists of text, endpapers and cover all inserted one within the other to form one section, and is ready for sewing. Use a darning needle and thread that is neither so thin as to be liable to cut the paper, nor so thick as to be clumsy, and of a colour that is either complementary to the colours used in the manuscript or inconspicuously neutral. Open the book and mark three points in the centre double spread: the first to range with the top of the first line, the second to range with the foot of the last line, and the third in the centre between the two. Start the sewing through the centre mark, taking care to keep the book evenly in the middle of the overlapping cover, and proceed so that when the job is done the thread forms a figure 8 with the final knot tied in the centre.

Fig. 50. Sewing a Single Section Book

The cover of strong paper may be left as it is, or in its turn can be wrapped in a coloured paper in much the same way as one sometimes wraps a school book to protect its cover. The allowance for the turned over edge of the wrapping need not be wider than three eighths of an inch. The coloured paper is

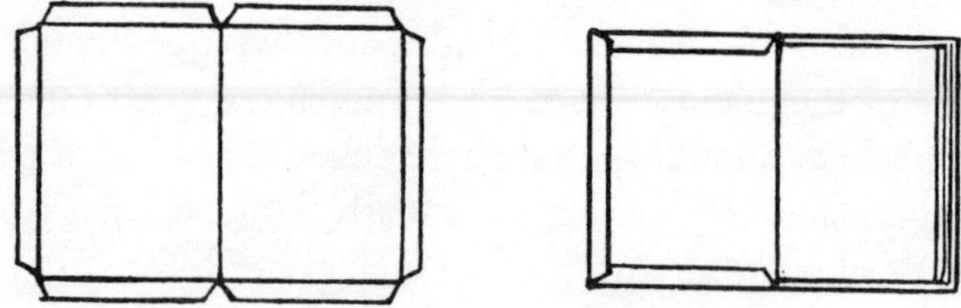

Fig. 51. Wrapping a Single Section Book

drawn over the cover of thick paper and only the three-eighths of an inch strip of turned in edge is pasted on to it. When this is dry the outer edge only of the first and last leaf is then stuck down lightly. This is to prevent cockling and is quite sufficient and strong if good paste is used. The book should then be placed under a weight so that everything lies quite flat. As pointed out before, it is important to avoid pasting down large surfaces. Without the bookbinder's skill and press there is always the risk of bad warping. For a thicker book it gives the wrapper more play if only its turned in fore-edge is pasted on to the cover.

A manuscript of several sections should be sewn on strips of vellum: three, four or five, according to the size of the book. These strips should be about five inches long and three-eighths of an inch wide. Again the upper and lower strips should range with or be related to the first and last lines of the page. When they are knocked level at back and head and the position of the strips marked with pencil on the spine of the manuscript, the sections of the book are sewn on to the

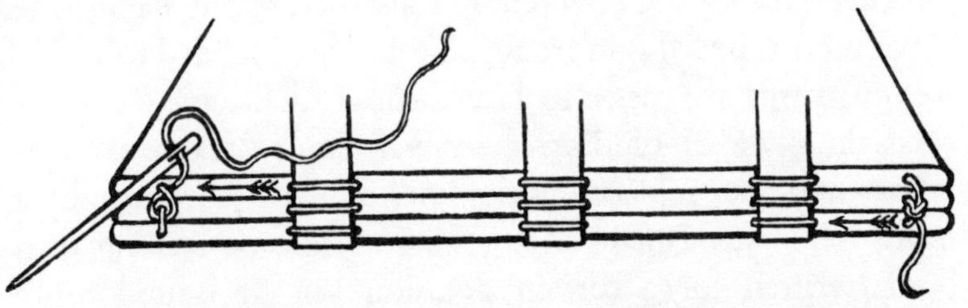

Fig. 52. Sewing several Sections, showing Kettle Stitch

vellum tapes. If no sewing frame is available the stiff vellum strips can be bent at right angles and rest or be fixed on a board with drawing-pins. Allowance has to be made when marking for the kettle stitch at head and foot of the spine. The kettle stitch bridges the gap between sections and thus ties them together, as shown in the diagrams. When the sewing is complete the strips of vellum are laced evenly through slits in the cover which is made of a stout handmade paper, that in its turn may be covered with coloured paper or even with silk fabric.

Paper covers can be decorated with designs in colour and gold. Shellgold can be applied with a brush and is therefore easier to work than leafgold. Marbled or paste paper may be found useful and attractive. On the other hand papers can be stained and even brushed with a wide brush in a streaky manner to procure a pleasant texture. A label with the title or any other suitable lettering can then be added. The paper of the label should preferably be thinner than the cover paper and again, if the edges only are pasted down, cockling should not occur. A mixture of paste and thin hot glue dries more quickly and helps towards the same end.

The kind of binding described, if well executed, can be considered as final, and it gives calligraphers the chance at least to produce a book from beginning to end. Calligraphers should experiment on these lines to test the possibilities of structure and design, keeping in mind that the best materials should be used even if they are covered. For instance, strong handmade paper used as board is more flexible and less inclined to crack. Vellum strips are easier to lace through than tape. In some cases the style of binding described can be taken as temporary and later replaced in the bookbinder's workshop by a more solid one. But in many cases a piece of writing or a book written for a certain occasion can be bound more quickly by the scribe himself, and, if carefully worked out, the result will show a pleasant and lasting unity.

Bibliography

Notes on the list of books

The following list of books comprises those consulted by the writers of the essays. A few general handbooks and historical manuals have also been included for the student. The books have been divided into several sections for easy reference. The date of the latest edition is given except in the case of books on heraldry where the dates are those of first publication.

FORMAL WRITING, ILLUMINATION AND LETTERING

Writing and Illuminating and Lettering, Edward Johnston. Pitman, 1954.
Manuscript and Inscription Letters, Edward Johnston. Pitman, 1928.
Lettering for Students and Craftsmen, Graily Hewitt. Seeley Service, 1930.
Lettering, Herman Degering. Ernest Benn, 1929.
The Elements of Lettering, J. H. Benson and A. G. Carey. McGraw-Hill Book Company, 1950.
The Alphabet Source Book, O. Ogg. Dover, 1947.
Twenty-six Letters, O. Ogg. Harrap, 1949.
Calligraphy's Flowering, Decay & Restauration, Paul Standard. Sylvan Press, 1949.
Calligraphy Picture Encyclopaedia, Alkmaar. Holland, 1951.
Lettering of Today, edited by C. G. Holme. Studio Publications, 1937, revised edition 1941.
Modern Lettering & Calligraphy, edited by R. Holme and K. M. Frost. Studio Publications, 1954.
'Revival of Writing and Lettering,' *Journal of the R.S.A.,* M. C. Oliver, 22 September, 1950.

TOOLS AND MATERIALS

Ancient Egyptian Materials and Industries, A. Lucas. Edward Arnold, 1948.
A Guide to Greek and Roman Life. British Museum Publication, 1908.
Painting Materials, R. J. Gettens and G. L. Stout. D. Van Nostrand, New York, 1943.
Die Handzeichnung ihre Tecknik und Entwicklung, Joseph Meder. A. Schroll, Vienna, 1923.
Les Outils de l'Ecrivain, S. Blondel. Paris, 1890.
The Pencil since 1565, C. C. Fleming New York, 1936.
Pencils. The Royal Sovereign Pencil Co. (Pamphlet.)
Papermaking, the history and technique of an ancient craft, Dard Hunter. Pleiades Books, 1947.
Modern Papermaking, R. H. Clapperton and W. Henderson. Blackwell, 1952.

'Parchment and Vellum,' Sir Edward Maunde Thompson. Article in the *Encyclopaedia Britannica*, 1945 Ed.

'Paper,' C. J. J. Fox. Article in the *Encyclopaedia Britannica*, 1945 Ed.

PIGMENTS AND MEDIA

Books obtainable from most Libraries:

Materials of the Artist & their Use in Painting, Max Doerner. George G. Harrap, 1949.

The Artist's Handbook of Materials & Techniques, Ralph Mayer. Faber and Faber, 1951.

The Chemistry of Paints and Painting, Sir Arthur Church. Seeley Service, 1890.

The Student's Cennini, Viola and Rosamund Borradaile. Dolphin Press, 1942.

Books obtainable from special Libraries:

The Book of the Art of Cennino Cennini, Lady Christina J. Herringham. George Allen and Unwin, 1899.

'Il Libro dell'Arte de Cennino d'Andrea Cennini,' *The Craftsman's Handbook*, Daniel V. Thompson, Jr. New Haven, U.S.A., 1933.

De Arte Illuminandi, anonymous fourteenth century treatise; trans. Daniel V. Thompson, Jr. Yale University Press, 1933.

The Materials of Mediaeval Painting, D. V. Thompson, Jr. George Allen and Unwin, 1936.

Books referred to but generally unobtainable:

Papers of the Society of Mural Decorators and Painters in Tempera. 3 vols. 1901–1907, 1907–1924, 1925–1935.

Schedula diversarum Artium by Theophilus, Robert Hendrie. John Murray, 1847.

De Clarea of the so-called anonymous Bernensis MS. Berne A 91.17. trans. D. V. Thompson, Jr. Harvard University, July 1932.

The Art of Limming, reproduced in facsimile from the original printed in London 1573. Ann Arbor. Edwards Brothers, 1932.

A Treatise concerning the Arte of Limning, writ by Nicholas Hilliard. London, 1642.

Introductory note on Nicholas Hilliard's Treatise concerning the Art of Limning, Philip Norman. Walpole Society, 1912.

Liber de Coloribus Illuminatorum sine Pictorum. Sloane MS. No. 1754. Treatise of Peter St. Audemar 1300. Trans. D. V. Thompson, Jr. *Speculum* Vol. 1, 1926. Cambridge, Mass.

Original Treatises on the Arts of Painting, Mary P. Merryfield. John Murray. 1849. Bolognese MS. *Segreti per Colori*.

A Few Notes on the Composition and Permanence of Artists' Colours. Winsor and Newton, 1948.

INK

Inks, Composition and Manufacture, C. Ainsworth Mitchell. Griffin, 1937.

Ink, C. Ainsworth Mitchell. Griffin, 1922.

Royal Society of Arts Journal, Cantor Lecture, January, 1922. C. Ainsworth Mitchell.

Libro nuovo d'imparare a scrivere tutte sorte sorte lettere, etc., G. B. Palatino. Rome, 1540.

Bibliography

Printing Ink, Frank B. Wiborg. Harper, 1926.
'The Analyst, 1930.' *Medico-Legal and Criminal Record,* A. P. Laurie.
'Pharmaceutical Formulas,' *Chemist Recipe Book,* Vol. 2, 1898. Reprint 1946.
Pigments and Mediums of the Old Masters, A. P. Laurie. Macmillan, 1914.
Outlines of Paint Technology, Noel Heaton. Griffin, 1928.
Workshop Receipts, W. E. Spon, 1930.
The Pen's Transcendency, Edward Cocker, 1660.
Theophilus. Translated by Hendrie in 1847.
Elements of Drawing, John Ruskin. Dutton, 1907.
The Library Handbook of Genuine Trade Secrets and Instructions. Foyles, 1923.
The School of Arts or Fountain of Knowledge, London, 1820.
The Art of Illuminating, M. D. Wyatt and W. R. Tymms. Day, 1860.
Guide to Illuminating on Vellum and Paper, G. A. Audsley. Rowney, 1911.
Brief Description of Tinctures and Materials of Heraldic Blazoning. Winsor and Newton.
Article on Inks, *Encyclopaedia Britannica,* 14th Edition, 1929.
Article on Inks, *Chambers Encyclopaedia.*
Article on Inks, *Everyman's Encyclopaedia.*

CURSIVE HANDWRITING

The New Handwriting, M. M. Bridges. Oxford University Press, 1898.
Handwriting: Everyman's Craft, Graily Hewitt. Kegan Paul, Trench, Trubner, 1938.
A Handwriting Manual, Alfred Fairbank. Faber and Faber, 1954.
Dryad Writing Cards, Alfred Fairbank. Dryad Press, Leicester, 1935.
Society for Pure English Tracts, *English Handwriting,* Nos. XXIII (1926) and XXVIII (1927), edited by Robert Bridges. Oxford University Press.
Written by Hand, Aubrey West. Allen and Unwin, 1951.
Sweet Roman Hand, Wilfrid Blunt. John Barrie, 1952.
Articles by James Wardrop on Renaissance calligraphers in *Signature,* Nos. 12 (First Series) and 2, 5, 8 and 14 (New Series).
Three Classics of Italian Calligraphy. Dover Publications, Inc., New York. 1953. (Facsimiles of writing books of Arrighi, Tagliente and Palatino.)
Italic Handwriting, Some examples of Everyday Cursive Hands. Newman Neame Ltd., 1954.
The First Writing Book. An English Translation and Facsimile of Arrighi's *Operina,* John Howard Benson, Oxford University Press. 1955.
Italic Handwriting, Tom Gourdie. The Studio Publications, 1955.
Bulletin of the Society for Italic Handwriting, edited by Dr. W. N. Littlejohns. First issue 1954.
An Anthology of Italic Handwriting, Alfred Fairbank and Berthold Wolpe. Faber and Faber (in preparation).

HERALDRY

For the further study of heraldry in general:

The Stall Plates of the Knights of the Order of the Garter, W. H. St. John Hope. Constable, 1901.
**Heraldry for Craftsmen and Designers,* W. H. St. John Hope. Pitman, 1913 (E).

Bibliography

*_A Grammar of English Heraldry,_ W. H. St. John Hope. Cambridge University Press, 1913 (E).

*_A Manual of Heraldry,_ Charles Boutell. Warne, 1863 (E).

*_A Complete Guide to Heraldry,_ A. C. Fox-Davies. Nelson.

Decorative Heraldry, G. W. Eve. Bell, 1897.

Heraldry as Art, G. W. Eve. Batsford, 1907.

Heraldry of the Church, Rev. E. E. Dorling. Mowbray. 1911.

*_Simple Heraldry,_ I. Moncrieffe and D. Pottinger. Nelson, 1953.

The following books contain illustrations of heraldic illumination:

Illustrated Catalogue of the Heraldic Exhibition, Burlington House. Society of Antiquaries, 1896.

*_Scots Heraldry,_ Innes of Learny. Oliver and Boyd, 1934.

*_Heraldry in England,_ Anthony Wagner. King Penguin, 1946.

[Dates, where given, are those of first publication, but later editions may be consulted where marked (E).]

Note: Those books marked with an asterisk are chosen for the general reader rather than the specialist.

THE BINDING OF MANUSCRIPTS

Bookbinding and the Care of Books, Douglas Cockerell. Pitman, 1948.

Some Notes on Bookbinding, Douglas Cockerell. Oxford University Press, 1929.

The Preservation of Leather Bookbindings, H. J. Plenderleith. British Museum pamphlet. H.M.S.O., 1946.

Bookbindings. Victoria and Albert Museum pamphlet. H.M.S.O.

Decorated Book Papers, Rosam and B. Loring. Oxford University Press, 1952.

A History of English Craft Bookbinding Technique, Bernard Middleton. Hafner Publishing Co., New York and London.

The Repairing of Books, S. M. Cockerell. Sheppard Press, London.

HISTORY OF LETTERING AND ILLUMINATION

The Story of the Alphabet, E. Clodd. Georges Newnes, 1900.

The A.B.C. of Our Alphabet, Tommy Thompson. Studio Publications, 1942.

The Alphabet throughout the Ages and in all Lands, David Diringer. Staples Alphabet Exhibition, 1953.

Introduction to Greek and Latin Paleography, E. Maunde Thompson. Oxford Clarendon Press, 1912.

Ancient Writing and Its Influence, B. L. Ullman. Harrap, 1932.

An Illustrated History of Writing and Lettering, Jan Tschichold. Zwemmer, 1947.

A History of the Art of Classical and Mediaeval Writing, William A. Mason. U.S.A., 1920.

Guide to the Exhibited MSS. in the British Museum.

The Legacy of the Middle Ages, C. Crump and E. F. Jacob. (Chapter on Handwriting by Professor E. A. Lowe.) Oxford University Press, 1926.

Codices Latini Antiquiores, Vols. 1–6. Professor E. A. Lowe. Oxford University Press.

Ancient Books and Modern Discoveries, Sir Frederic G. Kenyon. The Caxton Club, Chicago, 1927.

Bibliography

English Court Hands, 1066–1500, Sir Hilary Jenkinson. Cambridge University Press, 1915.

The Later Court Hands in England from 15th–17th Centuries, Sir Hilary Jenkinson. Cambridge University Press.

Penmanship of the 16th, 17th and 18th Centuries, Lewis F. Day. Batsford, 1911.

The Writing Masters and their Copybooks, Sir Ambrose Heal. Cambridge University Press, 1931.

A Book of Scripts, Alfred Fairbank. Penguin Books, 1955.

Schatzkammer der Schreibkunst, Jan Tschichold. Verlag Birkhauser, Basel.

Meisterbuch der Schrift, Jan Tschichold. Otto Maier Verlag, Ravenbsurg, 1952.

'Calligraphy,' James Wardrop. *Chambers Encyclopaedia,* 1950.

'Calligraphy,' Stanley Morison. *Encyclopaedia Britannica,* 1945.

La Lettre Ornée dans les Manuscripts du VIII–XII Siècle, E. Van Moé. Paris, 1949.

English Illuminated MSS from the 10th to the 13th Century, Dr. Eric Millar. Paris and Brussels, 1926.

English Illuminated MSS of the 14th and 15th Centuries, Dr. Eric Millar, 1928.

Illuminated Manuscripts, J. H. Middleton. Cambridge University Press, 1892.

English Illuminated Manuscripts, E. Maunde Thompson. 1898.

Illuminated Manuscripts, J. W. Bradley. Methuen, 1905.

Illuminated Manuscripts, J. A. Herbert. Methuen, 1911.

English Illumination, O. E. Saunders. Pegasus Press, 1928.

The Sequence of Mediaeval Art, Walter Oakeshott. Faber and Faber, 1950.

'Painting in Britain: The Middle Ages,' Margaret Rickert. *The Pelican History of Art.* Penguin Books, 1955.

'Les Principaux Manuscripts à Peintures du Lambeth Palace à Londres.' [In the *Bulletin de la Société française de Reproductions de MSS à Peintures.*]

Durham Cathedral Manuscripts, R. A. Mynors, 1939.

The Winchester Bible, Walter Oakeshott. Faber and Faber.

The Book of Kells, described by Sir Edward Sullivan. Studio Publications, 1942.

APPENDIX TO BIBLIOGRAPHY

FORMAL WRITING, ILLUMINATING AND LETTERING

A Book of Sample Scripts, Edward Johnston. Victoria and Albert Museum. 1966.

Calligraphy Today, Heather Child. Studio Books, 1963.

Lettering Today, Editor John Brinkley. Studio Vista, 1964.

Pen Lettering, Ann Camp. Dryad Press, 1958.

ABC of Lettering and Printing Types; A—Lettering, B—Printing Types, C—An historical Survey. Eric Lindegren 1960.

HERALDRY

Heraldic Design, Heather Child. G. Bell and Sons, 1965.

The Armorial Bearings of the Guilds of London, John Bromley and Heather Child. Frederick Warne and Co., 1960.

Heraldry in the Victoria and Albert Museum, H.M. Stationery Office, 1960.

CURSIVE HANDWRITING

The Bulletins and *Journals* of the Society for Italic Handwriting. First Issue 1954.

Juan de Yciar. Fascimile of the 1550 edition of Arte Subtilissima. Introduction by Reynolds Stone, Translation by Evelyn Schuckburgh. Oxford University Press, 1960.

Bibliography

A Newe Booke of Copies. 1574. Introduction by Berthold L. Wolpe. Oxford University Press, 1962.

Beacon Writing Books. A series of nine. Alfred Fairbank, Charlotte Stone and Winifred Hooper. Ginn and Co. Ltd., 1959–61.

The Irene Wellington Copy Book. Parts 1 to 111. James Barrie, 1957.

Guide to Italic Handwriting, Fred Eager. Italimuse Inc. Caledonia, New York, 1957.

Italic Lettering and Handwriting, Lloyd J. Reynolds. Reed College, Portland, Oregon, 1963.

HISTORY OF LETTERING AND ILLUMINATING

Writing, David Diringer. Thames and Hudson, 1962.

A Study of Writing, I. J. Gelb. Univ. of Chicago Press, 1952.

Album of Dated Latin Inscriptions, Arthur Gordon. *Parts 1–111.* 1958–1965. Univ. of California Press, 1958–1965.

Codices Latini Antiquores. Vols. I to XI, E. A. Lowe. Oxford University Press. 1934–1966.

Lettering, Hermann Degering. Ernest Benn, 1929–1965.

English Uncial, E. A. Lowe. Oxford University, Press, 1960.

Two Thousand Years of Calligraphy, Dorothy E. Miner, Victor J. Carlson, and P. W. Filby. Waters Art Gallery, Baltimore, 1965.

Palaeography, Julian Brown. Encyclopedia Britannica.

Palaeography, Richard W. Hunt. Chambers Encylopedia.

English Manuscripts in the Century after the Norman Conquest, N. R. Ker. Oxford University Press, 1960.

English Vernacular Hands from the Twelfth to the Fifteenth Centuries, C. E. Wright. Oxford University Press, 1960.

The Handwriting of English Documents, H. C. Hector. Edward Arnold, 1966.

The Origin and Development of Humanistic Script, B. L. Ullman. Rome, 1960.

Renaissance Handwriting: An Anthology of Italic Scripts, Alfred Fairbank and Berthold Wolpe. Faber and Faber, 1960.

The Script of Humanism, James Wardrop. Oxford University Press, 1963.

The Italic Hand in Tudor Cambridge, Alfred Fairbank and Bruce Dickins. Cambridge University Press, 1963.

Humanistic Script of the Fifteenth and Sixteenth Centuries, Alfred Fairbank and R. W. Hunt. Bodleian Library, 1960.

Calligraphy and Palaeography; Essays presented to Alfred Fairbank, Editor A. S. Osley. Faber and Faber, 1965.

The Illuminated Book; its History and Production, David Diringer. Faber and Faber, 1967.

Ornament in Medieval Manuscripts, Lucia N. Valentine. Faber and Faber, 1965.

Illuminated Manuscripts in the Bodleian Library. Part 1, German, Flemish, French and Spanish Schools. Oxford University Press, 1966.

Early Gothic Illuminated Manuscripts, D. H. Turner. British Museum, 1965.

Romanesque Illuminated Manuscripts, D. H. Turner. British Museum, 1966.

Illuminated Manuscripts Exhibited in the Grenville Library. British Museum, 1967.

Medieval Manuscript Painting, Sabrina Mitchell. Weidenfeld and Nicolson, 1964.

English Romanesque Illumination. Bodleian Picture Book No. 1. Bodleian Library.

Byzantine Illumination. Bodleian Picture Book No. 8. Bodleian Library.

Bibliography

English Illumination of the Thirteenth and Fourteenth Centuries. Bodleian Picture Book No. 10. Bodleian Library.

All the Titles in the Faber Library of Illuminated Manuscripts.

English Drawing of the Tenth and Eleventh Centuries, Francis Wormald. Faber and Faber.

The Master of Mary of Burgundy, Otto Pächt. Faber and Faber.

The Trajan Inscription in Rome, E. Catich. Catfish Press, 1961.

Edward Johnston. Priscilla Johnston. Faber and Faber, 1959.

Index

Index

Index

Index

Index